Rethinking Peace and Conflict Studies

Titles include:

Chandra Lekha Sriram
PEACE AS GOVERNANCE

Stephan Stetter
WORLD SOCIETY AND THE MIDDLE EAST
Reconstructions in Regional Politics

Rethinking Peace and Conflict Studies
Series Standing Order ISBN 978–1–4039–9575–9 (hardback) &
978–1–4039–9576–6 (paperback)

You can receive future titles in this series as they are published by placing a standing order. Please contact your bookseller or, in case of difficulty, write to us at the address below with your name and address, the title of the series and one of the ISBNs quoted above.

Customer Services Department, Macmillan Distribution Ltd, Houndmills, Basingstoke, Hampshire RG21 6XS, England

Conflict Transformation and Social Change in Uganda

Remembering after Violence

Susanne Buckley-Zistel

Otto-Suhr-Institut für Politikwissenschaft, Free University Berlin, Germany

First published 2008 by
PALGRAVE MACMILLAN
Houndmills, Basingstoke, Hampshire RG21 6XS and
175 Fifth Avenue, New York, N.Y. 10010
Companies and representatives throughout the world

PALGRAVE MACMILLAN is the global academic imprint of the Palgrave
Macmillan division of St. Martin's Press, LLC and of Palgrave Macmillan Ltd.
Macmillan® is a registered trademark in the United States, United Kingdom
and other countries. Palgrave is a registered trademark in the European
Union and other countries.

ISBN-13: 978–0–230–53762–0 hardback
ISBN-10: 0–230–53762–6 hardback

This book is printed on paper suitable for recycling and made from fully
managed and sustained forest sources. Logging, pulping and manufacturing
processes are expected to conform to the environmental regulations of the
country of origin.

A catalogue record for this book is available from the British Library.

Library of Congress Cataloging-in-Publication Data
Buckley-Zistel, Susanne, 1969–
    Conflict transformation and social change in Uganda : remembering
    after violence / Susanne Buckley-Zistel.
        p.   cm. — (Rethinking peace and conflict studies)
    Includes bibliographical references and index.
    ISBN 0–230–53762–6 (alk. paper)
    1. Social conflict—Uganda.   2. Social conflict—Uganda—Teso Region.
    3. Conflict management—Uganda.   4. Social change—Uganda.   I. Title.
    HN794.Z9S623 2008
    303.6'2096761—dc22   2008016309

10   9   8   7   6   5   4   3   2   1
17   16   15   14   13   12   11   10   09   08

Printed and bound in Great Britain by
CPI Antony Rowe, Chippenham and Eastbourne

To Coady and Ben

Contents

Abbreviations

CA	Constituent Assembly
CP	Conservative Party
DANIDA	Danish International Development Agency
DP	Democratic Party
FOBA	Fight Obote Back Again
GTZ	German Technical Co-operation
ICC	International Criminal Court
ICTR	International Crime Tribunal for Rwanda
ICTY	International Crime Tribunal for the Former Yugoslavia
IMF	International Monetary Fund
LC	Local Council
LDU	Local Defence Unit
LRA	Lord's Resistance Army
NRA	National Resistance Army
NRM	National Resistance Movement
NV	New Vision
PCT	Presidential Commission for Teso
RC	Resistance Council
RDC	Resident District Commissioner
RPA	Rwandese Patriotic Army
RPF	Rwandese Patriotic Front
UNLA	Uganda National Liberation Army
UNLF	Uganda National Liberation Front
UPA	Uganda People's Army
UPC	Uganda People's Congress
UPDF	Uganda People's Defence Forces
UPF	Uganda People's Front

Glossary

Region	People
Region	*People*
Teso	Iteso (general and plural), Etesot (sing. male), Ateso (sing. and plural female) and Kumam
Kitgum	Acholi
Gulu	Acholi
Karamoja	Various Karamojong communities
Ankole	Banyankole (plural), Munyankole (sing.)
Buganda	Baganda (plural), Muganda (sing.)
Lango	Langi

Interviewees

Interviewee	Date	Place	Organisation	Position
Janet Abaru	24.03.2000	Kamuda, Soroti district		Peasant
Max Acharu	10.04.2000	Kumi		Elder, former LC4 chairman
Terence Achia	14.04.2000	Moroto town	Local Council Moroto district (LC5)	Chairman
Edegu Adiolo	22.03.2000	Arapai, Soroti district	Local Council (LC3) for Arapai	Chairwoman
Mary Adongo	24.03.2000	Kamuda, Soroti district		Peasant
Basil Ajotu	10.04.2000	Kumi		Elder
Grace Akello	06.01.2000	Portsmouth	Government of Uganda	Minster of State for Entandikwa; MP for Wera, Katakwi district; former Secretary of PCT
Nico Akwang	22.03.2000	Arapai, Soroti district	Local Council (LC3) for Duburo, Soroti district sub-county	Chairman
Lakere Alamo	24.03.2000	Kamuda, Soroti district		Peasant
Ruth Aliu	05.04.2000	Kampala	Parliament of Uganda	MP, member of Teso Parliamentary Group

(Continued)

Interviewee	Date	Place	Organisation	Position
Peter Ayopo Amodoi	13.04.2000	Moroto town	Karamoja Resource Centre	Researcher/ policy advisor
Amudo Areni	24.03.2000	Kamuda, Soroti district		Peasant
Alfred Aruo	16.03.2000 and 01.05.2000	Soroti	Teso Cultural Union	Officer
Georg William Ayora	24.03.2000	Kamuda, Soroti district		Peasant
E.A. Brett	21.02.2000	London	DESTIN, London School of Economics	Lecturer
Aidan Colours	13.04.2000	Moroto town	Lutheran World Foundation	Project director
Joanna de Berry	09.08.2000	London	London School of Economics	Former PhD candidate
Nicolas de Torrente	11.02.2000	Kampala	London School of Economics	Former PhD candidate
James Eceret	09.02.2000	Kampala	PCT	Economist
Musa Echweru	26.03.2000	Soroti	Government of Uganda	RDC Nebbi district; former youth organiser in Teso insurgency and responsible for international relations and supply of arms
Frida Ediamo	25.02.2000	Soroti		Elder; former UPC politician
Simon Peter Egadu	13.04.2000	Moroto town	Karamoja Projects Implementation Unit	Deputy co-ordinator

xiii

Ateker Ejalu	05.04.2000	Kampala	New Vision	Chairman; former Minister of State for Special Duties responsible for Teso insurgency
John Ekanu	09.04.2000	Soroti	Pentecostal Church	Reverent
Janet Ekere	07.04.2000	Kalaki, Soroti district		Business women
Mary Epechu	24.02.2000	Soroti	Teso Initiative for Peace	Youth and Gender Officer
Stephen O. Esunget	21.03.2000	Soroti	District Population Officer	Demographer
Paul Etjan	05.04.2000	Kampala	Parliament of Uganda	MP for Tororo; former Deputy Prime Minister under Museveni; former UN delegate; Minister under Obote II and Amin
Michael Griffith	12.01.2000	London	Index on Censorship	Writer; former OXFAM Karamoja
Mzee Guidon	10.04.2000	Kumi		Retired civil servant, father to Kenneth Olumia
Betty Ikarit	19.04.2000	Soroti	CBS	Social worker, youth officer
Lucy Ikomu	10.04.2000	Kumi		Elder, former teacher
Geresom Illukor	08.04.2000	Kumi	Church of Uganda	Retired Bishop of Teso

(Continued)

Interviewee	Date	Place	Organisation	Position
Peter Kalagala	23.02.2000	Soroti	Government of Uganda	RDC Soroti district
Ian Legett	11.01.2000	Oxford	OXFAM	Emergency programme officer
Teko Lokeris	14.04.2000	Moroto	Karamoja Projects Implementation Unit	Conflict resolution programme officer; son of present Minister for Karamoja Peter Lokeris
David Mafabi	05.04.2000	Kampala	Pan African Movement/ Pan African Development, Education and Advocacy Programme (PADEAP)	Policy advisor; former rebel SPLA commander, Sudan; former communication officer under Obote II
John Maitland	15.01.2000 and 20.05.2000	London and Kampala	Uganda Development Trust	Co-Director; former Teso Relief Committee; former director of Ngora hospital, Kumi district, Teso
Andy Morton	13.01.2000	London	Christian Aid	Researcher; Amnesty International Uganda researcher during Teso insurgency
Moses Mudong	13.04.2000	Moroto	KISP (Karamoja Initiative for Sustainable Peace)	Elder; father of former Minister for Karamoja David Pulkol
Issah Musulo	17.04.2000	Soroti	World Vision	Programme manager

Edith Naser	01.05.2000	Soroti	GTZ/PCY	Project manager
Michael Obwaatum	28.03.2000	Kumi town, Teso	Government of Uganda	Deputy RDC, Kumi; former Head of Communications, Rebel High Command, Teso
Patrick Oguang	28.03.2000	Kumi town, Teso	Red Cross	Field officer
George Oguli	24.02.2000	Soroti	PCT	Commissioner, Soroti district
George Ojamunge	28.03.2000	Kumi town, Teso	Red Barnet	Kumi Children's Project
Edmund Okella	20.03.2000	Soroti	Teso College, Aloet	Teacher
Joseph Okello	02.05.2000	Serere, Soroti district	Local Council, Soroti district	Youth Counsellor
Francis Okello	17.04.2000	Soroti	Teso Initiative for Peace	Project manager, retired teacher
Pius Richard Okiria	24.02.2000 and 15.03.2000	Soroti	Teso Initiative for Peace and Catholic Dioceses, Teso	Director of TIP and priest
Thomas Okoth	14.04.2000	Moroto	Government of Uganda	RDC Moroto district
Peter Okwi	22.03.2000	Arapai, Soroti district	Local Council (LC3) for Tuburu, Soroti district sub-county	Chairman
Kenneth Olumia	24.02.2000	Soroti	ETOP (Teso Weekly Newspaper)	Editor-in-Chief
Egoing James Peter Olupot	01.05.2000	Kumi town, Teso	CARE	Security guard, former rebel and amongst the last four to continue the struggle until 1994
John Olweny	08.02.2000	Soroti	DANIDA	PCT programme officer

(Continued)

Interviewee	Date	Place	Organisation	Position
Omeda Omax	13.03.2000	Kampala	Government of Uganda	Minister of State for Transport, Labour and Environment; former rebel commander Serere district, Teso
Moses Omiat	21.03.2000	Soroti	SODANN	Programme manager
Fidel Omunyokol	20.03.2000	Soroti		Journalist
John Oryokot	16.03.2000	Soroti	Parliament of Uganda	MP for Kaplebyong, Katakwi district
Sam Otai	27.03.2000	Soroti	UPDF	Military officer; former 2nd Commander in Rebel High Command
John Emilly Oteka	24.02.2000	Soroti	Soroti District Local Council (LC5)	Chairman
Peter Otim	14.03.2000	Kampala	Centre for Basic Research	PhD student
Owmony Owjok	20.03.2000	Arapai, Soroti district	Government of Uganda	Minister of State for Northern Uganda Reconstruction Programme (NURP)
Moses Owor	28.03.2000	Kumi	Care International	Monitoring and evaluation specialist
Dennis Pain	13.01.2000	London	Department for International Development	Africa advisor; author of 'Bending of Spears'; former resident of Uganda

Okwir Rabwoni	04.05.2000 and 16.05.2001	Kampala and London	Pan African Movement/ Pan African Development, Education and Advocacy Programme (PADEAP)	former MP for Youth of West Uganda
Stella Sabiiti	09.02.2000	Kampala	CECORE (Centre for Conflict Resolution)	Director

Acknowledgements

This book has been a long time in the making and would not have been possible without the support and inspiration of a number of colleagues and friends. Of these I only want to mention a few: Francis Akello, Siraji Aluma, Shane Brighton, Gerald Duda, Joanna de Berry, Nicolas de Torrent, Fatima Touré, Vivienne Jabri, Mama Café, John Maitland, Claire Moon, Edith Naser, Okwir Rabwoni, Tina Silbernagl and the Teso Initiative for Peace (TIP). The main part of this book was written as a doctoral thesis at the London School of Economics between 1997 and 2002 and I am most grateful to Mark Hoffman for his supervision. Moreover, I would like to thank Oliver Richmond for suggesting to publish the book in his series as well as the editors and reviewers of Palgrave Macmillan for their useful suggestions.

I am furthermore profoundly indebted to many people in the Teso sub-region as well as in Uganda more widely – it is their information and insight which made it possible to illuminate the background of the insurgency that is central to this book. In particular, my fieldwork in Teso owes much to the help and support of Alfred Aruo, who also acted as my advisor and interpreter on many occasions, and especially to Father Richard Pius Okiria's assistance and friendship. I also want to express special gratitude to the numerous Iteso and Kumam who shared their time, experience and wisdom with me. This is a book about people, even if their voices are not always heard, and I owe it to them.

The empirical part of this book would not exist without the logistical, practical and spiritual support of Justice Africa, London, and the Pan African Movement, Kampala. David Mafabi and Bernard Tabaire have been particularly helpful with advice and insights. In addition, I owe Tajudeen Abdul-Raheem much gratitude for hosting me in Kampala, introducing me to people significant for my research (and social life) and especially for putting my Euro-centric views into perspective. Most importantly, I am profoundly in debt to Alex de Waal who has been of tremendous personal and intellectual support while writing my doctoral thesis, and without whose help many aspects of this project simply would not exist.

Furthermore, I would like to thank the *Sonderforschungsbereich* (SFB) 'Governance in Areas of Limited Statehood', Free University Berlin, for a visiting fellowship which allowed me to update the volume as well as the *Deutsche Stiftung Friedensforschung* for funding relevant new parts of my research. And, lastly, I would like to thank Coady for his valuable support over the years, and him and Ben for rendering my life more beautiful. I dedicate this book to them.

Introduction

What lies in-between war and peace is rarely the subject of academic analysis. In the spotlight of public attention, peace accords are signed, new governments sworn in and institutions built to channel conflicting interests in a post-conflict environment. Yet this formal termination of a violent conflict only marks the beginning of a long and winding road from war to peace. Only too often are peace agreements reached for the country to plunge back into violence once a war-torn society endures stress or is incited by manipulative leaders. After the experience of violence, what is overlooked in many incidences are the concerns of the people who were personally affected by the fighting and who have to find their way in the newly achieved peace. Even though post-conflict peacebuilding has become increasingly popular for academics and practitioners alike, the question remains how societies transform their antagonistic relationships into mutual acceptance. After hardship and horror, how can they continue living on the same ground and share the same means? How can the parties break out of the confinement of their group identity that has become so meaningful in times of fighting? Moreover, at the community level, after the violence, the fabric that once made up social life and that provided some reference as to what is right or wrong lies in shambles. Physical scars are visible, personal ones remain hidden, and the destruction of the infrastructure is often devastating. How can people start making sense of their lives again? And how does this uncertainty after a crisis affect their relationship to the former enemy?

This book argues that the termination of a violent conflict and the possibility of its long-term transformation need to be situated in the wider social and historical context of the parties involved. To be sustainable, a transformation requires the alteration of the exclusive boundaries that demarcate 'us' from 'them', and simultaneously it requires changes in

1

the composition of the own identity group and its relation to the enemy. Much of this process takes place in the way the past is remembered and the future anticipated. The book therefore shows how remembering after violence constructs a collective identity which may or may not render future reconciliation possible. With reference to the termination of a violent conflict in Uganda, I show how one of the parties, the people who live in the Teso sub-region, draw on particular memories of the past and turn them into narratives about their experience of the insurgency. This is conditioned by the way the conflict was terminated, as well as by their subsequent experience of their opponent, the government of Uganda. At present, this particular memory perpetuates the antagonistic relationship between the parties to the conflict, standing in the way of sustainable peace.

The Teso insurgency

When Yoweri Museveni's troops seized power in Uganda in 1986, they took over a country with a devastating record of human rights abuses, a derelict economy and a past marked by violence and suffering. For more than two decades, Uganda had been subjected to the ferocious dictatorships of Milton Obote and Idi Amin so that, in 1986, hopes were high that Uganda would now finally return to peace. However, although large parts of the country supported Museveni and his National Resistance Movement (NRM), rebels in the north as well as in the north-east, areas from which Obote and Amin had recruited their soldiers, continued to violently resist the change of leadership. The Acholi people in the north and the Iteso and Kumam in Teso in the north-east of the country were perpetrators as well as victims of atrocious human rights abuses. The protracted nature of the conflict manifested itself in extra-judicial killings, rape and abduction. The people from the Teso sub-region, which then covered the districts of Soroti, Kumi and Katakwi, were also subjected to cattle rustling by their Karamojong neighbours, magnifying their plight. Allegations were voiced that the National Resistance Army (NRA) was involved in these assaults, and soon the confidence of the Kumam and Iteso towards the Museveni government and its armed forces was thoroughly undermined. 'In those days, we were all rebels' people in Teso say today.

To end the hostilities, in a rather exceptional manner for the Great Lakes Region of Africa, the Teso insurgency was mediated through the collaborative effort of local initiatives, women, indigenous mediators, churches and not least Museveni's Presidential Commission for Teso. Fighting ceased in 1992, and today the people of Teso have no apparent intention to take up arms again. Nevertheless, resentment still lingers. The termination of the conflict has not led to long-term social change, people still feel marginalised and despite the promised economic development by Museveni the region is prone to hunger and poverty. The Teso case thus raises critical questions about the impact of the termination of a violent conflict on its long-term transformation.

Yet why does peace in Teso remain shallow? In this book I argue that the way people remember the insurgency perpetuates their animosity against the government, standing in the way of future reconciliation. This particular recollection is informed by the negative experience of an other – that is, the Government of Uganda – which, to the very day, has failed to advance development and progress in the region. In this context, remembering the insurgency allows for constructing a collective Teso identity, which is clearly demarcated from other identity groups in Uganda, providing reassurance and comfort after the experience of the violent conflict.

The argument thus draws a link between the mediation of the violent conflict in Teso and the present *status quo*. In this sense, it illustrates how identities are being constituted between past, present and future, as well as the experience of an other. Situated in the framework of hermeneutics, it draws on the use of narratives to depict how subjectivity is established performatively, as well as how it is mediated in the encounter with difference – it argues that there is a dialectic relationship between the experience of an other and the constitution of the self. Rather than attempting to paint a broad picture, the approach taken is that of focusing on the local, Teso specific characteristics of past, present and future. The book thus tells a different kind of peace story.[1] Importantly, in comparison with other, better documented conflicts in Uganda, most notably of the Lord's Resistance Army (LRA) in the northern districts of the Acholi, the Teso insurgency has so far not been the subject of academic analysis. One of the central arguments of this book is that Teso has been neglected politically and economically by the Ugandan government, and in a sense, this can also be said about the interest of national and international scholars thus far.

Analysing the termination of violent conflicts and social change

The objective of this book is to analyse what impact the termination of a violent conflict has on the transformation of the antagonistic relationship between the parties to the conflict and if and how it leads to long-term social change.[2] It is situated in a post-positivist or inter-pretative approach to social sciences which focuses on the discursive construction of identity in relation to difference, as it has become increasingly popular in International Relations (IR) theory over the past decade.[3] Due to its relevance for violent conflicts, the debate has been extended to conflict analysis, and the 1990s saw a proliferation of liter-ature on how social realities like 'enemies' are created in discourse and language.[4] One important aspect emerging out of these discussions is that these 'realities' are not misperceptions, but part of what constitutes a particular collective identity. For instance, in a series of case studies on US foreign policy David Campbell shows how securing US national iden-tity relies on finding an outside enemy.[5] Identity is thus constituted in relation to difference, and the boundary that demarcates self and other potentially gives rise to conflict. While these approaches to conflict stud-ies have been very valuable for understanding how violent conflicts are constructed discursively, there has so far been no attempt to analyse how peace is constructed discursively. It is here where this book seeks to make a contribution.

The importance of discursive approaches for peace studies has been questioned by John Vasquez's remark that knowing how war was 'invented' by people does not tell us how to bring about peace.[6] This book responds to Vasquez's challenge by providing a framework as well as an empirical analysis of the transition from war to peace. It argues that, even though it might not bring about peace, a discursive approach helps to analyse the 'invention' of peace in discourse and whether it promotes or obstructs the transformation of the antagonistic relation-ship between the parties to the conflict. Significantly, under the concept discourse I do not only understand text or speech, but the totality of socially constructed rules that together constitute a more or less coher-ent reference for what can be said or done.[7] In other words, discourses are a system of meaningful practises that form the identity of subjects and social relations.[8]

In this book, the particular approach to discourse analysis is taken via the notion of hermeneutics. Hermeneutics translates 'understanding' or 'interpretation' and depicts how identities change in the process of understanding each other, for instance, as parties to a conflict in the course of a mediation process. In other words, hermeneutics refers to the constitution of shared meaning among participants to a conversation. If successful, the hermeneutic encounter produces agreement about the issue at stake and, simultaneously, it changes the party's understanding of each other. In the case of ending violent conflicts, this might lead to a transformation of the relationship between the parties from antagonism to mutual acceptance.

The structure of the book

According to recent figures, about half of all peace accords have lead to renewed violence.[9] These sobering statistics are particularly relevant for Africa where wars continue to have a detrimental impact on the population and its welfare. This book therefore begins with a description of contemporary violent conflicts in Africa. In contrast to recent contributions that situate the occurrence of war in rational behaviour and the strive for economic gain, it argues that violent conflicts need to be considered in their historical and social context and that, as a consequence, efforts to terminate a conflict need to take these aspects into account. In Africa, this often includes, *inter alia*, the social and political cleavages created by former colonial powers through their 'divide and rule' politics.

Against this backdrop of violent conflicts in Africa, Chapter 1 proceeds by analysing three different approaches to terminating violent conflicts – conflict settlement, conflict resolution and conflict transformation – in order to assess whether they take the wider context of the conflicts and their parties into account. Despite many similarities, the approaches differ significantly, in particular, regarding their understanding of the causes of violent conflicts, as well as their assumptions about the best strategies for external conflict management, its effects on the parties, and its impact on the wider conflict. In essence, conflict settlement refers to strategies that seek to terminate a violent conflict by creating a win–win situation, in most cases using interest-based negotiations between key stakeholders, leading to an agreement over the interest at stake and thus to an outcome which is considered to be to the benefit of all. In contrast, conflict resolution understands conflicts to occur not simply due to incompatible interests but also due to structural inequalities. As a result, its aim is not simply to accomplish the interests of the parties, but to change social, political and economic structures more widely. Critically, I argue, both approaches are inadequate for addressing violent conflicts as a social phenomenon since their understanding of the causes of a conflict does not take wider social dynamics into account. Moreover, they tend to de-politicise the context in which violent conflicts occur and they rely on cultural assumptions that might not be relevant beyond Western horizons.

In contrast, approaches to conflict transformation go one step further in that they recognise that conflicts due not simply occur due to incompatible goals and unequal structures, but that these are outcomes of historical processes which define the identities of the parties involved and which call for more substantial social change. Moreover, they suggest that for the ending of violent conflicts to be sustainable it is best to use local approaches, rather than supposedly universal blueprints. Following this, Chapter 1 continues with an exploration of traditional conflict management in Africa. The chapter also discusses its underlying values, strategies and objectives and closes by asking how its effect on the transformation of a conflict can be assessed.

To respond to this question is the objective of Chapter 2 where a general framework for analysing conflict transformation is developed. To this end, the first part of the chapter discusses post-positive contributions to conflict studies that focus on the emergence of violent conflicts, or what I call the 'invention of war'. The second part, then, introduces the notion of hermeneutics and argues that it provides important insights relevant for analysing the transformation of violent conflicts, or the 'invention of peace'. The argument takes a lead from what Vivienne Jabri calls 'discourse on peace'.[10] For Jabri, '[t]he legitimisation of war is situated in discursive practices based on exclusionist identities', and she asks whether it is possible 'to conceive of peace as situated in a critical discursive process which, rather than reifying exclusion, incorporates difference?'[11] Of importance is here Jabri's implicit request to *change* the discursive practises of inclusion and exclusion. Since the legitimisation of war is situated in discourse, discourse is also the site for legitimising, or inventing, peace. Hermeneutics, I argue, can help to better understand these processes.[12] It is based on the work of Martin Heidegger and Hans-Georg Gadamer and signifies the 'fusion of horizons', that is the accomplishment of understanding and meaning in communication. Horizons are the particular backgrounds in which the parties to a conflict are situated, and which determine the way they understand themselves as well as their opponent, or their other. According to hermeneutics, when encountering an other in the process of understanding, people question, and potentially alter, their horizons and consequently their interpretation of self and other. Two intertwined movements are at play in hermeneutics. Simultaneously, the parties to a conversation reach back to their past to evaluate their horizons and they cast themselves forward into the future of anticipated meaning, or in the case of violent conflicts potential reconciliation, with the other. Our identity is thus negotiated in the constant backwards and forwards movement of the hermeneutic encounter in which meaning is accomplished. Nevertheless, hermeneutics has been subjected to various forms of criticism. Of significance for this book is the allegation that it searches for truth and deeper meaning in communication and hence introduces a sense of closure. In response, philosophers such as Gianni Vattimo have suggested a more generous understanding of Heidegger's and Gadamer's work which is not based on the quest for truth. For Vattimo, hermeneutics simply refers to 'the ontology of the actual'.[13] It describes an interactive, fluid, rather than a teleological process.

One significant value of hermeneutics for peace and conflict studies is its recognition that identities are constituted with reference to past and future, as well as the encounter with an other. Conditioned by their experience of their (former) enemy, the way the parties to a conflict remember their past determines how they anticipate their future, and *vice versa*. Remembering the past is reflected in the particular narratives on which people draw in order to make sense of their lives. They do so not as individuals, rather their memory is determined by their social environment.[14] It is thus produced by, as well as productive of, a collective identity in the present. Hence, remembering is selective: some incidences are chosen to be remembered whereas others are chosen to be forgotten. However, if the past can be selectively remembered or forgotten it suggests that 'remembering is not the negative form of forgetting. Remembering is a form of forgetting'.[15] Forgetting does therefore not mean to fail to remember, it is not amnesia, but rather a way of *remembering differently*. At a collective level, a change in remembering the past therefore manifests itself in *re-membering* a community, that is, re-assembling it in a different way. The identity of the community changes in the light of different interpretations of its past.

Regarding the transition from conflict to peace, a number of important aspects can be drawn out of the hermeneutic process. Firstly, it implies that a process of conflict transformation entails changes in the identities of the parties to the conflict. When changing the way the parties see themselves as well as the former enemy, the structures and cleavages that provoked the conflict are being renegotiated. An assessment of conflict transformation should, therefore, ask if and how this is happening in a post-conflict society. Secondly, the process of changing is conditioned by the way communities remember their past (and hence re-member the community) as well as how they anticipate their future. The analysis of transformation processes needs to take this into account through asking what stories are narrated about the experience of the violent conflict and what anticipations are articulated for the future. Thirdly, processes of conflict transformation are always susceptible to power hierarchies which determine the outcome. Hence, political, social and economic power relations need to be included in the analysis. And fourthly, a conflict transformation process should not introduce a new sense of closure to the detriment of diversity since this can potentially lead to a new conflict. If and how this is the case after a violent conflict should therefore be assessed.

After having developed the theoretical framework, the book analyses the transitions from conflict to peace in Teso. The exploration of the insurgency begins in Chapter 3 with a rather traditional account of the history of Uganda. In addition to providing a background for readers unfamiliar with Ugandan politics, it seeks to map the social dynamics that developed over time and constituted the antagonism between the people of Teso and the government of Uganda under Museveni. Beginning with British colonial rule, I argue, some parts of Uganda have been privileged over others, leading to resentment and deep cleavages. This led to a number of violent conflicts in various parts of countries, including in Teso.

One method of traditional conflict management in Africa, as explored in Chapter 1, is consensus building through mediation. This was used by various actors to terminate the Teso insurgency, albeit in a modernised and at times informal manner. Chapter 4 analyses if and how the different forms of agency of the mediators worked together to impact on the structures of inclusion and exclusion that ran through Uganda at the time. More precisely, it asks if and how the mediation efforts changed the antagonistic attitude of the people of Teso towards the Ugandan government. I argue that the work of the Presidential Commission for Teso, introduced by Museveni in 1991, played a particularly significant role in 'bringing the rebels out of the bush'. Through the promise of economic development, the Commission facilitated the people's re-evaluation of their initial reasons to take up arms. This re-interpretation of their past with a view to future prosperity led the people from Teso to accept the government's gesture of peace.

What makes the Teso case significant for a book on conflict transformation is that both parties to the conflict, the Museveni government and the people from Teso, reached out to each other in order to end their violent dispute.[16] Peace in Teso did not simply occur due to the victory by the national army over the insurgents, rather it was the result of a collaborative process. The mediation took place in communication, for instance, through seminars and workshops organised by the Teso Commission, and it changed the way people in Teso perceived themselves as well as their other, the Museveni government. The Teso case thus held out the prospect of providing valuable insights into the fusion of horizons. And yet, in the course of the empirical research it became apparent that peace remained shallow. The mediation which ended the insurgency had been successful in bringing the insurgents 'out of the bush', but the resentment that started the fighting lingers to this day. People still feel excluded, and despite the promise of development by Museveni the region remains impoverished. So, has the relationship between Teso and the Museveni government been transformed as a result of the mediation process?

In order to respond to this question, the book turns to the present day remembering of the Teso insurgency. After having explored its historical and social backdrop in Chapter 3, a very different approach towards history and the cause of the insurgency is taken in Chapter 5. Based on the hermeneutic recognition that identities are situated between past and future, and that the interpretation of the past is reflected in the narratives people choose when referring to it, a selection of different stories about the beginning of the fighting is provided. They present the replies offered in response to my question: '*What caused the insurgency?*' In order to assess the long-term impact of the mediation efforts, the chapter analyses how identities have been constructed in the process of remembering – and hence narrating – the past of the insurgency in one way, while forgetting others. Significantly, today one particular narrative is dominating, almost to the exclusion of competing accounts. In this version of the beginning of the insurgency, the Iteso and Kumam are described as the innocent victims of government politics – an account which allows for a particular ordering, or re-membering, of the Teso community, as well as for a number of political claims towards the present government.

The assessment of the long-term impact of the Teso mediation on social change is continued in Chapter 6. It first describes the responses to the only war memorial to commemorate the insurgency – a mausoleum close to the trading centre of Mukura in Kumi district – and then explores the significance of the invention of the new cultural leader of the Iteso, *Papa Emorimor*, in order to highlight an innovative way of changing the role of the Iteso in the wider Uganda. Being central to the hermeneutic process of retrieving the past and considering a particular future, both examples, albeit different in scope, serve to illustrate how the people of Teso are dealing with their past today, and how this shapes their prospects for the future. The chapter draws the conclusion that many years after the end of the insurgency, Teso still has not

reconciled with the Museveni government. Even though the mediation restored relationships and harmony, it re-stored them, that is,
re-established the initial antagonistic relationship rather than transforming the conflict. The Mukura memorial, in particular, produces and
reproduces the antagonism between the Iteso and the government. Only
the invention of *Papa Emorimor* bears the potential for transforming
the pre-conflict order since it empowers Teso, turning it into a more
proactive player in national politics. The two examples thus reflect
two tendencies in Teso today: anger about the past, on one hand, and
preparation for a more empowered future, on the other.

Against the backdrop of prevailing poverty and resentment in Teso,
Chapter 7 asks what went wrong in the process of mediation which
promised to be so successful in transforming the conflict at first. With
the aid of the hermeneutic framework of analysis and its four interrelated aspects – change of identities, remembering, closure and power –
it draws together the various strings of the book, highlighting the obstacles and shortcomings of the mediation process which led to the present
status quo. In sum, despite the accomplishment of a consensus in the
mediation process, the way the people from Teso and the Museveni
government relate to each other today has not changed. Rather, it is
still marked by the same power asymmetries which gave rise to the
insurgency and which manifested themselves in the mediation process,
leaving the people of Teso with resentment and bitterness towards its
(former) enemy, the Museveni government. By drawing on a particular interpretation of the past which narrates the Museveni government
as perpetrator and the people of Teso as victims, future reconciliation
seems far off. The hermeneutic process of retrieving the past in light of
an anticipated future has led to a writing of local Teso history which
remains uncontested. A sense of closure limits what is possible in the
future.

While the book is primarily concerned with the analysis of conflict
transformation the final chapter opens up the scope through comparing different instruments of dealing with the past of a violent conflict
in order to redress the antagonistic relationships between the parties to
the conflict and to lead to a more sustainable peace. Transitional justice,
reconciliation initiatives and unification policies are all vehicles to contribute to social change after the experience of violence. However, they
all follow different objectives and strategies, and have different impacts
on the relationship between the parties, so that their application or combination has to be carefully considered. Most importantly, this requires
taking the needs and wishes of the people affected into account.

Methodology

The empirical argument of this book relies on research conducted in Teso and other parts of Uganda in 2000. This posed the obvious and unavoidable challenge of seeking to understand social and political processes in a culture different from one's own. Culture can be understood as an environment of 'a constantly evolving setting, within which human behaviour follows a number of particular courses'.[17] In this sense, it is one of the main contentions of this book that actions, for instance, the emergence, support and ending of violent conflicts, can only be understood through the particular socio-historical background of the conflict and the people involved. In order to incorporate this aspect in the analysis of the mediation of the Teso insurgency and its aftermaths I chose an ethnographic approach. In addition to interviews with various stakeholders, including political and clerical leaders, soldiers and ex-combatants, national and international NGO staff and journalists, I used Participatory Action Research (PAR) as a method to draw attention to 'local, discontinuous, disqualified, illegitimate knowledges'.[18] The aim of PAR is to comprehend conflict in its social, political and cultural context; it is an interactive and participatory process that facilitates the understanding of an environment different from one's own. Through active participation in the research environment, the analyst, seeking to interpret the unfamiliar, evaluates, and possibly alters, concepts and conceptions deriving out of her or his own background.[19] PAR is thus a methodology which seeks to bridge the gap between different cultural contexts, yet despite all ambitions, this can of course only happen to a limited extent.

1
Violent Conflicts and Their Termination

According to the Human Security Report (HSR) published in 2006, the number of violent conflicts waged around the world has declined since the beginning of the 21st century, and this trend has been by far greatest in Sub-Sahara Africa.[1] Even though the number of armed struggles that broke out in the 1990s doubled compared to the previous decade, their termination has increased as well. Significantly, and in contrast to the 1970s and 1980s, many conflicts were ended through settlement rather than victory, which marks a considerable turn. As for the 1990s, the HSR identifies 42 violent conflicts which were ended by negotiation and 23 by victory, as well as of 17 negotiated settlements and four victories in the period from 2000 to 2005. Many of these negotiated settlements occurred against the backdrop of UN peacekeeping missions which rapidly expanded at the time. While these numbers are encouraging they do not allow for much triumphalism. Even if settled conflicts last on average three times longer than those which ended by victory, they are nearly twice as likely to start up again within the first five years.

Against the backdrop of these sobering statistics it is important to ask how the termination of a violent conflict can lead to a more sustainable peace? One crucial aspect lies in the impact of the termination of a conflict on the communities concerned. With special reference to intrastate conflicts in Africa, this chapter therefore assesses three different approaches to terminating violent conflicts – settlement, resolution and transformation – in order to explore how they link the termination of a conflict with long-term social change.

Violent conflicts in Africa

In African societies – as in all others – what causes conflicts is complex and multi-faceted. At the micro level, conflicts between individuals, families and lineages erupt over personal differences and quarrels, marital disputes, rituals or over the competition over scarce resources such as land and pasture. At the macro level, conflicts often occur between governments and opposition groups as well as on the clan and village level.[2] Against the backdrop of widespread poverty in Sub-Sahara Africa, conflicts over belonging and identity frequently merge with attempts to control often-scarce economic resources.

Nevertheless, violent conflicts in Africa have undergone significant changes since the end of colonialism and the accompanying liberation struggles, and they continue to change over time, often in relation to changing global contexts. Robert Luckham argues that since the 1990s, the scale of violence has increased dramatically, in particular regarding atrocities committed against civilians.[3] Large-scale terror campaigns including killing, rape, displacement and the destruction of living spaces are common characteristics of wars such as in Sudan, Angola, Rwanda, Burundi, Somalia, Sierra Leon and Liberia. In addition to immediate war-related fatalities among combatants and non-combatants, many people die due to the immediate consequences of war, such as poverty and malnutrition, AIDS infections due to rape or poor sanitary conditions during displacement, encampment and detention. Furthermore, conflicts in Africa tend to be geographically unequally distributed, frequently affecting one part of a country or a region more than another and they often either have a 'war next door' or have a 'war before'.[4] This is tragically exemplified by the war in the DR Congo (1998–2003) in the Great Lakes Region, where eight African nations and some 25 armed groups were involved, causing the death of an estimated four million people.

Despite much literature on the causes of conflicts in Africa, they remain intractable and difficult to predict.[5] Some analysts argue that changes in the working of the global economy after the Cold War have led to so-called new wars.[6] They suggest that conflicts are no longer fuelled not only by grievances and a sense of injustice regarding the treatment of a particular social group but also by greed. This greed manifests itself in the exploitation of natural resources, taxation of humanitarian aid, the funding of combat by diaspora communities aboard and the like.[7] Consequently, they argue, waging warfare is less an outbreak of hatred and resentment than an acquisitive desire to maximise gains. It is thus a rational choice.[8]

Other features of 'new wars' include the pursuit of identity politics and the exclusive claims to power on the basis of tribe, nation, clan or religious identitites, often build on communities that are 'invented' rather than 'discovered'.[9] In contrast to 'old wars', the aim is often no longer the victory on the battlefield, but to create a pure and unified nation. Since, with the exemption of Rwanda, this does not necessarily lead to a genocide the terms 'ethnocide' and 'politicide' have been coined to describe the deliberate destruction of social groups who share either cultural or political characteristics. Dafur in Sudan serves as a sad reminder of what consequences these strategies can have.

Yet, despite the relevance of the concept of 'new wars', the emergence and continuation of civil wars in Africa remains much more complex. In addition to economic gains, the rationale – rather than rationality – to fight is highly dependent on cultural, personal and historical aspects, which cannot be explained by the 'new wars' framework. It is therefore important to understand the role played by social processes in intra-state conflicts. In many cases, they point to a degree of continuity with 'old wars' and require a highly nuanced understanding of how various old and new aspects work together to make people take up arms.[10] Instead of simple explanations, as argued by Paul Richards, violent conflicts must be considered as a social process in which the boundaries between war and peace are constantly renegotiated.[11] War belongs within a society where it is one among many closely intertwined aspects of social reality. The occurrence of a violent conflict is deeply embedded in the historical and social continuities that run through a society and that influence the mutual perception of the parties to the conflict.[12] Consequently, the emergence of violent conflict has to be situated in the precise social context from which it emanates.[13]

In Africa, this often runs along cleavages introduced by colonial powers. Against the backdrop of limited resources and manpower to fully administer the conquered territory, many colonial administrations opted for a 'divide and rule' policy according to which they selected one part of a society, elevated its status and used it to govern the rest of the polity. As a result, this so-called strategy of indirect rule left deep cleavages between privileged and suppressed sections of the population that – in many cases – have not been overcome to date. In the post-independence period, these cleavages often formed the basis of party politics and political alliances, firmly establishing the divisions in the political structure of the societies. In present history, they give rise to the contestation of citizenship rights for some parts of a society as well as to power struggles.

Among other factors, they lie at the heart of the genocide in Rwanda, as well as the violent conflicts in Uganda, Burundi and Nigeria, to name but a few.

This brief sketch of violent conflicts in Africa indicates that, in order to be sustainable, it is important that efforts to end a war take the transformation of these cleavages into account. Consequently, approaches to terminating conflicts must consider the historical and social situatedness of the conflict, as well as the perpetuating factors such as economic gains and interest and how they influence each other. The following section analyses if and how different theoretical and practical efforts to end violent conflicts have taken notice of these concerns.

Different approaches to terminating violent conflicts

The way we see the world shapes how we respond to it. In other words, our actions are informed by our understanding of social and political processes. This epistemological question about the source, nature and limits of our knowledge is, of course, also relevant to the various approaches to terminating violent conflicts that have emerged over the past decades. Their objective is to end protracted, often intra-state and ethnic conflicts through third party intervention, and they developed out of the necessity to provide an alternative to state-centred high politics.[14] In contrast to state-centred strategies, which involve political and military leaders and use coercive measures such as sanctions and arbitration, they focus on the role of individuals (even though these may include civil and military leaders) in conflicts by seeking to change their negative perceptions about each other. For the sake of illustration, in this chapter conflict settlement, conflict resolution and conflict transformation serve as examples for three different strategies for terminating violent conflict. As we shall see below, despite many similarities the approaches differ significantly, in particular, regarding their understanding of the causes and nature of violent conflicts, as well as their assumptions about what an external conflict resolution intervention should entail, what effects it has on the participants of the intervention, and how the intervention impacts on the wider conflict.[15]

Conflict settlement and conflict resolution

Conflict settlement refers to strategies that seek to terminate a violent conflict through creating a win–win situation. For supporters such as Roger Fisher and William Ury conflicts are caused by the pursuit of incompatible interest and goals, for instance, scarce resources or terri-tory, and they can be resolved through reaching an agreement about these interests that is to everybody's benefit.[16] The objective of conflict settlement is, therefore, to change a zero-sum game into a win–win situa-tion. The main targets in conflict settlement efforts are political, military and religious leaders – with experts and academics playing the role of facilitators – who are assumed to be rational cost-benefit calculators who modify their behaviour once they realise it is to their advantage. Con-flict settlement focuses on outcomes, such as the end of direct violence, yet it is hoped that the secession of fighting leads to a more permanent peace.[17]

One practical example of conflict-settlement approaches is Principled Negotiation, which is built on four principles.[18] The first is to separate the people from the problem, both geographically and personally. Nego-tiations often take places in secluded environments among leaders and key stakeholders in order to create some distance to enable the partic-ipants to see the conflict in a different light. Ideally, this helps them to listen actively to the concerns and interests of their opponents, to consider their own and their opponent's position more 'objectively' and to make emotions explicit and legitimate. This is based on the rationale that once each side is able to articulate its central interests and compre-hends those of its opponent a creative solution to the problem can be achieved.[19]

Secondly, Principled Negotiation focuses on interest, and not posi-tions. Positions are understood as short-term representations of the parties' interests, rather than fundamental, long-term interests them-selves. The workshops serve to move beyond mere positions to find out what the underlying interests actually entail. Since interests can be multiple, shared, compatible and conflicting the workshops seek to identify those which are compatible and shared in order to create a com-mon ground among the participants. Furthermore, focusing on interests potentially moves the discussions away from the past, which is often laden with emotions and resentment, to the present and future, making it easier to find solutions satisfactory to all.

Before seeking an agreement, thirdly, the participants to the work-shops develop a multitude of options which can then be evaluated according to whether they fulfil all parties' interests. The final choice of appropriate options, so the fourth principle, needs to be based on objec-tive criteria, that is, standards independent of the will of either party. A good outcome is then less defined in terms of the ability of the parties to compromise, but rather in terms of the extent to which all interests have been considered appropriately.[20] As free agents, the parties to the conflict can then make rational choices about what were initially apparently incompatible options following which both parties to the conflict gain from creating a win–win situation. Regarding the wider impact of conflict-settlement approaches in societies in conflict, one intended side effect of the workshops is skills training, that is, to build the analytic capacity of the parties to identify mutual interests and to devise solutions which offer mutual gain.[21] When the participants return to their communities it is assumed that they apply and spread their newly acquired skills so that a larger group of people benefits from the training.

In contrast, conflict resolution stands for process-oriented efforts to address the underlying structural causes of violent conflicts. In contrast to the conflict-settlement approach, theorists and practitioners such as John Burton and Ronald Fisher argue that conflicts do not only arise due to incompatible interests, which can be negotiated, but also due to non-material, non-negotiable human needs – for instance due to marginalisation, discrimination and inequality – and that these have to be addressed when trying to end a conflict.[22] Conflict is thus not considered to be *per se* negative but a positive effort to change an existing *status quo* and instead of terminating a conflict, the objective is to render it non-violent. Conflict-resolution approaches thus initiate a process, rather than simply producing outcomes, because they address the underlying inequalities and injustices in order to achieve long-term social justice.[23]

One particular approach to conflict resolution is based on the notion of 'human needs'. According to Burton, individuals and groups strive for the fulfilment of their needs which, if not satisfied, lead to instability, the violent pursuit of fulfilment and in worst cases to protracted social conflict.[24] This derives from the view that in order to survive, humans need a number of essentials that go beyond food and water, including safety and security, love, self-esteem, recognition, personal fulfilment, identity, culture, freedom and distributive justice. Even though the length and composition of this list varies with the person advocating for the approach, all elements have in common that they are non-negotiable, that is, they are essential and will be pursued with all possible means.[25]

Importantly, needs are not subject to scarcity and can, in theory, be granted to all. In fact, the more the needs of one party are satisfied, the more likely is the other party to enjoy the fulfilment of its needs.[26] In conflict-resolution workshops based on human needs, the mediators first analyse the conflicting issues of the parties to the conflict to assess the underlying needs violation. They then bring the parties to the negotiating table to discuss these issues in order to reach an agreement as to what the 'real' problems are, to recognise each other's needs, and acknowledge the cost of their conduct so far in terms of needs violation. Conflict resolution thus takes the shape of analytical problem-solving workshops aimed at reaching a shared acceptance of the core needs of all participants as well as at exploring ways to meet these needs through joint actions.[27] In an ideal case, the workshops reveal an outcome which is acceptable to all parties.[28]

Compared to a settlement approach, conflict resolution broadens the scope of actors involved in the termination of a conflict. In addition to leaders it incorporates civil society representatives, academics and other individuals who are capable of promoting a process of change. Regarding the impact of conflict-resolution workshops on the wider community, it is thus anticipated that the new insights trickle down to the constituencies. Nonetheless, it remains a short-term intervention aimed at mainly stimulating rather than directly encouraging wider processes of social change.

This brief description of conflict-settlement and conflict-resolution approaches reveals many parallels, most notably the secluded setting of the workshops, the role of the mediators as facilitators, the understanding of the agency of the participants as being rational and autonomous, as well as their focus on individual representatives of the parties to the conflict, rather than on the society more widely. However, it also exposes significant differences, for example, how the termination of the conflict is envisaged. While a settlement approach refers to behavioural change, that is, the parties finding a way to reach agreement, resolution goes further in that it requires a change in attitudes of the participants, ideally making a new outbreak of violence unlikely.[29] However, conflict settlement and conflict resolution have come under severe criticism from academics and practitioners alike. Four aspects are particularly important and shall be addressed in the following: their assumption about the impact of the workshops on the wider society, their de-politicised analysis of the context in which violent conflicts occur, their understanding as to what causes a violent conflict and their underlying cultural assumptions.

Regarding the first aspect, it has been argued that the strategy of conflict settlement and resolution workshops to physically and mentally remove the participants from the conflict context to enable them to acquire a more distant, and by implication more objective, understanding of their own and their opponent's perspective is counterproductive for the trickle-down effect on the parties' constituencies.

Both approaches anticipate that the workshops have an impact on the wider communities through the newly learned skills of the participants, including their ability to detach themselves from stereotypes and to see the conflict in a new light, which are all requirements to reach a settlement or resolution as the outcome of a workshop. However, how can these new skills contribute to the over-all ending of a conflict 'if they are indeed de-linked from the socio-political environment at all the levels at which protracted conflict is extant'?[30] In order to guarantee the trickling down of skills and decisions it is thus important to involve the wider community.

In a similar vein, secondly, both conflict settlement and conflict resolution situate the agency of the parties to the conflict in ahistorical and apolitical contexts. The objective of the workshops is to generate new insights and mutual understanding in order to settle or resolve a particular conflict. This assumes that the parties act as rational agents – as cost-benefit calculators – when assessing their needs or interests and when agreeing on an outcome of the workshops that is to everybody's advantage. Yet, although at least the conflict-resolution approach considers factors external to the workshop – such as injustices and inequalities as causes for conflicts – the impact of these structural power imbalances on the agency of the parties to the conflict and their performance within a workshop remain neglected. But the ability to settle or resolve a conflict is strongly conditioned by the role the parties play in the society at large. It is marked by structures of domination, discursive frameworks and modes of legitimisation which enable and constrain their agency when settling or resolving a conflict, consequently impacting on the nature of the outcome.[31] Deeply rooted structural forces such as race, ethnicity, gender or class influence the parties' understanding of the context of the conflict, their linguistic and material resources drawn upon when articulating their position and when understanding their opponent's, and their capacities to engage with their institutional backdrop.[32] In the context of third party interventions, such inequalities are not only of pertinence to parties in conflict, but they also influence the capacities of external intervenors.[33] To end a violent conflict, then, it is important to take the socio-political context of both agents and structures into account.

This leads to the third criticism. Both conflict settlement and conflict resolution understand conflict as arising due to incompatible goals, such as access to resources, power or the fulfilment of needs, which can be revealed and addressed through negotiation and ultimately settled or resolved. Terminating violent conflicts is then a scientific rather than normative endeavour.[34] However, as argued by Norbert Ropers, conflicts are not simply about issues, but also about the relationship between the parties to the conflict. They 'typically operate at two levels: the more or less openly negotiated level of political demands and interests, and a deeper level of collective experiences, stances, and attitudes integral to the formation of identity'.[35] The latter dimension determines the relationship between the parties and is deeply embedded in collective memory and enshrined in social practice.[36] An important role in shaping the interest and relationship aspects of conflicts is played by events in which one or all groups have been the victims of despotic rule, expulsion, military conquest or some other form of violence. If conflict settlement or resolution are confined simply to an apparently 'reasonable' balance of interests, the danger remains that the neglected 'deeper dimension' of collective experience, traumas and attitudes will manifest itself as an inexplicable 'irrational' derangement, such as the outbreak of violence.[37] Consequently, when working towards ending a violent conflict it is paramount to address the relationship between the parties to the conflict also.

Lastly, the fourth criticism refers to the underlying cultural assumptions of conflict settlement and resolution. Provocatively, they have been accused of trying to socially engineer societies in conflict along the model of Western societies, the latter of which is held to be universal.[38] For instance, Paul Salem argues that for the Western community of conflict-resolution theorists, conflict is an overwhelmingly negative phenomenon, 'notable only for its harmful side-effects of violence, suffering, and general discomfiture'.[39] In contrast, an Arab position might hold that these side-effects are not nearly as significant as the value of the struggle itself, if it succeeds. Moreover, both conflict resolution and conflict settlement are based on the assumption that facts and values can be separated from each other. This is not necessarily the case outside Western mindsets where agency is less understood as autonomous and rational. As a result, terminating violent conflicts is not simply a matter of changing perceptions, attitudes and behaviours, but it is situated within wider social structures or cosmologies including moral, religious and ideological aspects. Norms and values play an important role for the kind of ending that it envisaged.

Moreover, approaches to conflict settlement and conflict resolution maintain that the interests or needs of the parties can be identified, isolated and eventually addressed individually. In contrast, a more holistic worldview suggests that conflicts are highly interrelated and that they cannot be isolated from each other.[40] A similar criticism holds for the role of the third party which, in Western approaches, is merely seen as a detached facilitator who assists the parties to the conflict in bringing to the fore all interests and needs that remain so far unsatisfied. In cultures less atomised than the West, a facilitator has a much more powerful role. She or he is considered to be an authority which can actually resolve the conflict at stake. Leaders or elders are therefore looked upon as being able to and responsible for ending the violence. Regarding the participants in the workshops, not many outside the West see themselves as individuals who are bound to one another and the state by an agreed-upon system of rights and duties. Instead, they belong first and foremost to their communities where they abide to their particular rules and rituals.[41]

A further culturally informed aspect is the strife of both conflict settlement and conflict resolution to reach an agreement between the parties to the conflict. In non-Western contexts, however, where governmental authority and the rule of law are not always guaranteed, this can potentially turn into a rather precarious and insecure situation for the parties since they have to give up some control and autonomy and accept mutual interdependence. The unpredictability of this situation, that is, the limits to one's freedom of action without fully trusting the other party to fulfil its promises, renders the parties vulnerable. It may thus be preferable to uphold a conflictual, but nevertheless known, situation than to create a less conflictual but more unpredictable, volatile one.[42]

The above criticism is substantial and shakes the very foundation of conflict-settlement and resolution approaches. What is common to all points is that they do not consider violent conflicts as social phenomenon, as for instance suggested by Richards above. In this sense, they focus too strongly on agency without adequately considering the structures in which these agents are situated.[43] To combine the two levels of engagement, structure and agency, has been central to debates in social sciences for some time. It is furthermore, albeit not explicitly, key to an alternative approach to terminating violent conflicts which can be called conflict transformation and which tries to respond to the criticism levelled against settlement and resolution.

Conflict transformation

Conflict transformation refers to approaches that seek to encourage wider social change through transforming the antagonistic relationship between the parties to the conflict. Based on the understanding that conflicts do not simply occur due to incompatible interests and unmet needs, it situates them in the historically and socially defined relations between the collective identities of the parties to the conflict. Problems of inequality and injustice are highlighted by socially and culturally constructed meanings and suggest it is at this level where interventions seek to take place.[44]

Conflict transformation does not only seek to re-establish the *status quo ante* but it is a long-term outcome, process and structure oriented effort with a strong emphasis on justices and social change.[45] Academics and practitioners such as John Paul Lederach, Johan Galtung and Adam Curle, in particular, stress the necessity of transforming structural and asymmetric power imbalances between the parties in order to move to a sustainable peace.[46] This may include the transformation of actors (through changes within parties or the appearance of new parties), issues (by altering the agenda), rules (through changes in the norms and rules governing the conflict) and structures (by changing the relationship and power asymmetry).[47] The framework has since been expanded by the categories transformation of contexts (through changes in the international and regional environment) and transformation of personnel and elite (through changes in their perspectives and will as well as gestures in conciliation).[48] From a more practical viewpoint, the notion of social change may also include a long-term perspective of the promotion of human rights and inclusive governance, sustainable development and security sector reform.[49] In this sense, the aim is to turn peace into a social phenomena emerging through and constitutive of social practices which renders peace an institutional form that is largely seen as an acceptable form of human conduct.[50] To conceive of conflicts as social and historical constructs presents new and important opportunities for their transformation since it follows that conflict can be un- or de-constructed, that is, their meaning can be transformed. Through such a process the parties to the conflict are able to change their antagonistic relationship into one which allows for mutual acceptance.[51] Importantly, this also requires transforming the contexts in which these meanings are situated. We shall return to this point in the following chapter.

Differing from conflict settlement and resolution, conflict transformation is not confined to workshops with leaders but to different interventions at all levels of society. According to Lederach, actors and approaches to conflict transformation can be conceptualised in the form of a pyramid.[52] At the top of his structure, he places top leaders as well as high-level negotiation as a means to address the conflict. This is followed by mid-level leaders and a problem-solving approach in the middle, and grassroots leaders and local peace constituencies at the bottom. In order to be successful, Lederach argues, conflict transformation has to happen on all levels simultaneously; that is, they have to be interdependent.

Importantly, and in contrast to conflict settlement and resolution, transformation approaches build on culturally appropriate models of conflict mediation aimed at empowerment and recognition.[53] Hence, culture does not become an obstacle but a critical resource.[54] Since societies have their own coping and survival mechanisms and techniques for managing conflicts it is widely accepted that efforts to transform violent conflicts should include, respect and promote resources from within a society and that peacebuilding efforts should build on existing cultural frameworks. The importance of culture is threefold: it constitutes different values, norms and beliefs for socially appropriate ways of dealing with conflicts and disputes, including their management or resolution; it affects significant perceptual orientations towards time, risk or uncertainty, power and authority; and it comprises different cognitive representations or discursive frames such as schemas, maps, scripts or images, bound up in metalinguistic forms such as symbols or metaphors.[55]

Traditional conflict management in Africa

In recognition of the importance of culture, under the umbrella of conflict transformation, traditional approaches to terminating conflicts have become increasingly popular among academics and practitioners alike. If effective, they provide people affected by violent conflict with the means to solve their own problems. In Africa, this has given rise to the notion of an 'African renaissance' and to the promotion of local and indigenous conflict management projects by both governmental and non-governmental actors.[56] Crucially, they are not situated in modern thought and practice and they do not draw a clear line between agency and structure but follow a more holistic approach. In addition, as discussed in the following, they do not understand the individual as an autonomous, rational actor but as a member of a community from which it cannot be separated and to which it is responsible for its actions, as much as the community is responsible for an individual.

According to William Zartman, '[c]onflict management practices are considered traditional if they have been practiced for an extended period and have evolved within . . . societies rather than being the product of external importation'.[57] However, in much of the developing world, colonialism – and subsequent Western influence – had a devastating impact on local cultures and the availability of traditional knowledge. Harmful for traditional structures were, *inter alia*, the competing and at times conflicting values and norms introduced by Western-style education and governance systems, the promotion of Christianity or Islam,

the introduction of the centralised modern nation-state and of capitalist market economies, as well as the increase in mobility due to
the provision of transport and telecommunication. But colonialism did
not only destroy the cultural foundations on which traditional dispute
mechanisms were built, it also co-opted them to serve the interests of
the colonial administration, corrupting indigenous traditions.[58] As a
consequence of the destruction of traditional values, traditional conflict-
management mechanisms have lost some of their strength so that
current efforts to revive their effectiveness are confronted with semi-
functioning structures. It is, however, important to acknowledge that
there cannot be a romantic return to a past before external influences
but that, as always and everywhere, local traditions develop over time
through internal and external stimuli. There is no clear demarcation
between 'the realm of the exogenous "modern" and the endogenous
"traditional", rather there are processes of assimilation, articulation,
transformation and/or adoption in the context of the global/exogenous –
local/indigenous interface'.[59] Present efforts to revive traditional conflict
management have to take their historical adaptation, modernisation
and sometimes institutional formalisation into account. Traditional
hence signifies the heritage of the past which has been modified and
transformed over the course of time.[60]

Moreover, restoring to the past is always selective and determined by
the needs and perspective of the present. This juncture between old and
new renders it possible to extend traditional approaches with modern
aspects such as gender equality and the respect for human rights, that
is 'to create a framework that is a hybrid between indigenous African
traditions and modern principles to ensure the human dignity and
inclusion of all members of society – women, men, girls and boys'.[61] Traditional conflict management can hence turn into a holistic approach
in which traditions are combined with best current practise in conflict
transformation.[62] This might, nevertheless, lead to their manipulated
application to serve the interests of power holders as it is, for example, the case with the local village tribunals *Gacaca* which have been
re-invented by the Rwandan government to prosecute the offenders of
the 1994 genocide.[63]

Despite regional differences and cultural, ethnic and linguistic diversi-
ties there is a striking similarity between the nature of traditional conflict
management across the African continent. This is due to commonalities
in social formations in African societies based on what is occasionally
referred to as preliterate worldview or thought system.[64] When conflicts
are solved at the community level, the selection of a disputing mode

is informed by ongoing, long-term relationships.[65] As argued by Ernest E. Uwazie, the disputants consider the network of socio-economic relations in which they are embedded and chose a way of solving the conflict which does not upset the *status quo*. In this sense, the past and the historical context in which disputants are situated is as important as their anticipation for the future:

> Mediation is most likely to succeed between disputants whose various residential and kinship ties require them to deal with one another in the future. In other words, it is a phenomenon of communities. When social relationships are enduring, disputants need to find a settlement to continue to live together amicably.[66]

Traditional practice highlights the need of the socio-political community to assert itself, its identity and its control of its norms.[67] The importance of norms and values in mediation derives from the fact that they guide behaviour and expectations. Guy Oliver Faure categorises them into three cross-cultural aspects: relationship, restitution and identity.[68] Regarding the first aspect, he states that in a mediation process the quality of a relationship between the parties to the conflict has to be preserved to a mutually satisfying level, even if this is to the detriment of the outcome about the issue at stake. The communal management of the conflict is often more important than the actual outcome of the process.[69] For the mediators, the objective is hence less to find a solution to a problem than to manufacture consensus between the participants. In other words,

> a poor settlement between the parties to the conflict or a mediation, even costly, is more advisable than an arbitration that would be viewed as a sign that harmony has definitively been broken. . . . Harmony is such a crucial value that a hostile attitude between disputing parties can be as much penalized as the crime at the origin of the conflict. Thus, relations among members of the same community are never framed or dealt with according to a zero-sum logic.[70]

Restitution, the second aspect, is a necessary mechanism by which to restore harmony. The objective is restorative justice, that is, to restore social relationships and harmony. By contrast, the punishment of the offender, as practised in the Western punitive justice systems, would be understood as a further injury to the community. In traditional conflict management in Africa, justice therefore forms a significant part of a mediation, but as compensation and not as retribution for an offence.[71] Traditional conflict management does not understand a dispute to exist between two parties, but between the culprit and the whole community, that is, harm has been done to the whole group. As a consequence, apologies have to be performed publicly, in front of all community members who bear some responsibility regarding the role a culprit plays in their society. Thirdly, in traditional societies, to preserve a community's identity is often what is really at stake in a mediation process, in particular, since the identity of an individual is defined via that of his or her community. In other words, identity is conferred ascriptively by family, village or tribe. Mediating conflicts thus takes on the form of reconciling divergent interests in order to maintain the physical existence and spiritual well-being of the entire community.

One of the key functions of traditional conflict management is to structure the actors' actions. Faure distinguishes three categories of structural elements by which to understand traditional mediation: cognitive aspects, the role of parties to the process and their approaches to the problem.[72] Regarding the first element, cognition organises thinking, introduces meaning and structures behaviour. It thus governs the conduct of the mediators. Different from Western, modern societies, in non-modern societies people think mainly in global, holistic terms, that is, all elements of a situation are captured simultaneously under the shape of a whole that is non-fractional. The latter is expressed differently in different cultures. In Africa, it is, for instance, captured in the concepts *Kparakpor* in Yoruba, *Ubuntu* in the Zulu and *Ujamaa* in Kiswahili which all emphasise association and relationships.[73] Differing from modern cultures, this mode of reasoning does not pose opposites or dichotomies, such as good/evil, strong/weak, right/wrong, where one always excludes the other, but opposites are unified in a holistic worldview, rending it particularly useful when dealing with complexity, such as during a mediation process.[74] Based on this form of reasoning, mediators often apply metaphors and images as a means of portraying complexity. Myths and tales provide the social fabric in which the participants are situated and to which they conform as a real and imagined community. Rituals and symbols serve to reinforce norms and values, but potentially also power relations.

As for the nature of the parties involved, in traditional conflict resolution, actors do not participate as individuals but as members of a particular tribe, clan, village, age group or other community.[75] Even the mediators are part of a whole and cannot be disassociated so that, as a consequence, they do not reflect their own personal interests but that of their community. Due to their ascribed wisdom based on age and experience, elders play a particularly strong role as mediators; their authority provides them with the clout necessary for making decisions.[76] A further aspect of traditional conflict resolution is that meetings are always held publicly so that all members of a community can witness the proceedings. The community thus also has a stake in the outcome of the mediation, increasing its weight. As a consequence, if a culprit repents, perjury is not only an offence to the victim but to the whole community.

Lastly, the overall organisation of mediation sessions forms a further structural component affecting and governing the entire relationship-building process.[77] Typically, traditional societies operate in concentric circles to slowly identify the scope of the mediation. The conversations move slowly from the periphery to the core, until the issue of dispute gradually surfaces. As a result, the process itself is foreseeable for the parties, giving them time and allowing them to save face, if necessary. 'The washing of dirty laundry' in public may lead to shame and compromise the position of the parties and it undermines the prestige and honour of the family head or a community leader.[78]

Yet, traditional conflict management is not necessarily a benign and just mechanism. In contrast, the mediating role of conventions, norms as well as moral principles also serves to uphold political authority and social order, including harmony within a social system.[79] This can be achieved through 'implicit sanctions' through, that is, 'the subtle but pervasive means by which members of . . . [a community] are moulded into complying with rules of social control – the moral code, the normative order, and the belief and value system'.[80] By, for instance, creating an image of social harmony on the basis of myths, beliefs and values as part of an ongoing process of socialisation, conformity to the rules is produced and the continuity of the community ensured. As a result, community members are complying with the rules of conduct, the dispute settlement and the outcome of mediation process. In many cases, the failure to comply equals an assault on the whole community, leading to strong condemnations and sanctions by other community members.[81] This mechanism is enhanced by the fact that there is a strong degree of social and economic dependence between the community members, which, in rural areas, in particular, is necessary for survival.[82]

Against this backdrop, what is the benefit of applying traditional methodologies such as mediation as a means of conflict transformation? Firstly, traditional approaches promise a higher degree of local ownership, and thus potential success, than external efforts. For many communities, external conflict transformation efforts are perceived as intrusive and ignorant of indigenous concepts of justice and peace. In contrast, the local conflict mediators are generally more sensitive to the community's needs and have more credibility and hence impact. To try to resolve a conflict inside of a community renders it possible that the conflict strengthens rather than undermines a group's unity and solidarity.[83] Secondly, traditional approaches often follow a different rationale than Western problem-solving approaches and are therefore more suitable for the local cultural context. All over the continent, people have deep-rooted cultural norms and values, and in many of the conflicts in Africa this cultural heritage plays a critical role. Central to many efforts is the use of mediation in order to reach a consensus, to restore relationships and order, as well as to contribute to the reconciliation between the parties to the conflict.[84] Thirdly, in contrast to the criticism levelled against conflict settlement and conflict resolution, traditional conflict management is not detached from its wider social impact but rather placed right in the middle of social relationships. Its understanding of the occurrences of violent conflicts is not limited to interests, goals and needs, but it situates their emergence within the social network that constitutes the community.

In this sense, at least three of the four criticisms voiced against the conflict-settlement and conflict-resolution approaches – that is, their assumption about the impact of the workshops on the wider society, their understanding as to what causes a violent conflict, and their underlying cultural assumptions – are irrelevant for traditional conflict management. However, regarding the fourth criticism discussed above, the question remains if and how traditional approaches consider the wider political contexts which influence its participants and whether they can contribute to long-term social change. Do they lead to a transformation of the conflict, that is, do they change the antagonistic relationship between the parties to the conflict? Can they address the historically and socially defined relations between the parties which led to the emergence of the violence in the first place?

In addition, the approaches to traditional conflict management discussed above are employed to solve community conflicts, as opposed to intra-state conflict, and many of them only deal with mid-level crimes. Murder, war crimes or even genocide are too serious an offence to be dealt with by traditional mediation, even though these mechanisms have been amended in individual cases, such as the *Gacaca* tribunals to prosecute genocide-related crimes in Rwanda, and possibly in the future the *mato oput* in northern Uganda to deal with the atrocities committed by members of the Lord's Resistance Army against the Acholi. It is hence important to assess to what extent local conflict management mechanism are able to deal with violent conflicts and if and how they need to be enlarged by modern aspects, turning them into hybrids between the old and the new, the local and the global. But how to measure their success?[85] In order to be able to analyse the potential and limits of traditional conflict management for intra-state conflicts it is first of all necessary to develop a theoretical framework for the assessment of conflict transformation and social change. And it is to this matter that we shall now turn.

2
Inventing War and Peace

After a violent civil conflict has been terminated, for instance, by negotiation or traditional meditation, the parties to the conflict continue sharing the same territory. They are faced with the challenge of having to acquire a mode of relating to each other, which replaces the violence of the past. Yet how do they alter their antagonistic relationship into mutual acceptance? How does the termination of a violent conflict lead to actual long-term transformation and social change? And how can this be analysed? In order to respond to these questions it is first of all necessary to develop a theoretical concept for analysing change after violent conflicts. To this end, built on recent post-positivist contributions to IR theory, this chapter seeks to develop a framework for analysing the emergence, or invention, of peace.

The importance of post-positivism for peace studies has been questioned by John Vasquez's remark that an analysis based on the discursive construction of reality 'maintains by its very logic that, because war was invented, it can be disinvented by people. "Knowing" this, however, does not tell us how to bring about peace'.[1] In this chapter I challenge this rejection of post-positivism's value for peace studies and argue that it offers valuable insights into the construction of antagonistic relationships which are useful for understanding how such relationships can be un-constructed. To this aim, this chapter is split into two sections: the first section introduces the notion of post-positive conflict analysis in general and the 'invention of war' in particular. The second section, then, explores the notion of hermeneutics and suggests to use it as a foundation on which to build a framework for assessing how war can be 'disinvented' by people.

Inventing war

According to Vivienne Jabri, '[i]dentities are constructed representations of the "self" in relation to the "other" '.[2] Implicit in this statement are at least two assumptions worth investigating more closely: first, Jabri suggests that identities are not realities waiting to be possessed, but rather that they are constructed over space and time, and second, she points to the relationship between identity and difference as the locus of conflict. Regarding the first point, it is central to Jabri's argument that identities do not derive from biological proclivities, but rather from being situated in a particular discourse. This social and historical context provides 'a variety of pre-existing experiences, implicated in human conduct through practical and discursive consciousness' out of which the individual actively selects particular modes of representation.[3] It is hence not autonomous agency or rational choice that guides the selection; rather it is the individual's belonging to a spatio-temporal community that defines who she or he is and how she or he acts. In her argument, Jabri borrows from Anthony Giddens's structuration theory that suggests that social practice is ordered across space and time. Again, social action is not the result of the actor's rational choice, but rather derives from her or his situatedness in a particular set of structures, or rather structural properties, in the form of '[r]ules and resources, or sets of transformation relations, organised as properties of social systems'.[4] In Giddens's structural properties 'structure only exists internal to . . . practice and as memory traces orientating the conduct of knowledgeable human agents'.[5] However, Giddens does not suggest that structural properties determine agency. Rather, social systems, which provide the structural properties, consist of reproduced relations between actors that have been organised as social practices.[6] For Giddens, all social life is generated in and through social *praxis*; where social *praxis* is defined to include the nature, conditions and consequences of historically and spatio-temporally situated activities and interactions produced through the agency of social actors.[7] There is therefore an important circular movement between agency and structure which forms the main contention of structuration theory:

> Crucial to the idea of structuration is the theorem of the duality of structure . . . The constitution of agents and structures are not two independently given sets of phenomena, a dualism, but represent a duality. According to the notion of the duality of structure, the structural properties of social systems are both medium and outcome

of the practices they recursively organize. Structure is not 'external' to individuals... Structure is not to be equated with constraints but is always both constraining and enabling.[8]

In other words, the moment of the production of action is also the moment of the reproduction of structural properties simultaneously, even in times of the most radical change.[9] Yet, this is not to suggest that structures are merely constructed by action, but rather that actions reproduce them as conditions, as rules and resources, that makes agency possible. So one important insight that derives from Giddens's structuration theory is that structural properties come into existence through agency as much as agency is constituted through structural properties. And yet, in order to have some impact on structural properties one single act is insufficient – only through repeated action, over space and time, is the agent able to exercise some influence. As we will see in the course of this book, repetition has a significant ontological impact.[10] The identity of agents is informed and conditioned by the prevailing structural properties of a particular discourse. And yet, since it is agency which shapes the structural properties, non-conformist action might become powerful by gradually transforming the prevailing 'reality' into a different one over time. This might happen through constantly judging and acting, that is, through the permanent provocation of wide-ranging structural practices.[11]

Returning to Jabri's notion of identity construction, the argument adopted in this book is that agents are historically situated and that their actions are enabled and constrained by the particular structural properties, or discourses to use a synonymous term. This recognition has an impact on both the way people invent as well as un-invent war. Against this backdrop, the existence of belligerence and hatred can be considered as a structural property which has developed in a community over time and which can potentially be un-made. This, however, requires change.

The second assumption implicit in Jabri's argument above is that there is a 'relation' between the construction of self and other. Even though Jabri's text reveals little about this relation, I would like to suggest that unravelling the construction of identity along the line of identity/difference provides valuable insights into the emergence and ending of conflicts and, therefore, merits closer attention. According to William E. Connolly, the importance of the other for the self is that the self simply would not exist without the other. Without difference there would be nothing to contrast ourselves from. In Connolly's words:

An identity is established in relation to a series of differences that have become socially recognised. These differences are essential to its being. If they did not coexist as differences, it would not exist in its distinctness and solidity.[12]

Difference is hence indispensable for identity. '[T]he constitution of identity is achieved through the inscription of boundaries which serve to demarcate an "inside" from an "outside", a "self" from an "other", a "domestic" from a "foreign" '.[13] Social systems are constructed along the line of inside/outside where exclusion at each level influences the other and is shaped by it.[14] The spatio-temporal representation gives us a particular identity since we have to draw lines between where we stand and where there is space for somebody else. Here and there, now and then, us and them become meaningful in light of this 'affective geography' where loyalty and allegiance is ascribed to those we associate ourselves with.[15] Hand in hand with this process of identity creation, however, goes the claim for legitimacy and the notion of rights for 'since we have come to exist we believe that we have a right to exist'.[16] This right to exist can only be challenged by somebody who is not a member of my particular identity group – it can only be the indispensable other who has the ability to deprive us of our identity.

So far we have established that the existence of a self is ultimately linked to an other. Inside the spatio-temporal boundaries, identity is produced and reproduced through routinised practice. Agency is meaningful for it is conducted along the lines of collective memory traces which allow for knowledge among the members of a discourse. This raises the question how the construction of the self influences the relationship between identity and difference? In order to explain conflict as being situated in the prevailing discursive and institutional continuities of a community, Jabri introduces the notion of conflict as 'constructed discourse'. Again in accordance with Giddens's structuration theory, she suggests that conflicts are not events that suddenly occur, but rather that they are situated in a discursive environment. Pre-existing structural properties supply the necessary foundation to justify and legitimise the emergence of and involvement in conflicts. Myths, memories and symbols not only provide the ground from which identity is drawn, but they also narrate the tale of the other as enemy and threat.[17] These exclusive discourses about the inside/outside split of community boundaries are likewise embedded in discursive and institutional continuities and serve as a justification for the practice and politics of exclusion.[18] But where do these exclusive discourses originate? Why was the other created as an enemy? Is it simply the existence of difference which provides the basis for conflicts?

In an attempt to respond to these questions, Campbell argues that '[t]he problematic of identity/difference contains...no foundations which are prior to, or outside of, its operations'.[19] Instead conflict arises on the level of the boundaries which are supposed to provide distinctness and solidity for the respective identities, and which are not always originally clear cut. As Connelly notes '[if] there is no natural or intrinsic identity, power is always inscribed in the relation an exclusive identity bears to the difference it constitutes'.[20] This power is manifested in turning the indispensable other into the evil other. 'Identity requires difference in order to be, and it converts difference into otherness in order to secure its own self-certainty.'[21] Connolly hence argues that

> the paradoxical element in the relation of identity to difference is that we cannot dispense with personal and collective identities, but the multiple drives to stamp truth upon those identities function to convert difference into otherness and otherness into scapegoats created and maintained to secure the appearance of a true identity. To possess a true identity is to be false to difference, while to be true to difference is to sacrifice the promise of a true identity.[22]

Hence, according to Connolly, communities which are uncertain about their own identity have a tendency to affirm this identity through increasing the difference between members and non-members leading to an exaggeration of the differences. Devoid of pre-existing coherent identities, the individual or the community is inclined to demarcate itself from the other.[23] This boundary drawing between self and other is thus central to post-positivist conflict analysis. In consequence, the promotion of peace has to tackle the prevailing social continuity of exclusion by changing the nature of the boundaries between inside and outside.

Emergence and support of violent conflicts

In linguistic terms Jabri locates the support for post Cold War conflicts in the 'discourse of origins' where elites 'hark back to a distant past in order to mobilise a bounded, exclusionist present'.[24] She argues that authorities and elites hold the power to control which discursive and institutional practices prevail inside of a community when she writes that

[t]he ability to consolidate and reproduce authoritative power is dependent on the capacity to manipulate the memory traces of a community and control information gathering and dissemination which generate and reproduce the discursive and institutional continuities which 'bind' societies.[25]

The 'binding' of societies can be based on a hegemonic discourse which does not allow for dissident voices, and it may consist in demonising anybody who is not a part of this 'we-group'; a process of boundary drawing and demarcation is set in motion. Due to the overlap of signification, legitimisation and domination, plural communication is no longer possible, it is distorted and becomes exclusive. Jabri makes special reference to the state, a highly administered social system, as central to both the reproduction of war through the manipulation of the public discourse, as well as through the institutionalisation of the war process.[26]

Yet, the difficulty with Jabri's argument is that it credits too powerful a role to elites. Her argument resonates with David Keen and Mats Berdal's study of conflicts in Sub-Sahara Africa, according to which a range of elites initiate violence in order to deflect political threats.[27] They suggest that the growing internal and external pressure for democratisation puts the mere existence of dictatorial governments in jeopardy, and in order to secure their position governments frequently incite violence along ethnic lines. Due to a general lack of disciplined and effective counter-insurgency military forces, there is a tendency to oppose the flaring-up of rebellion through the mobilisation of 'top-down' violence, 'with elites taking advantage of the fear, need and greed of ordinary people to recruit civilians'.[28] Ethnic identities provide a useful vehicle for motivating violent conflict; existing discursive and institutional provisions are deployed to cut a gap through a community serving as a 'regressive political function'.[29]

Similar to Jabri, for Keen and Berdal the authority held by elites provides the necessary power to steer the perception, or discourse, of a community into a particular direction. However, the frequent occurrences of insurgencies, as opposed to government led wars, suggest that there are also actors outside of governmental institutions. Moreover, as central to the previous chapter, the occurrence of violent conflicts is internal to societies, and not external to them.[30] To solely attribute the potential of manipulating discourses into violence and exclusion to governments and elites reduces the multiple and diverse agents in a social field. As a consequence, it is not the case that 'anything goes' when it comes to manipulation. Unless it is in line with a generally prevailing sentiment in the population, propaganda and hate speech incited by individuals does not necessarily lead to widespread violence. For here, too, agency is constrained (and enabled) by structure. The genocide in Rwanda, for instance, an often cited example to illustrate the degree to which people can be manipulated into committing the most horrendous crimes against humanity, was based on ethnic polarisation first politicised through German and Belgian colonial rulers and then radicalised after independence. In addition, it was carefully prepared over many years, and it occurred not only in the middle of a civil war and the corresponding extreme polarisation, but also in the context of a flawed peace process. The action of killing was thus situated in a 'long-duree' of fighting and hatred and not merely the result of a spontaneous Hutu conspiracy.

Despite these critical remarks there remains a powerful role for discourses in the emergence of violent conflict. In response, much of post-positive conflict analysis is concerned with exploring how rituals of power have arisen, taken shape, gained importance and affected politics.[31] Campbell, for instance, draws on Jacques Derrida's notion of *deconstruction* to illustrate the workings of power relations. Deconstruction is perhaps best explained through what it is not: it is not the negative task of demolition, and it is also not a simple dismantling of an entity into small parts.[32] Furthermore, deconstruction is not criticism in a general or Enlightenment sense of faultfinding, nor is it a scientific or philosophical method based on a metaphysics which can be applied to a particular case.[33] Deconstruction can be explained as the reading of a text in a way that 'opens up the blind spots or ellipses within the dominant interpretation'.[34] Generally, texts are written in ways that exclude alternative perspectives; they make claims to reflect a particular reality authentically so that they introduce a sense of closure, which stifles alternative interpretations. Deconstruction reveals these limits and invites plural, alternative interpretations. Drawing on the deconstruction of texts, Campbell shows how narratives about the violent conflict in Bosnia reflect particular accounts of Bosnian history which are conditioned by a selective understanding of ontological presumptions about ethnicity, nationalism, identity, violence and so on.[35] Ignorant of their ontological selection, the texts introduce closure on a multiple interpretation of history through developing a particular truth, or meta-narrative, devoid of contestation. The value of deconstruction is hence to open monopolistic accounts and to reveal their contingent character.

Ultimately, Campbell's use of deconstruction seeks to challenge 'the relations of power which, in dealing with difference, move from disturbance to oppression, from irritation to repression, and . . . from contestation to eradication'.[36] He calls for a different configuration of politics in which the overriding concern is the 'struggle for alterity', in which eradication is replaced by the nourishing and nurturing of antagonism, conflict and plurality.[37] In other words, Campbell is concerned with celebrating difference through 'the proliferation of perspectives, dimensions and approaches to the very real dilemmas of global life'[38] and he seeks to 'contest the drive for a new normative architecture – especially in form of newly minted codes and principles – as a necessity for responses to the context of crisis'.[39] The importance of deconstruction for conflict analysis is that it allows for opening up closed discourses as multiple sites in which difference is not suppressed but appreciated. Its emancipatory potential is to challenge prevailing boundaries, that is structures of inclusion and exclusion, drawing attention to what has been stifled and offering an opportunity for silenced voices and opinions to emerge. The question remains, however, whether challenging structures and meaning is sufficient in war-torn societies. Once the prevailing power structures have been contested, maybe even violently, are they to remain open? In fact, can they remain open? Is nurturing antagonism, conflict and plurality possible, or indeed desirable? Despite appreciating Campbell's concern with challenging boundaries and opening up closed discourses this book argues that, regarding violent conflicts, he does not recognise that people need a sense of identity, a sense of belonging, a sense of limits and boundaries. Not for reasons of 'human nature' or 'human needs', but simply because, otherwise, sociality would be impossible. For interaction to be meaningful, shared concepts or 'language games', are required.[40] This is of particular importance for the time after a violent conflict when a new, peaceful future has to be developed and when the social structures that formerly made up the world and provided meaning are destroyed. For '[w]ars unmake worlds, both real and conceptual'.[41] Worlds cannot be simply recreated but have to be created anew since recreation would merely reproduce the tensions that led to the violent conflict.[42] After the violence, the creation of new identities can happen in antagonism or mutual acceptance of the other party to the conflict, perpetuating or reducing the potential for future violence. Often, though, antagonism prevails since the experience of bloodshed and loss has marked people deeply, rendering group identity even more relevant than at the beginning of the hostilities. Hence, in many cases after a war both parties to the conflict end up trapped in collective identities.[43] This resonates in Vakim Volkan's concept of 'chosen trauma' according to which a group draws a traumatic event into its very identity in order to reproduce its collective identity.[44] The repetition of narratives about the traumatic event constructs the group's identity in opposition to the identity of the opponent who caused the trauma, and as such becomes a social reality for those who participate in this discourse. A common identity, a 'we-feeling', is shared between the people who recall the same painful past, rendering their social interaction meaningful, while reproducing their boundary towards the outside.[45] This maintenance of antagonist relationships keeps societies vulnerable to future violence.

The potential for reproducing antagonistic relationships between the parties to the conflict shows that, even though the cessation of fighting is often considered as the endpoint of a peace process, it marks nothing more than a beginning.[46] In cases where the parties to the conflict continue living in close proximity to each other, such as *inter alia* in Rwanda, Burundi, Sierra Leone, Bosnia-Herzegovina, Northern Ireland, Guatemala or El Salvador post-conflict transformation requires some form of invention of new structures to prevent a new outbreak of violence. For 'wars . . . only really end when they are *transcended*, when they . . . [go] beyond the traditional currency of victory and defeat; when the defeated side . . . [accepts] that the victory of its enemy . . . [is] also its victory as well'.[47] In an ideal case, the transcending of a war does not simply result in the new distribution of power; rather, it *challenges and changes* the power structures themselves. It does not merely invert the power asymmetries but moves the parties to the conflict to a different level in which the power structures are newly defined and no longer rely on the exclusion of one party at the expense of the other. Conflict is then positive, for it challenges boundaries, *and* it is also positively constructive for it leads to newly invented ways of relating to each other. To move from conflict to peace it is thus not sufficient to deconstruct exclusive power structures, leading to plurality and diversity, but it is at the same time also necessary to *change* these structure and antagonisms, moving the parties to a new level beyond enmity. This has so far been largely ignored by post-positive approaches to conflict studies and shall be addressed in the following section.

Inventing peace

To return to Vasquez's remark at the outset of this chapter the central objective of this book is to analyse ways to un-invent war and to invent peace. The attempt to 'invent peace' is inspired by Jabri's remark, and subsequent question, that

[t]he legitimation of war is situated in discursive practices based on exclusionist identities. Is it therefore possible to conceive of peace as situated in a critical discursive process which, rather than reifying exclusion, incorporates difference?[48]

Jabri suggests that a 'discourse on peace' should transform the symbolic and institutional orders which underpin a violent conflict. She calls for a 'counter-discourse which seeks to understand the structurated legitimation of violence and challenges the militarist order and exclusionist identities which encompass it'.[49] The significance of her quest lies in her argument that by changing the way we talk to and about each other we alter the wider discursive settings – as well as ourselves. Since this aspect is central to the notion of hermeneutics, the notion shall be explored at greater length.

Hermeneutics

The word hermeneutics has its etymological origin in ancient Greek and signifies translating, interpreting and making intelligible. The concept derives from the messenger Hermes who was tasked with dispatching messages between the gods of Greek mythology. Even though the term hermeneutics has been in use since the 17th century it was the German theologian Friedrich Schleiermacher (1768–1834) who published the first significant exegesis on the subject. To him, hermeneutics was the tool through which to understand the meaning of the Bible as well as of legal texts. Wilhelm Dilthy (1833–1911), in reference to Schleiermacher's approach, developed the term *hermeneutic circle*, which later provoked the German philosopher Martin Heidegger (1889–1976), and subsequently his student Hans-Georg Gadamer (1900–2002), to provide an alternative account of the 'art of understanding' which Gadamer then labelled *philosophical hermeneutics*.[50] Since Heidegger's and Gadamer's departure illustrates aspects significant for the present context it is necessary to explain the concept in more detail.

In his major work *Truth and Method* Gadamer lays out the fundamental ideas behind his notion of hermeneutics. The somewhat misleading title, however, does not introduce the quest for an authentic, universal truth and a methodological guideline for action.[51] Rather, Gadamer emphasises that 'hermeneutic reflection' only serves to lay open alternative ways of knowing, that is, truths which would not have been noticed otherwise.[52] Hermeneutic reflection refers to the complex process set into motion when we encounter something or somebody new and strange which we seek to understand, for instance somebody we find ourselves in conflict with.[53] Once understanding has been accomplished the shared meaning about an issue at stake is however not more 'true' than the assumption we had before the encounter. Rather, this newly acquired truth is merely different, and there is no hierarchy of different truths. As a result, hermeneutics opens the door for a pluralism of interpretation and the competition of different truths. In the process of understanding, a number of influential factors are at work which impact on the outcome of the encounter. In the following section I broadly lay out the central arguments.

Central to the idea of hermeneutics is that a part can only be understood in relation to the whole and the whole only in relation to its parts. There is thus a circular movement.[54] For instance, the interpretation of a text invokes a circular movement between its overall interpretation and the specific details that a particular reading offers. The new details potentially modify the overall interpretation which in turn sheds light on new parts significant for understanding. In this process, understanding becomes more and more profound.[55] For Schleiermacher, who first theorised hermeneutics, yet without explicit reference to the term 'hermeneutic circle', this suggests that a text can only be understood by the interpreter when she or he fully grasps what the author had in mind. For him, hermeneutic interpretation requires the mental retracing of the writer, as well as her or his situatedness in a historical context. In this traditional conception of hermeneutics, understanding is only possible through the reconstruction of the author's subjective and objective circumstances. Schleiermacher's notion of the hermeneutic circle is hence formal and methodical; for to him understanding is the reproduction of the initial production, and it results in a divine act in which the interpreter is able to place herself or himself entirely into the author, or the other. Through Schleiermacher's, and later Dilthy's, model of hermeneutics a positivist notion of understanding is suggested where the interpreter and the interpreted remain distinct entities. Yet, due to a particular understanding of subjectivity and rationality, they are able to completely step into the other's position. To this end, methods such as psychoanalysis and historical or bibliographical research help to produce a true and authentic picture of the text and its author.

As mentioned by way of introduction, Gadamer discarded Schleiermacher's formal interpretation of the hermeneutic circle.[56] In the process of understanding, Gadamer argues, we do not place ourselves into the author's mental situation, nor into their subjective circumstances, but only into her or his opinion. As for the objective circumstances, Gadamer criticises Schleiermacher in that he only recognises the author's historical contextualisation, yet disregards the situatedness of the interpreter herself or himself. We, as interpreters, always also bring our own historical context into the encounter with the text, or the other, and hence every interpretation, and understanding, can ultimately only happen from the vantage point of our own situatedness. Understanding is thus contingently dependent on both the interpreter's and the text's spatio-temporal background.

In his re-interpretation of the hermeneutic circle, Gadamer refers to Heidegger's notion of hermeneutics as discussed in *Being and Time* where the latter argues that understanding is always determined by the interpreter's preconception. In the process of interpretation we do not simply try to paint an accurate picture of the author, nor do we try to understand the text through the author and the author through the text (as subject to the traditional conception the hermeneutic circle) so that accomplished understanding dissolves the circle in complete knowledge. Rather, completeness can never be achieved; there is a constant interplay between the spatio-temporal background of the interpreter and the author, that is, the other in which the interpreter understands herself or himself, and *vice versa*. This process is set into motion through comparing commonalties and then questioning difference. I will return to this point in more detail below. For now it suffices to say that our anticipation of meaning is not guided by a form of sublime subjectivity, but rather that when interpreting a text we always bring ourselves in. Through firstly recognising what we have in common with the other's tradition this communality is always under construction. Thus it is not merely a precondition for understanding, but it is always produced in the process of understanding itself. The hermeneutic circle for Heidegger and Gadamer is hence not formal, as it is for traditional approaches, but it describes an ontological structural moment of understanding.[57] Where for Dilthy and Schleiermacher hermeneutics meant the art of understanding, for Heidegger and Gadamer it is understanding itself.

Fusion of horizons

The redefinition of the hermeneutic circle by Heidegger and Gadamer has significant consequences for ways of approaching otherness. By analogy, when engaged in a dialogue with our 'enemy' we only understand an argument, that is, a part, in relation to her or his historical, social or geographical background, that is, the whole. Statements and utterances have no universal validity which makes them universally intelligible. They are invested with meaning due to the speakers spatio-temporal background, or what Gadamer calls 'tradition'. Traditions can be understood as an ongoing outcome of historical lives, as the representation of mean-while nameless authorities,[58] or as the historical environment through which we know ourselves. We cannot divest ourselves from tradition. Our understanding of the world is thus ultimately linked to our traditions, which exercise a form of authority on our being, on our view of the world and our view of the other. The way we are, the way we understand, the way we relate to our environment is conditioned by our past. As a consequence, the individual cannot, when making judgements, refer back to some pre-social rationale, but only to what Gadamer calls prejudices, that is, judgements that have been made before the evaluation of all circumstances. And yet this does not necessarily mean that these prejudices are wrong. But rather

> [p]rejudices are not necessarily unjustified and erroneous, so that they inevitably distort the truth. In fact the historicity of our existence entails that prejudices, in the literal sense of the word, constitute the initial directness of our whole ability to experience. Prejudices are biases of our openness to the world. They are simply conditions whereby we experience something – whereby what we encounter says something to us.[59]

The 'literal sense' of the word Gadamer is referring to derives from the German word for prejudice: *Vorurteil*. *Vor-urteil* means at the same time prejudice and pre-judgement, a judgement we have made prior to being more knowledgeable about the circumstances.[60] We might have strong prejudices against our 'enemy', yet only pre-judgements/prejudices enable us to commence evaluating something new and strange. *Vorurteile* are situated in a particular bounded community through which our being has been constituted. They are at the same time a limitation and a necessity to understanding; they enable and constrain the way we conceive of our 'enemy'.

Gadamer's claim, that in the process of understanding our traditions always have an effect upon us, leads him to develop the term *Wirkungsgeschichte*, or 'effective history', that is, the operative forces of traditions.[61] Traditions are the materialisation of effective history. Effective history is thus our own history which has an effect on the way we are. Therefore, to think truly historically means to include our own history, to render ourselves (as an individual, community, etc.) conscious of the effects of the distinct past. In other words, understanding, in its essence, is a process of *wirkungsgeschichtlichem Bewusstsein*, of 'effective historical consciousness', for it requires the revelation and consideration of our history.[62] Nevertheless, '[e]ffective-historical consciousness is inevitably more being (*Sein*) than consciousness (*Bewusstsein*)',[63] it has strong ontological implications.

To exist historically means that our knowledge of ourselves can never be complete for every finite present has its limitation which is represented in what Gadamer calls 'horizons'. A '[h]orizon is the range of vision that includes everything that can be seen from a particular vantage point'.[64] The term is used to indicate the limitation of thinking to a finite entity. Yet, as a consequence, people are not static, but dynamic for they change over space and time. In Gadamer's words:

> Just as the individual is never simply an individual because he [sic] is always in understanding with others, so too the closed horizon that is supposed to enclose a culture is an abstraction. The historical movement of human life consists in the fact that it is never absolutely bound to any one standpoint, and hence can never have a truly closed horizon. The horizon is, rather, something into which we move and that moves with us. Horizons change for a person who is moving.[65]

It is of major importance not to misunderstand Gadamer in this aspect. When he suggests that we retrieve our past, and that we question our prejudices, he does not suggest that there is a true self which can be discovered. Hence, Gadamer's truth is relational, and in the process of understanding, it is related to the other and to the anticipation of understanding the other in the future. In the process of understanding, Gadamer consequently suggests, we question our own horizons and interrogate our prejudices and prejudgements. In doing so we find out which prejudices about our 'enemy' are wrong and which ones are right. At first sight, the categories 'wrong' and 'right' suggest some deeper 'truth' which calls for uncovering – like a true 'evil spirit' of our 'enemy' which is said to be intrinsic to her or his race, ethnicity or genes. However, in Gadamer, truth never gains absolute, authentic terms, but is rather relative to the experience of being confronted with the strange and different.[66]

When encountering our 'enemy', in the process of reaching understanding, as depicted in Gadamer's hermeneutics, simultaneously two distinct, yet intertwined, movements take place: one movement is the retrieval of the past, the other the casting forward into a future. It is fair to say that Gadamer is generally more concerned with the first and Heidegger with the second movement, yet since the movements form an entity I discuss them here together.

Firstly, to render us conscious of our own effective history is a process of retrieving the past. Assumptions and positions, taken for granted and 'naturalised' over time, are questioned. Habits and routines, part of our day-to-day conduct, are re-evaluated. More precisely, the way we think about our 'enemy', the resentment we harbour, is brought under scrutiny. The way we have seen ourselves, thought of ourselves and represented ourselves is challenged through excavating our past in the light of the 'enemy'. From the moment we retrieve our past, and become conscious of our effective history, we become aware of the silent influences, *Vorurteile*, that guide us. Once conscious we might consider our prejudices and prejudgements as inappropriate and unsuitable and discard some of our assumptions or positions, habits or routines. In doing so, in discarding features that were intrinsic to our identity, we change. Questioning past horizons, evaluating previously uncontested features of our tradition and potentially discarding them, alters the way we are. Retrieving the past, therefore, has a significant impact on the present for it defines who we are now. Our present identity is a product of the way we conceive ourselves in the light of our own horizon. Yet, we can only interpret the past in the light of today.

The second movement referred to above is to cast ourselves forward into a future. The way we see ourselves in the future reflects back on how we conceive ourselves in the present. To cast ourselves into the future means, for instance, to anticipate that an understanding with the 'enemy' will be reached, that there will be some form of reconciliation in the time to come. Thus, to anticipate the accomplishment of understanding in the future, that is the creation of shared meaning, demands a particular attitude in the present. At the same time, through reaching out to a future we reflect back on our presence. When encountering the alien and strange we are confronted with assumptions, positions, habits and routines different from our own. It is the wish, and therefore the anticipation, of accomplishing understanding about the issues that differ that leads us to the self-critical process of evaluating our own horizons, that is, of retrieving our past as mentioned above. Essential to retrieving our past is thus to reach forward into the future and to anticipate a certain state of shared understanding with the other, such as the possibility of future reconciliation after a violent conflict.

It is important to state that both parties, in the process of understanding, evaluate their horizons and potentially discard particular features. In so doing they alter their horizons, and who they are, and eventually fuse their horizons. 'Understanding...is always the fusion of horizons which we imagine to exist by themselves.'[67] In the process of fusion we enter into a communion with our 'enemy' in which we do not remain who we were, in which we might adopt some of the 'enemy's' views as much as the 'enemy' might adopt ours. This is not to suggest that a process of unification takes place, which deletes all forms of difference.[68] For example, in the context of discussing religion Gadamer suggests that although many non-western cultures have successfully adopted a global, Western-centred market economy, which entails a very substantial element of modernity derived from Judeo-Christian religion, the non-western cultures have simultaneously maintained their own forms of religion. They have, on the level of global economy, evaluated their traditional approaches, realised that they will benefit from adapting to Western practice, and ultimately altered their routine. Yet only in the field of economy – not in other spheres of their culture. Hence, the fusion of horizons should not be understood as the assimilation of difference. Rather, in the process of hermeneutics, as depicted by Gadamer, we actually appreciate difference in its purest form for we respond to it through questioning ourselves. The communion into which we enter with the 'enemy' is as contingent as our previous identity; it is not an all-absorbing sameness, but a consensus reached about a particular issue at stake. Nevertheless, it provides us with meaning and (contingent) truth.

In summary, two movements, two dynamics, are at play in philosophical hermeneutics. Simultaneously, we reach back to our past to evaluate our effective history and we cast ourselves forward into the future of anticipated meaning, or potential reconciliation with our enemy. Our identity is therefore negotiated in the constant backwards and forwards movement of how we conceive of our history and how we conceive of our future. This conception is also very much conditioned by our experience of the other. To return to the beginning of this section, the backwards and forwards movement is what is illustrated in the *hermeneutic circle*. We understand the part in relation to the whole, that is, the self in relation to the other, and the whole in relation to the part, that is, the other in relation to our self. The hermeneutic circle is not a formal template, but rather it describes the ontological structural moment of understanding.[69] Hermeneutics symbolises not the art of understanding, rather it is understanding itself. Hermeneutics is the ontology of the present, its truth or meaning, as much as it is the ontology of the identities involved.

Critique of authenticity

The accomplishment of shared meaning in the hermeneutic process of fusing horizons has been accused of introducing closure by providing authentic meaning. One of the most pronounced critics of hermeneutics is Michel Foucault. In his words hermeneutics seeks

> re-apprehension through the manifest meaning of discourse of another meaning at once secondary and primary, that is, the more hidden but also more fundamental.[70]

Being an outspoken opponent of the search for the truth, Foucault argues hermeneutics searches for a deeper and truer truth as the outcome of the process of questioning, and ultimately fusing, horizons. He particularly rejects the existence of 'meaning' which allows, as discussed above, for understanding and some form of truth about an issue at stake. For him, without using these words though, the establishment of more fundamental meaning would lead to a sense of closure introducing new boundaries of inclusion and exclusion. Although, after a violent conflict, these boundaries might be more benevolent and hence preferable to the boundaries which were challenged by the conflict, they nevertheless introduce new static structures into the social reality which might provoke future contestation, potentially leading to new fighting. Closure puts a lid on the constant interpretations of past, present and future and prevents the continuous negotiation of self and other necessary for a diverse and vibrant society with space for contestation and dissent.

Foucault's view that hermeneutics introduces authenticity and closure is widely shared, yet it is also contested. For the Italian philosopher Gianni Vattimo, for instance, hermeneutics depicts the 'ontology of the actual'.[71] Vattimo argues that Heidegger's intention in *Being and Time* was not to establish a new and better meaning of Being because all other philosophical approaches were insufficient, although he recognises that one could, and may, interpret his text in this way. Yet, if one follows the course Heidegger took after *Being and Time*, Vattimo contends, the striving for a deeper meaning would be revealed as contradictory.[72] In Heidegger's writing the positivist notion of 'truth as correspondence' is not simply rejected due to some inadequacy, which needs correction. His project is far more ambitious. For Heidegger, 'Being is event', although Heidegger himself never explicitly makes use of this notion.[73] Thus Heidegger is driven by the motivation not only to deconstruct truth as correspondence and to propose a more adequate conception, but he also aims 'to "respond" to the meaning of Being as event'.[74] When conceiving of Being and truth as an event as opposed to a category which corresponds to an authentic reality it is important to differentiate *truth as opening* and *truth as correspondence*.[75] 'Truth as correspondence' refers to a truth as opening in terms of 'a historico-cultural horizon shared by a community that speaks the same language, and within which specific rules of verification and validation are in force'.[76] Truth as opening is then not true because it conforms to certain criteria, but because it is truly 'original' for it summons the horizons which provide the backdrop for all verification and falsification.[77] The question in hermeneutics is not simply related to encountering the unknown, but it simultaneously questions the taken-for-granted and what has become a habit. As such, it opens up horizons in order to keep them open.[78] The 'hermeneutic experience of opening' is consequently an aesthetic event, a poetic creation.[79] Vattimo concludes that therefore

> the truth of the opening can...only be thought on the basis of the metaphor of dwelling....I can do epistemology, I can formulate propositions that rate valid according to certain rules, only on the condition that I dwell in a determinate linguistic universe or paradigm. It is 'dwelling' that is the first condition of me saying the truth. But I cannot describe it to a universal structural and stable condition.[80]

Truth as opening understood as dwelling resembles Gadamer's notion of belonging to, and being imbedded in, a particular tradition for it is only then that we share certain concepts, or even words, and understanding occurs. It is here where we can speak the 'truth'. Yet Vattimo emphasises that this does not mean being passively subjected to a particular system or structure, but rather that '[d]welling implies...an interpretative belonging which involves both *consensus and the possibility of critical activity*'.[81] This is similar to Gadamer's reference to the ability to question our own horizon.

The rejection of an accommodation of truth in a deeper origin is what leads Vattimo to coin the phrase 'the nihilistic vocation of hermeneutics'.[82] Hermeneutics, as the locus of dwelling, turns into the ontology of the locus and its population. It turns into the 'ontology of the actual'.[83] A particular identity prevails at a particular time and place. Not forever, not everywhere, but nonetheless there. Hermeneutics is the arresting of the flux, the fragile existence of something which ceases to be in the very moment of its origin.[84]

To sum up, in order to understand each other, and this is what hermeneutics stands for, it is necessary to have a shared notion of truth. This is not only a prime requirement for co-existence after a violent conflict, but even for simple communication. Some form of boundedness is necessary to make sense of the world. And yet, being bounded does not mean being confined. Understanding merely suggest dwelling in a here and now, for a spur of a moment – before again drifting apart. In philosophical terms the truth which is brought about in the process of a hermeneutic encounter, in the process of fusing horizons, is at the same time always contested from outside and inside alike. It is never there to stay for it is itself not the representation of an authentic origin. Rather, it is contingent in its existence – and in its disappearance.

At this point it is necessary to ask what implication the notion of truth as opening has for conflict transformation processes? As emphasised in the discussion of deconstruction's value for conflict studies above, hermeneutics does not establish a new 'normative architecture... as a necessity for responses to the context of crisis',[85] but only contingent truths. At the same time, though, it enables to challenge and to change the structures that have given rise to the conflict without introducing new, impermeable boundaries which might again call for violent conflict. Hermeneutics as a framework of analysis thus enables to conceptualise how an antagonistic relationship between the parties to a conflict changes into mutual acceptance. Since hermeneutics emphasises the importance of time in the constitution of identities the following looks at this aspect more closely.

Remembering and identity

After violence, both parties remain confined to their collective identities which provided meaning during the conflict. Victors may collectively 'suffer' from amnesia and forgetting of atrocities committed, while victims might refuse to accept defeat through constant reference to the injustice endured at the hands of the victors.[86] These experiences shape memory and future realities, as illustrated by the case of Teso in this book. But here we might ask: What does it mean to remember some things and not others?

Remembering is traditionally associated with securing past experiences.[87] The past is understood as a former reality to which we have unhindered access so that it appears in our mind in the same manner as we experienced it originally. In other words, the memory of a moment is an identical copy of the moment itself. Nevertheless, more recent academic scholarship questions this assumption when it suggests that 'the present moment is nothing like the memory of it'.[88] An alternative understanding of memory, and history, has been introduced by the German philosopher Friedrich Nietzsche. According to him, the act of historicising, the rendering conscious of the past, leads to a 'degree of sleeplessness, of rumination, of the historical sense, which is harmful and ultimately fatal to the living thing, whether this living thing be a man, or a people or a culture'.[89] Not to be able to forget, that is not to 'feel unhistorical', prevents people from happiness.[90] Nietzsche therefore suggests liberating ourselves from these past pressures which encumber our steps as dark, invisible burdens: 'the unhistorical and the historical are necessary in equal measures for the health of an individual, of a people and of a culture'.[91] The importance of being unhistorical, or forgetting, becomes apparent in Nietzsche's discussion of horizons. He suggests that human beings need to be rounded up and enclosed by horizons since for him it is a universal law that 'living beings can be healthy, strong and fruitful only when bounded by a horizon'.[92] The line of the horizon is drawn through remembering and forgetting the past, through enclosing some moments into the horizon while leaving out others.

Forgetting in Nietzsche hence signifies a break with a particular historical consciousness, a break necessary to leave behind painful experiences which prevent us from overcoming present deadlocks. If one follows Nietzsche's advice, one could argue that the shared, collective knowledge of a community's past includes remembered as well as forgotten aspects. Remembering and forgetting are constitutive of an identity. As described by Ernest Renan in his famous essay *What is a Nation*: 'The essence of nations is that all individuals have many things in common, and also that they have forgotten many things.'[93] At first sight, since the objective of this book is to assess the transition from conflict to peace, Nietzsche's forgetting seems both, useful and necessary. It is therefore important to ask whether forgetting past atrocities opens up new prospects for a peaceful future.

Despite recognising that forgetting is necessary for 'happiness', I would like to suggest that, for Nietzsche, breaking with the past requires a rather drastic obliteration of events. Nietzsche's notion of forgetting suggests the oblivion of crucial experiences. This strategy proves problematic in, for instance, a post-conflict society where people have suffered atrocities and pain, and where forgetting, deleting or obliterating takes away people's legitimate urge to articulate grievance and to have their traumas recognised. As such it belittles their agony. In addition, in most cases, violence has left obvious reminders such as the loss of family members, houses and homes which call for endless remembering. Nietzsche's invitation to forget seems necessary, yet his strategy appears unfeasible.

There is, however, an alternative to Nietzsche's conception of forgetting which recognises the validity of remembering while at the same time allowing for breaking, or rather transforming, the boundaries of horizons.[94] It recognises that present consciousness, in fact the present identity, by necessity derives from remembering the past (which is still in accordance with Nietzsche's suggestion) and yet contains a form of forgetting that does not lead to a state of oblivion or amnesia. Rather, it recognises that forgetting itself is simply a way of *remembering differently*. Here, 'remembering is not the negative form of forgetting. Remembering is a form of forgetting'.[95] When, for instance, Gadamer writes that '[o]nly by forgetting does the mind have ... the capacity to see everything with fresh eyes, so that what is long familiar combines with the new into a many levelled unity',[96] he does not call for oblivion in order to determine the boundaries of a horizon, in the way Nietzsche does. Gadamer rather suggests opening our horizon to the interpretation of somebody else's experience in order to re-evaluate our own horizon and to potentially change the way we interpret, and thus remember, an event. In doing so, Gadamer recognises that there cannot be a true interpretation of our past. Remembering is rather a re-fashioning of the past, in fact, it is a re-membering of thoughts, or, put another way, it is an opportunity to construct a new 'ordering' of contingent historical events. The crucial difference between Gadamer and Nietzsche is that while Nietzsche seems to suggest blanking-out past experiences, Gadamer asks for re-interpreting the incidence. One could paraphrase Nietzsche as suggesting 'forget the past, it did not happen', and Gadamer to say 'look at your past, are there not different ways of interpreting it?' To return to the assessment of the transition from war to peace in post-conflict societies, one could illustrate their difference by either suggesting to forget what caused an insurgency or to remember it in a way that considers the responsibility of all parties involved. This would then not only lead to an exclusive blaming of the other side but also to assessing one's own accountability.

In other words, it can be argued that to remember the past differently is to re-member.[97] The remembering of the past by a community previously exposed to violent conflict re-members the members of this community, it re-organises social life, that is, it assembles the community and its members in a different way. Through re-membering differently we re-constitute our previous horizons and simultaneously the narratives we draw upon to constitute our own identity as well our opponent's. This re-construction bears the potential to assemble not only our thoughts and perceptions in a different way, but also war-torn communities *per se*. It allows for a redefinition of the collective identity which is not based on antagonism against an outside (former) enemy. Where there was an exclusive boundary between identity/difference before, this border might become more permeable. As such, it opens up possibilities for a peaceful co-existence.

In this sense, according to Gadamer '[t]he true locus of hermeneutics is the in-between'.[98] By analogy the time and space after a violent conflict can be described as the time 'in-between': in-between war and peace, in-between friend and enemy, in-between the parties to the conflict, in-between territorial boundaries. 'In this situation past and future are equally present precisely because they become equally absent from our sense.'[99] This notion of in-betweenness is what Hannah Arendt calls 'the odd time in-between', where the threads of traditions are broken and a gap becomes vacant in which action and change may occur.[100] This gap, she suggests, is no longer a condition peculiar to thought, but provides a tangible reality for political action. Arendt's notion of the gap serves as a useful metaphor for a site on which to locate conflict transformation. The end of a war provides a distinct point in time to accommodate this odd time in-between, the gap.

A hermeneutic framework for analysis

By way of conclusion, the question arises: What value the introduction of hermeneutics has for peace and conflict studies? First of all, it is important to remember that hermeneutics is not a method that can simply be applied to 'invent peace', to use Vasquez's term. Rather, it is the description of a process that happens when two or more parties reach understanding and can thus be used as a framework for analysing the transition from conflict to peace. Even though hermeneutics in itself does not resolve conflicts it enables us to analyse if and how conflicts have been solved well. As argued above, after a violent conflict war-torn societies need some form of new boundaries and identities. To conceptualise how understanding is accomplished, or horizons fused, to use Gadamer's terminology, permits comprehending the formative and transformative processes through which the parties to the conflict have to go in order to 'invent peace'. The particular focus on ontology and identity inherent in a hermeneutic approach reveals what mitigates or exacerbates the 'fusing of horizons'. To be able to identify these successes and failures might lead to the articulation of particular policies and strategies to enhance a conflict transformation process.

Another valuable insight gained by hermeneutics is the importance that the 'retrieval of the past' and the 'casting forward into the future' have on how people perceive themselves today. *Vorurteile* – that is, prejudices and prejudgements – rooted in our traditions determine our interpretation of the other with whom we are in conflict. In the hermeneutic encounter, we question and potentially discard (some of) these *Vorurteile* and change both our relationship to the other and ourselves. The assessments of our *Vorurteile* and the subsequent change can be positive, leading to a reduction of hostility and a process of reconciliation, but it can also be negative and re-enforce or even harden the frontiers. Both scenarios took place in Teso, as we shall see in the following chapters, albeit at different times. This highlights Vatimo's argument that horizons do not fuse into an everlasting unity, but rather that they involve consensus and critical action.[101] Attempts to introduce closure thus potentially collapse since one party to the conversation – or meditation, as in our case – might feel overpowered and challenge the new 'order' and boundaries established and maintained as an outcome of the process.

With identities being constituted between past and future – as well as the encounter with an other – remembering and forgetting play a significant role. *Inter alia*, remembrance is fixed in (sometimes oral and local) history as well as memorials. Consequently, their assessment provides valuable insights into the present constitution of an identity group. Central is the question how the interpretation of the past is conditioned by the encounter with the other and whether it leads to a re-membering of the community so that it no longer constitutes itself in opposition to the former enemy. Has it led to a reduction of the boundaries between self and other and to the potential for peaceful coexistence? The same can be said about visions for, or an image of, the future. Here, too, we ask in a dialectic manner whether the parties to the conflict have a positive or a negative outlook and how this is informed by yet at the same time informs their relationship to the other party to the conflict.

In this chapter I have argued that current post-positivist IR scholarship which calls for the challenging of boundaries which give rise to violent conflict is a valuable contribution to peace and conflict studies. However, I contend that it is necessary to move the project one step further to include how this challenging can lead to the actual *changing* of structures and identities without establishing new boundaries of inclusion and exclusion. This, I propose, takes place in the hermeneutic encounter. In summary, a framework of analysis can be drawn out of the fusion of horizons which is relevant for understanding the successes and obstacles in the transition from violent conflict to peace.[102] Firstly, hermeneutics suggests that a process of transformation leads to changing the identities of the parties involved. Through altering the way the parties see themselves as well as the former enemy, the exclusive structures which gave rise to the conflict are being renegotiated. An assessment should therefore ask whether and how this is happening in a particular war-torn society. How do people explain their own identity group in relation to others? Secondly, the process of changing is subject to how communities remember their past (and hence re-member the community) as well as how they anticipate their future. Research into transformation processes should therefore take these aspects into account through asking what tales are being told with reference to the beginning and experience of the violent conflict? And how do people envisage their future? Thirdly, a transformation process is always susceptible to power hierarchies which determine the outcome. An analysis therefore has to include the evaluation of political, economic and social power relations in both discourse and institutions. And fourthly, the transformation must not introduce a new sense of closure which eradicates diversity, potentially leading to a new conflict. Questions to be raised are whether the shared meaning developed in the process is homogenising or whether it allows for difference. Is the end of reconciliation to make everybody the same, or are communities able to thrive in their diversity?

Based on this framework of analysis the remainder this book investigates to what extent the mediation efforts that terminated the Teso insurgency have led to a re-membering of the Teso society. Do people still define themselves in opposition to the Museveni government? Through analysing how the people of Teso narrated the local history of the causes of the insurgency as well as what role the Mukura war memorial and the newly invented tradition of the cultural leader *Papa Emorimor* play for the constitution of Teso identity, the following chapters shall help us to understand whether peace has been invented successfully.

3
Effective History and the Beginning of the Teso Insurgency

Wirkungsgeschichte, the effect of history, is central to this chapter on the historical background to the Teso insurgency which lasted from 1987 to 1992. In addition to analysing the local developments of the violent conflict it seeks to situate its occurrence in a wider, national context. As argued in Chapter 1, despite some relevance of the concept of 'new wars', the emergence of civil wars in Africa – and elsewhere – remains complex and multi-faceted. In many incidences, the motivation to pick up arms is embedded in cultural, personal and historical aspects so that violent conflicts should be considered as social processes.[1] This also holds true for Uganda where social cleavages and boundaries have been shaped over time and predisposed the country to conflict. Crucial here was, in particular, the experience of British colonial rule due to which people developed alliances and antagonisms that are still of relevance today. In order to explore these developments, this chapter is split into two parts: the first provides an overview of the population groups that live in the region of Teso, the second situates the insurgency into regional and national historical developments from a Teso perspective. Since the people of Teso have never played a major role in national politics, even though they benefited from some governments more than from others, their existence has been largely ignored by historians and anthropologists, leading to a gap in the literature. Nonetheless, despite the poor documentation, a few observations can be made in relation to general trends in the country, which had, and continue to have, repercussions for Teso.

The Teso region of Uganda

Officially recognised today as a sub-region, Teso consists of four districts: Soroti, Kaberamaido, Katakwi and Amuria, as well as formerly

Kumi, and it is inhabited by two different ethnic groups: the Iteso, who derive from the Karamojong, and the Kumam, who are of Luo decent. While they share many cultural traits, their languages and cosmologies differ and even though the two peoples have been living in the same region for generations they still maintain their individuality and distinction. Conflicts between the ethnic groups occur sporadically, however, they are hardly ever violent in scope. Only during the insurgency did the differences lead to mutual persecution and cut a rift through the society that has not yet been reconciled.

Originally, the Kumam and Iteso were cattle herding people. However, especially due to the introduction of cash crops during colonialism, their tradition has gradually changed towards farming and agriculture. The insurgency disrupted this process violently, it left the Iteso and Kumam with merely 7 per cent of their cattle, and Teso has been struggling to find a middle-way between agriculture and livestock since.[2] Compared to western and central Uganda the agricultural and farming conditions of Teso are rather harsh, the climate is hot with little rainfall, and food scarcity after poor rainy seasons is common. The seasonal cattle rustling by the neighbouring Karamojong warriors frequently disrupts the local economy, standing in the way of growth and prosperity.

According to local mythology narratives, the Iteso are decedents of the Turkana who still live in Kenya today. Before the advent of colonialism,

> [t]he Turkana, the Iteso and Karimojong [sic] were living peacefully together in northern Kenya. Whether because of the difficulties in finding pastures, or because of the severity of the winters, they decided to disperse. The Turkana said 'Caves are enough shelter for us, and enough protection from our enemies.' Turkana means 'cave'. The Karimojong said 'We will keep moving until we become withered old men.' *Amojong* means 'old', and *akikar* means 'thin', so that Ngikarimojong means 'those who have become dried up with age'. The Iteso said: 'nor will we close ourselves up in caves until the tomb claims us'. *Ates* means 'tomb', and so they became the Ngiteso, 'those of the tombs'.[3]

Hence the Turkana, so the narrative continues, stayed in Kenya, while the Karamojong and the Iteso moved into what is now known as Uganda. From there, only the Iteso continued their journey westwards until they reached what today referred to as Teso, their exodus is said to have happened between 1600 and 1830.[4] While the story of origin of the people of Teso might sound romantic, it has great significance for the Iteso today. For even though, as the above narrative suggests, it is assumed that the Iteso and the Karamojong are related – 'the Karamojong', so they say, 'are our uncles' – there has always been at times a simmering, at times open degree of hostilities towards the Karamojong neighbours. Since the 'Karamoja problem' had a serious impact on the beginning and development of the insurgency, it is necessary to dwell on it in greater detail.

Karamoja is the largest sub-region of Uganda yet it has the lowest population. Its people are mainly semi-nomadic cattle herders who – if during dry the season water and pasture become too scarce for survival – move their animals to more fertile grounds such as Teso. Even though throughout recorded history the Karamojong have used grazing areas in what is now referred to as Teso sub-region the conflict between Teso and Karamoja over pasture has been intensified by colonial boundary drawing.[5] Significantly, contrary to the Iteso and Kumam, the Karamojong are pure cattle herders with almost no alternative economic or social base but their animals. In Karamoja, therefore, animals mean survival. Water and pasture become matters of security, the loss of animals is the loss of life.

Despite more than a century of engagement, Karamoja has been little affected by Western modernisation. This dates back to British colonialism which neglected the region considerably. Today this causes much resentment among the Karamojong who argue that the British deliberately created a 'human zoo' in which nature – including humans – was kept in its most original state. Furthermore, after independence Karamoja continued to be excluded from the Ugandan polity so that today, it differs significantly regarding its culture and customs, leading to its rather sceptical treatment by many Ugandans and non-Ugandans alike. Numerous myths about Karamoja distort the perception of, and attitude towards, the region.[6] For instance, the Ugandan media often portrays the Karamojong as 'naked savages' and frequently publishes pictures of Karamojong warriors drinking fresh blood from puddles in order to demonstrate their 'beastliness'. Against this backdrop, debates on how to 'civilise' Karamoja are fierce, and opposed by the view that the Karamojong should be granted the right to continue living their life their own way.

Tragically, though, among the most widely available modern objects in Karamoja are firearms, mainly AK47s, which are often used in cattle raids by young warriors. The availability of small arms in the region is due to a number of reasons. In the 1960s and 1970s the Karamojong were subjected to frequent raids by their armed Kenyan ancestors and neighbours, the Turkana, leading to their obtaining guns in the course of the battles. Moreover, when Idi Amin was defeated in 1979, his retreating soldiers left behind a large arsenal of about 30,000 guns which fell in the hands of the Karamojong.[7] In 1985 and 1986 more guns were acquired through the retreat of Obote's troops and the Uganda National Liberation Army (UNLA), so that the availability of guns today is estimated at about 80,000.[8] The supply of small arms is further enhanced by the trafficking of arms more generally throughout the Horn of Africa.

The availability of small arms, as well as the Karamojong warring culture, is a frequent source of conflict in the region. In many cases, the warriors protect as well as acquire cattle through raiding, a custom which predates colonialism. Yet, cattle rustling does not only occur inside of Karamoja but spills over into neighbouring districts such as Teso, occasionally causing the death of Teso herders and farmers.[9] In particular, non-armed communities, such as the Iteso and Kumam, have no chance to defend themselves, let alone to counter-raid in order to return their animals. While the Ugandan government initially ignored the devastating impact of small arms in Karamoja its current policy of disarmament has caused resentment by the Karamojong and criticism by Ugandans more widely. The government's use of heavy artillery and helicopters to intimidate the Karamojong is often rather aggravating and thus counterproductive since it perpetuates the view among Karamojong warriors that they need their guns for protection. Moreover, the weak enforcement of law and order in the region is an obstacle to holding individuals accountable for their offences and to deterring further crimes. As a consequence, the raiding by the Karamojong warriors remains one of the most serious challenges in northern Uganda.

Colonialism in Teso

As already suggested, in order to understand the dynamics of Teso today, it is necessary to understand their historical development. The sub-region was created in 1912 after five years of negotiation between the Iteso and the missionaries residing in Teso. According to Joan Vincent, the establishment of colonial rule saw the introduction of taxes; the growth of an ethnically heterogeneous and racially administered population; the creation of hierarchies of civil service chiefs;[10] mission education; as well as the growth of a small middle sector education.[11] Education, in particular, gained significance in Teso. Until today, the Iteso take pride in their training and education, which has become an important part of the regional identity.[12] Moreover, during and after colonialism, many Iteso gained access to influential administrative positions. As a consequence, today the people of Teso think back to the colonial period as 'the golden age', and it is against this backdrop that the present lack of development is measured.[13] The wealth accumulated in Teso during colonialism was mainly due to the introduction of cash crops – most notably cotton – leading to the development of a labour market in which 20 per cent of Teso men were employed.[14] As we shall see, this radical shift from farming to labour had significant implications for the historical and political development.

On a more general note, British colonialism in Uganda began with the Anglo-German Agreement of 1890 which brought Uganda under the sphere of British influence. Initially, the administration of the country was given to the Imperial British East African Company until, in 1893, Britain took full control of the country's administration and turned it into first a provisional and then an official British Protectorate in 1894.[15] The colonial period was terminated in 1962 when the British Parliament approved a constitution that handed over state power to elite groups 'best trusted to serve the British Interest'.[16] On the 9 October 1962, Uganda finally gained independence. Unsurprisingly, during the 68 years of colonial rule, the political landscape of Uganda had changed dramatically – the repercussions of which are still prevalent today. In this context, Jan Jorgensen has identified two areas in which the British administration had a lasting impact and which are of relevance for the present book: first, the political tension between the kingdom of Buganda and the colonial state of the Uganda Protectorate, and, second, the economic and political tensions due to land ownership and labour reservoirs.[17] In the following I address each of these points in turn.

The political tensions between the different regions in Uganda, firstly, result from a policy of inequality through indirect rule which was practised under colonialism and supported the kingdom of Buganda at the expense of the rest of the country. This established a power asymmetry which still affects the political landscape. The background for ruling indirectly was that

> [c]olonial governments in Africa did not wish to rule by a constant exercise of military force and they needed a wider range of collaborators than those Africans who were brought into the neo-traditions of subordination. In particular, they needed to collaborate with chiefs, headmen and elders in the rural areas.[18]

The attempt to avoid military force was however not an altruistic decision. Rather, it had proved impossible to control the large populations of people in colonised states. In Uganda, for instance, the first six years of British involvement led to three civil wars, which had a devastating impact on the economic benefits of colonising.[19] Consequently, the British realised that colonialism was impossible without the mediation of rules and laws through classes physically located in the colonies and thus opted for indirect rule by involving sections of the colonised population in governing the country.

The people of Buganda, the area around the capital Kampala, became the main vehicles for indirect rule; it was here where Uganda's administrative system was first introduced.[20] In 1900 the (B)Uganda Agreement was signed between the British administrators and the chiefs of Buganda, who were then already literate Christians and allegedly in full understanding of the terms of the treaty.[21] The agreement consisted of three parts: the fixing of Buganda's boundaries; the establishment of indirect rule through the Baganda king *Kabaka*,[22] as well as land settlement. Buganda became an independent province under the British Protectorate, equal in status to the other provinces. In return, the *Kabaka*, his chiefs and his people had to co-operate with the Protectorate governments.[23] Hence, the *Kabaka*, and this was an exception in British colonialism, remained the leader of his people.

The most radical deviation from British colonial practise was however the land settlement which allocated almost half of the land of Buganda to the *Kabaka* and his chiefs.[24] In response to obtaining land, the predominately protestant Baganda chiefs remained loyal to the colonial rulers. Over the years, the so-called Buganda system of administration was extended to other regions of the country so that land agreements and chief appointments of Baganda chiefs started reaching beyond the border of Buganda.[25] Teso, too, became the home of a number of Baganda whose interest was mainly in commerce and who, unlike the Iteso, were permitted to acquire land. The colonial administration benefited from the cultural proximity of the Baganda to the Iteso which turned them into 'intermediaries or brokers for the "civilising mission" of European Christianity and administration',[26] successfully establishing indirect rule. However, due to increasing disagreement and resentment between the Iteso and the Baganda, the colonial rulers were later forced to withdraw the Baganda.

Here, the question poses itself as to why the Baganda received special treatment from the British administration? The, albeit still limited, respect for the Baganda is apparent in the following quote:

> If there is any country forming part in the Uganda Protectorate which could do us any real harm it is Uganda itself – the kingdom of Uganda [i.e., Baganda]. Here we have something like a million fairly intelligent, slightly civilised negroes of warlike tendency, and possessing about 10,000 to 12,000 guns. These are the only people for a long time to come who can deal a serious blow to British rule in this direction.[27]

Furthermore, it has been suggested that the pride of their own monarchy led British colonial anthropologists to classify African societies into either centralised (monarchical) or stateless societies.[28] Against this backdrop, they felt that the monarchical societies resembled 'civilised' European states with a higher degree of cultural development while other societies were seen as savages. In the case of Uganda, the kingdoms of Buganda, Bunyoro, Toro and Ankole, all based in southwest and central Uganda, were thus considered more civilised than the north and the northeast.

It has been argued that the British administrators were furthermore concerned that at least some Africans should become members of the governing class of colonial Africa and they established institutions such as the King's College in Buganda.[29] The education of a political and cultural elite was valued highly, as apparent in the following quote:

> We felt strongly that if the ruling class in the country were to exercise in the days to come an influence for good upon their people and to have a sense of responsibility towards them, it was essential that something should be done for the education of these neglected children, on the soundest possible line... by the disciplines of work and games in boarding school so as to build character as to enable Baganda to take their proper place in the administrative, commercial and industrial life of their own country.[30]

Hence, the king of Buganda, *Kabaka* Mutesa, was inaugurated while still at school at King's College where he stayed until he finished his studies. In addition to his formal education through the British administration the *Kabaka* also joined the Cambridge Officer's Corps, and was later, thanks to the suggestion of King George VI, promoted to the rank of a captain, which was a very rare exception for an African.[31] The role of kingship in Buganda was thus adapted to the British idea of the Crown. As a culture which honoured and respected royalty 'British administrators set about inventing African traditions for Africans', they started codifying and promulgating traditions they considered valuable, thereby transforming flexible customs into hard prescriptions.[32] As for Uganda, it promoted the kingdom of Buganda and turned it into the centre of political power for the whole of the country. While the Baganda enjoyed privileges laid out in the Uganda Agreement of 1900, the rest of the country was governed under the Native Authority Audience of 1919.[33] This imbalance of power between Buganda and the other kingdoms, on one hand, and the rest of Uganda on the other, remains a locus for tensions until today. It introduced major cleavages into the polity.

The second area in which colonialism had a significant impact on present day Uganda was its unequal distribution of land and means of production in different regions of the country, creating economic and political tensions. The Buganda Agreement of 1900 shaped a class of Baganda notables and powerful landlords which resulted in an increasing class division among Ugandans. In an agricultural economy such as Uganda the ownership of land is crucial. Due to the commercialisation of agriculture and the inclusion of Uganda into the world economy a capitalist class developed. Landowners either received taxes from farming tenants or used their land for cash-crop production through paid labour.[34] In the early days of colonialism, while Buganda was economically prosperous from producing export products, cash-crops were discouraged in the northern regions and the land remained in the hands of the Crown. Rather, the north and north-east of the country was turned into a 'labour reservoir'.[35] West Nile, Acholi, Lango and Teso turned into recruitment grounds for not only soldiers, police officers and prison guards, but also administrators, clerks and farm workers. The employment in the security sector, in particular, had a significant impact on the identity of the Teso region, which still prevails today.

The private ownership of large areas of land in the hands of a minority eventually led to the first appearance of landless workers.[36] In addition, due to an increase of labour migrants from Rwanda, comprised of people fleeing the harsh Belgian colonial rule, the national recruitment process came to a sudden halt.[37] The abrupt increase in the number of available workers made parts of the labour force from northern Uganda redundant.

The process of land allocation coincided with the promotion of cash crops, particularly cotton, in Teso in the early 1920s. As we have seen above, the agricultural change from farming to cash crops marked a change in the social make-up and created an even larger workforce. Most Iteso stopped working in the army, the administration or on Baganda farms and started paid labour on Teso farms.[38] In addition, the introduction of oxen ploughs in the late 1930s led to significant changes in the farming of cash crops and to an increase in production and consequently in the wealth of landowners. Plough and oxen owners emerged as the 'Big Men' who owned large parts of land and employed workers for cultivation.[39] For Teso, at the time, cultivating cotton led to increasing prosperity, which today still marks a point of reference. Working in the civil sector remained, nevertheless, important so that in the 1950s traders, teachers and civil servants comprised a significant middle class.[40] Notwithstanding this, the majority of Kumam and Iteso belonged to the work force and, despite modest wealth, there was a large gap between the prosperity of the kingdoms in the south and the district of Teso, resulting in an understanding of Teso identity in opposition to the rich kingdoms. In this sense, too, British colonialism had a significant influence on the Teso identity. As a consequence, at the time of independence in 1962, Uganda was marked by a strong north–south divide. Buganda – as well as to some extent the kingdoms of Bunyoro, Toro and Ankole – were characterised by wealth, prosperity and a high level of education.[41] The rest of the country, however, became more and more impoverished. Even though, in 1962, Uganda was rated one of the most promising economies on the African continent, it remained highly unstable politically.

On the eve of Independence, five parties emerged as contenders for the future leadership of country:[42] the Uganda National Congress, which later turned into the Uganda People Congress (UPC), the Progressive Party (PP), the Democratic Party (DP) and the *Kabaka Yekka* ('*Kabaka* Only', KY). Significantly, the newly formed parties did not reflect a rise of national interest – or a national identity – but rather ethnic, religious and regional divisions. Among the parties that consolidated over time, the UPC had a strong socialist profile and was affiliated with the Northern regions, the DP was strongly Catholic and anti-communist and could draw on large support in Buganda, whereas the KY, established in response to the DP, was Baganda, strongly loyalist and did not recognise any person as superior to the king *Kabaka*. In 1962, the British colonial rulers handed over Uganda to the parties they thought were best suited to govern the country. Buganda and the *Kabaka* maintained a privileged status to the extent that Buganda was granted federal status in relation to the central government.[43]

Independent Uganda

In the first years after independence, Uganda's political parties operated in a multi-party framework. In 1962, the UPC, under the leadership of Milton Obote from Lango in the north, formed an alliance with KY in order to increase its strength against the DP in the first Ugandan elections. As anticipated, the UPC won the majority of the seats outside of Buganda while the KY emerged as the strongest party from inside.[44] Based on the Westminster model, the UPC/KY coalition formed the first government with Milton Obote as the Prime Minister and *Kabaka* Mutesa as President. The harmony between UPC and KY was, however, short-lived: within a few years the ideological and political discrepancies defeated pragmatism and led to a civil constitutional coup in 1966. The coup culminated in the Battle of Mengo, in which the army under Idi Amin defeated the Baganda, killing at least one thousand people and leaving a lasting hatred for Obote among the Baganda.[45] After the *Kabaka* had fled to the UK Obote imposed a unitary constitution, appointing himself as the President of Uganda. One year later, he abolished all kingdoms and rendered Uganda a republic. Uganda's new constitution eliminated the federal status and independent powers of the former kingdoms, as well as all Baganda privileges, and consolidated the power around the president. Obote justified this radical shift by arguing that this would de-ethnicise politics, although he achieved the opposite.[46] The dissatisfaction in Buganda, and in the southern regions in general, forced Obote to rely more and more on military force to secure his power. Moreover, he increasingly adopted left-wing policies culminating in his policy 'Move to the Left' in 1969. In 1970, he nationalised Uganda's 85 leading companies, an action which was not appreciated by the former British colonial rulers, abolished strikes and attacked feudalism as well as the Buganda hegemony.[47] Based on his anti-feudalist policies Teso turned into one of Obote's strongholds.

While Obote was preoccupied with introducing new politics to Uganda, as well as struggling against an increasing ethnic divide, the greatest threat to his presidency emerged from his own ranks. The creation of northern Uganda as a labour reservoir by the colonial administration had led to the fact that most of his soldiers derived from the north. However, despite regional similarities ethnic tensions between the different northern groups soon developed.[48] In particular, disputes grew between soldiers from Acholi and Lango (the latter Obote's ethnic group) on one hand, and the people from West Nile on the other, leading to increasing personal mistrust between Obote and his army commander from West Nile, Idi Amin.[49] In a surprising move, while Obote had left the country to attend a Commonwealth meeting in January 1971, Amin took over power.

In the first instance, particularly in Buganda, Amin's coup was welcomed.[50] He returned the dead body of the *Kabaka*, who had died in exile, released prisoners and was widely hailed as 'a man of peace'.[51] This situation was however short-lived and Amin started governing the country in a reign of terror and unimaginable cruelty.[52] After three months in power, Amin 'suspended all democratic rights, gave the army dictatorial powers of arrest and punishment, and set up a military tribunal to try political offenders'.[53] Contrary to most regions of Uganda, Teso was little affected by Amin's terror regime. People continued their lives without showing any political ambitions and successfully avoided falling into Amin's discredit.

The international community followed the developments in Uganda with shock and horror, yet it was a more immediate neighbour who came to the countries defence. Amin's politics finally went one step too far when he annexed 1800 square miles of Tanzanian territory, alienating President Nyerere who had already been an outspoken critic of the dictator.[54] In Tanzania, a group of exiled Ugandans formed the Uganda National Liberation Army (UNLA) and united with the Tanzanian People's Defence Force (TPDF). They invaded Uganda jointly in 1979 leading to Amin's flight to Saudi Arabia. Amin's defeat was followed by two short periods of governance. Yusuf Lule (UNLA) only stayed in office for 69 days until political intrigues, paired with his lack of experience in political leadership, led to his removal.[55] His successor Godfrey Binaisa fell prey to a bloodless coup by the military regime of Paulo Muwaga in 1980, which opened the path to general elections in the same year.

The main contending parties in the elections were the two major traditional parties, the DP with much support in the south and the UPC which could draw mainly on voters from the northern regions. In addition, the Conservative Party (CP) and the Uganda Patriotic Movement under Yoweri Museveni competed in the elections. When Obote's UPC won the election he became President of Uganda for the second time.[56] His success was, however, strongly contested by his opponents, accusing him of rigging the elections. Against this backdrop, Museveni – despite his party having performed rather poorly in the election – founded the National Resistance Movement (NRM), and its military wing the National Resistance Army (NRA), and launched an insurgency war in a region called Luwero, which soon became known as the Luwero Triangle or the Luwero war.

Two different accounts are on offer to explain the beginning of Museveni's guerrilla warfare.[57] First, people from the north argue that Museveni took up arms to end the succession of northern rule of the country. Since *Kabaka* Mutesa fled into exile, Uganda had been ruled by people from the northern districts. Museveni – himself from Ankole in the southwest – represented the section of the country which had been privileged by the colonial rulers but which had not been in power since independence. Second, and in contrast, the people around Museveni argue that Uganda had in the past suffered from oppressive regimes and that the elections had been seen as a window of hope for a democratic government, but that Obote's rigging of the elections had brought these ambitions to a halt. For them, NRM/A guerrilla warfare was hence the only alternative.

During the Luwero insurgency, the Kumam and Iteso fought side by side with the Acholi and Langi in Obote's UNLA. In line with colonial traditions and political affiliations Obote had recruited his army staff predominately among the northern and north-eastern ethnic groups. Yet, after several years of fighting against Museveni, Obote faced strong tensions inside his army and was accused by the Acholi of favouring his own ethnic group, the Langi. The tensions culminated in a military coup in 1985, which gave way to the military council of Tito Okello and Bazilio Olara Okello. However, with the Okello government in place disunity persisted in Uganda. The new government's instability forced it into negotiations with the NRM, resulting in the Nairobi Peace Accord in late-1985. Despite the Nairobi Accord, Museveni's troops launched a final attack in January 1986, which led to the successful seizure of Kampala and the subsequent installation of the NRM as the new government. By March of the same year, the NRA/M had gained control of the whole country. Defeated in their struggle the Kumam and Iteso UNLA soldiers retreated eastwards towards their homes where they sceptically awaited the course the new government would take. Many returned to their villages and families.

The beginning of the insurgency

Among the left-wing African elites Museveni's victory was celebrated and praised, as portrayed in the following words:

> The Uganda Revolution is... politically and morally the most signifi-
> cant event that has happened in Africa since the Ghana victory; and
> there is no doubt that in the next few years it will establish itself
> as having had a much more profound and far-reaching impact on

Africa's history than even Ghana's. Ghana was the first place, and Uganda the second in the long march to genuinely free Africa.[58]

For many at the time, Museveni personified the end of post-colonial influence and the beginning of a new area. Yet not everybody in Uganda felt liberated and armed resistance developed rapidly. In 1986, a group of UNLA soldiers fled to Sudan and regrouped as Uganda People's Democratic Army/Movement (UPDA/M); pro-Amin rebels gathered in West Nile and formed the West Nile Bank Front (WNBF); in western Uganda the Allied Democratic Front (ADF) came into existence; and in Acholi a women called Alice Lakwena started the Holy Spirit Movement which has now turned into Joseph Kony's Lord's Resistance Army (LRA). And yet, at least in the first phase of the NRM government a policy of reconciliation prevailed and the exiled political leadership was encouraged to return to Uganda.[59] The rationale was to 'bring the enemies in' and to give them a prestigious public office in order to prevent them from turning against the Movement. In the early stages, the NRM policy of reconciliation contributed significantly to taming potential political opponents.[60]

As for Teso, Museveni's takeover was initially welcome. The cattle raiding by the Karamojong warriors had accelerated in 1985–1986; allegedly, it had been supported by the Okellos who used it as a means of intimidating the Iteso and Kumam, and the new Museveni government was expected to put an end to the neighbours' assaults. From the NRM government's side there was also no initial antagonism against the Iteso and Kumam. The resentment was rather directed against the Acholi, as manifested in a radio speech by Museveni in which he explained that his quarrel was not with the Obote soldiers but with the 'Okellos'. 'Okellos' served as a synonym for Acholi.[61] Nevertheless, the positive climate changed within a few months and mutual mistrust grew gradually, in particular, because immediately after Museveni seized power he began to reorganise the public sector.[62] As a consequence, vast numbers of civil servants were made redundant, and since Teso had, during Obote's regime, provided a substantial portion of the police, prison and military staff, unemployment affected the region severely. Moreover, it was one of Museveni's priorities to reorganise the national army and to demobilise ex-combatants:

[W]e had realised that once we came to power it would be necessary to do away with the old colonial-style army which had been recruited along sectarian lines and manipulated by unscrupulous politicians and directors. Therefore, immediately after the fall of Kampala we started organising a new national army.[63]

The ex-combatants in Teso learned about their demobilisation through a radio announcement in 1986/1987 in which they were asked to report to the local administration to hand in their guns.[64] This message, however, provoked negative recollections: when Idi Amin came to power in 1971 he broadcast a similar announcement, and when the soldiers arrived at the administration offices to deliver their arms many were tortured or executed. Consequently, in 1986, the Kumam and Iteso ex-soldiers feared that these atrocities would be repeated, and that they would be punished for having fought Museveni in the Luwero Triangle. Instead of reporting to the authorities many kept their arms and hid in the villages.

Furthermore, in 1981 Obote had introduced a paramilitary police force, called the Special Forces, where 5000 of the 8000 recruits originated from Teso.[65] The Special Forces were under the direct control of the Minister of State of Internal Affairs, Col. Omaria, himself an Etesot. They had played an instrumental role in Obote's regime, and they were all well trained professional combatants. During the Luwero bush war the Special Forces became notorious for their brutality and aggression against the NRA and other insurgents. As a result, one of Museveni's first political decisions was to disband the Special Forces, yet many of its members struggled with the fact of being made redundant.[66] In addition, parallel to regular Kumam and Iteso soldiers and the Special Forces a third military group was demobilised. During Obote's regime a militia had been established with the objective to guard the borders between Karamoja and its neighbours in order to deter cattle raiding and to guarantee the safety of Kumam and Iteso farmers and herders. Museveni's interpretation of the militia was however different:

> During the Obote II regime, UPC politicians complicated the [Karamoja] problem further by creating a tribal militia in Acholi and Teso which, in turn, raided Karamoja and counter-plundered.[67]

Regardless of the moral integrity of the militia, its removal from the Karamoja border in 1986–1987 opened the way for the Karamojong warriors to enter and raid Teso to an extent previously unknown.

All in all, the scale of the demobilisation of combatants from Teso was considerable and left the Kumam and Iteso with a feeling of mistrust. Since many of them had played a significant role in the Luwero war they took a very personal stance in relation to the new government's actions and interpreted it as punishment for their support of Obote. Such was the atmosphere in Uganda and Teso at the beginning of Museveni's leadership. In north and north-east Uganda peace was very fragile. Although the NRM made an effort to assure people that its intention was to unite the country, it was unsuccessful in establishing trust. Armed warfare began in Teso and Acholi. While in Teso it continued until 1992, for the Acholi it still has not been terminated.

What actually caused the Teso insurgency is the subject of numerous different interpretations of the past which shall be recounted separately in Chapter 5. Importantly, though, the civil war was imbedded in social and historical continuities which can be traced back at least to colonialism, indicating a continuation with old wars rather than being a 'new war'.[68] Local support for armed struggle was vast – in fact in the whole of Uganda resistance against the NRA was the strongest among the people of Teso and the Acholi[69] – however not everybody was prepared to actively engage in the fighting. But those who were fit for combat were given little chance: either the rebels forced them to join the struggle in the 'bush' or they were forcefully recruited into the NRA. For an adult male to stay inactively in the village was impossible since he was immediately suspected of either collaborating with the army or with the rebels. Thus many men were drawn into combat even though they would not have participated out of their own initiative.[70] Those who did not want to be involved in the insurgency had no choice but to leave Teso for safer grounds. As we shall see later, the support of the society more widely was mobilised with reference to the cattle raiding of the Karamojong, alleging the involvement of the NRA. Even in churches, priests and clergymen used their position to insist on the necessity to fight against the government. This led to the shared belief that injustice was committed against the Iteso and Kumam and enabled the collective mobilisation of the population. As a result 'everybody was a rebel', either actively in the bush or in a supporting role such as through cooking and catering.[71] At least in the early days, women, children and elders, who remained in the villages, did their best to assist 'the boys'.

Militarily, the rebels had little chance to succeed against the NRA. In addition to the NRA's technical superiority, it pursued radical strategies such as a ruthless scorched earth policy, the splitting of rebel groups into small, regional units confined to their areas of operation, and the obstruction of arms supply from abroad, leaving the Teso rebels with little hope of victory. In Kumi, they forcefully encamped the civil population for six months to separate the rebels from the non-combatants.[72] In an environment of violent conflict the heavy loss of human and material capacities leads to two alternative conclusions: either the combatants feel that they have already lost a lot and that they owe it to the cause and their fallen comrades to continue. Or they realise that their chances for victory are too slim and that they should avoid increasing their loss and surrender. In Teso, the second sentiment prevailed so that the rebels, one after the other, came out of the 'bush'. It is estimated that the NRA itself absorbed 10,000 rebels. Many turned from fighting against the NRA on one day to fighting with the NRA on the next. Against this backdrop, the reasons generally given for the end of the violent struggle in Teso are twofold: first, it was recognised that the rebels were too weak to topple the government, and second, the suffering was so fierce that people were not prepared to endure it for much longer.[73] At first sight, these two explanations resemble a defeat and many people in Teso today indeed feel they were outplayed by the NRA/M. However, as we shall see in the following chapter, the end of the Teso insurgency was more nuanced than simple surrender and a number of actors, including the government and indigenous actors, contributed to the termination.

One of the central assumptions of this book is that violent conflict is deeply embedded in historical and social continuities that run through a society and that influence the mutual perception of the parties to the conflict. Consequently, this chapter has sought to situate the emergence of the Teso insurgency into the country's wider social and historical contexts, that is, its effective history. In particular, this implies understanding the impact of colonial, in particular indirect, rule on national cleavages and their cementation into party politics after independence. Against this backdrop, the end of the Teso insurgency needs to be considered to the extent to which it challenged and changed the structures of 'us' and 'them' that ran through the society. Did the termination of the fighting address these cleavages? Did it lead to social change? We shall turn to these questions in the following chapter.

Uganda under Museveni

Before continuing with the Teso insurgency it is insightful to briefly explore the wider national developments in Uganda. With Museveni's victory the country was subject to considerable change. Most importantly, with the stated objective to facilitate the democratisation process Museveni introduced an alternative governance and administration system. On a local, institutional level, the government set up a system of Resistance Councils (RCs) which operated on village, parish, sub-county, county and district level and which had special provisions for women, the youth and the military.[74] Instead of a multi-party system Museveni thus opted for a socialist-inspired no-party system. Through direct elections at the village and indirect at higher levels the population at large was drawn into the decision-making process, enabling them to influence communal politics. Although their executive power was limited, the RCs nevertheless provided some scope to criticise the activities of central and local authorities and, at least, in the early days after Museveni's usurpation of power, it was argued that the RC system had a crucial impact on the process of reconciliation and integration.[75] On a national level, multi-party politics was replaced by the NRM, or in short 'the Movement'. Museveni justified his Movement system by arguing that much of the violence in Uganda had been caused by competitive party politics reflecting the division of the nation, and that his Movement would lead to the integration of all citizens. Although political parties were allowed to exist, they were prohibited from organising public meetings, rendering them ineffective. Museveni appointed a broad-based and ethnically diverse government, including former opponents, yet accusations quickly abounded that the real power remained in the hands of his inner circle.

Even though the NRM initially referred to itself as interim administration it extended its transition status until 1996 when the first presidential elections were held, leading to a clear victory for Museveni.[76] Since parties were not allowed to contest in the elections, the campaign was between individuals as presidential contenders. In 2000, Ugandans had the opportunity to vote in a referendum on whether they wanted to keep the Movement system or resort to multi-party politics, and chose the former. Nevertheless, resentment about Museveni's strong position and his grip on power grew steadily, both among Ugandans and from within the Movement. His main contender in the 2001 election thus came from his inner circle: Kizza Besigye gained 28 per cent of the votes while Museveni gained 69 per cent. Even though Besigye had fought side-by-side with Museveni during the Luwero war, and had been close to his centre of power, he accused the Movement of being undemocratic, dishonest and corrupt. As the only viable alternative to Museveni, and despite originating from southern Uganda, he drew on wide support from the North. Against growing resentment towards the Movement system, violent protests in Kampala and considerable international pressure, Museveni called for a second referendum in 2005 in which voters overwhelmingly supported the return to multi-party politics. This coincided with the strongly Movement-influenced parliament approving a constitutional amendment which terminated presidential term limits, enabling Museveni to turn the Movement into a political party and to stand for a third term in office. In 2006, Museveni won Uganda's first multi-party elections since 1980 with 59 per cent of the votes, while Besigye gained 37 per cent. In the run up to the elections, Besigye was arrested, intimidated and obstructed, and his staff threatened and exiled.

From a developmental perspective, following Museveni's victory in 1986 Uganda's war-affected economy recovered significantly. His often very pragmatic approach led him to re-evaluate his initial, socialist-inspired economic agenda and to accept the support of the IMF and the World Bank to reconstruct the country. This has led to an increase in privatisation, even though transparency has often been overshadowed by corruption and nepotism. Nevertheless, against the backdrop of Uganda's violent past, the country is often hailed as the economic success story of Africa and it was the first country to benefit from the Heavily Impoverished Poor Country Initiative (HIPC) dept relief in 2000. Uganda's economic success is however not equally distributed. The northern and eastern regions, in particular, remain marginalised and impoverished, women remain traditionally excluded from wealth, class differences prove to be insurmountable, particularly when linked to landownership and education, and a clear urban/rural divide prevails.

The international community and violent conflicts in Uganda

For the past two decades, Uganda has been strongly favoured by many Western donors who therefore carry some responsibility for the development of the country. At the beginning of Museveni's presidency in the late-1980s, the international community showed little interest in assisting conflict transformation in post-conflict societies – the paradigm simply was not fashionable at the time. His early years did however coincide with the first efforts by IMF and World Bank, and subsequently other Western donors, to promote economic liberalisation in Africa. The considerable success of these programmes in Uganda turned it into an African role model and became rather important for international agencies: against the backdrop of less successful interventions elsewhere, Uganda served to prove that it was not the donors' liberalisation approach itself which was inadequate, but the manner in which it was executed in the respective countries.[77] However, international assistance was limited to particular regions, widening the wealth gap between the centre and the south on one hand and the north and the east on the other. Inadvertently, thus, the international community perpetuated the economic imbalance introduced by the colonialists, contributing to deepening the fissures between north and south.

Compared with the donors' strong influence on the economy, for a considerable amount of time they revealed little interest in interfering in the post-conflict reconstruction process. Satisfied with their achievements in the economic realm, they hardly ever criticised the government for its domestic politics. Many donors concentrated on technical, supposedly apolitical assistance in the field of institution building, while the division of the country and the ongoing conflicts in the north and east were ignored. Even though most donors disapproved with the Movement system, or at least its execution, and considered it to be undemocratic, they refrained from linking political change with development conditionalities.[78] Instead, some opted for a 'soft diplomacy' approach through informal dialogue.

With the democratisation process coming to a standstill at the beginning of the 21st century, the international community underwent a considerable shift. Individual donors started resorting to sanctions such as freezing pledged funds[79] (about half of Uganda's budget comes from international donors), for example, in response to the UN's accusations of Ugandan troops looting minerals in the DR Congo (2002),[80] after violent protests and the amending of the constitution to enable Museveni to stand for a third term in office (2005), and over the arrest of the presidential contender Besigye (2006).

The lack of donor interest in conflicts in Uganda is surprising if one considers that one of Africa's longest insurgencies has been talking place in the north of the country. In the region of the Acholi, where the LRA under Joseph Kony has been fighting the government to install a regime based on the Ten Commandments, about 12,000 people have been killed by insurgents and government troops. Moreover, many Acholi have died due to appalling living conditions in Internally Displaced People (IDP) camps, where about 2 Million people (90 per cent of the population) are forcefully encamped. Given that the Acholi, similar to the people from Teso, have been historically opposed to Museveni's government, its lack of initiatives to bring the violence to an end, or its at times disproportionate aggression against the LRA, have been widely interpreted as a strategy to keep the Acholi at bay. When in September 2002 the Ugandan government launched its military campaign *Iron Fist* to exterminate the LRA, the fighting accelerated dramatically, leading to the displacement of almost the entire Acholi population into camps. Moreover, for the first time the LRA ventured into the neighbouring sub-regions. As a result of these incursions, large sections of the Teso and Lango population were displaced into IDP camps in the districts of Lira and Apac in Lango, as well as of Kaberamaido, Katakwi, Amuria and Soroti in Teso.

At its peak, the camp population in northern Uganda reached a total of 1.7 million people.[81]

Only after considerable international pressure – in 2004, the UN Under-Secretary General for Humanitarian Affairs called the conflict the world's 'largest neglected humanitarian emergency'[82] and threatened to bring the case before the UN Security Council if the government remained idle – was a ceasefire agreement signed in August 2006. After more than two decades of violent conflict in the North, recent political developments have generated some optimism about the possibility of a peace accord between the LRA and the Government of Uganda. In 2006, talks in Juba resulted in a cessation of LRA hostilities and an improvement in the security situation of northern Uganda. As a result, in Lango since mid-2006 IDPs have started to return home, while Teso is experiencing some delay due to renewed cattle rustling by Karamojong warriors. However, negotiations have since come to a standstill, not least because the International Criminal Court (ICC) has issued arrest warrants for Kony and his inner circle on the charges of having committed war crimes, which has created an impediment in their willingness to surrender.

The threats by the UN Under-Secretary General to bring the situation of the Acholi in the North before the UN Security Council had a decisive impact in alerting donors to what has been happing before their eyes for almost 20 years, as well as on advancing peace talks with the LRA. Since then, there has been an increasing awareness among donors that the Northern and Eastern regions of the country have so far been largely excluded from their development assistance and some agencies have been taking steps to launch programmes, for example, to reduce the prevalence of Small Arms and Light Weapons (SALW) in Karamoja. After years of inactivity regarding Uganda's democratisation process, it appears that the international community has now realised its own responsibility and its potential to exert some pressure.

4
Mediation and the Creation of Peace in Teso

Central to the termination of the Teso insurgency were methods based on traditional conflict management. The mediations by various formal and informal agents were hybrids between customary mechanism as discussed in Chapter 1 and modernised and institutionalised practise. The objective of this chapter is to analyse these initiatives and to assess whether they led to the transformation of the violent conflict. In line with Giddens's structuration theory, it investigates whether the various agents who mediated the end of the insurgency were successful in changing the structural properties of inclusion and exclusion that gave rise to the insurgency. Did they have an impact on rendering the dichotomy between the Museveni government on one hand and the Iteso and Kumam on the other less exclusive? Did they re-member the Teso society? In order to reply to these questions, I first develop an understanding of mediation based on hermeneutics. This shall serve as a backdrop against which to evaluate the mediation process in Teso focusing on how it terminated the fighting, who the main agents were and if and how it changed people's motivation from war to peace.

Mediation as creation

As we have seen in Chapter 1, approaches to conflict settlement and conflict resolution are based on the assumption that conflicts are caused by the pursuit of incompatible goals and interests, or unsatisfied needs. In response, efforts to end violent conflicts take the form of problem-solving workshops where the parties to a conflict join together to find solutions and agreements which cover all interests and satisfy all needs. With the aid of a third party as facilitator, an atmosphere is created which allows the parties to the conflict to constructively manage their disagreements. Problem-solving workshops seek to create a non-distorted and reciprocal communication so that the participants can realise where their problems 'really' lie.[1] Consequently, they are situated in a political tradition which assumes a certain set of underlying normative principles including the rational agency of the parties to the conflict and that the parties can divest themselves of their particular social-historical background.

In Chapter 1, I showed that these principles have recently been challenged. In response to the shortcomings of problem-solving workshops, this book suggests an alternative conceptualisation of approaches to conflict management. Such a conception bears some similarity to what has been referred to as 'narrative mediation' in which the complex social contexts that shape conflicts are considered.[2] Focusing on the constitutive properties of conflict stories, narrative mediation does not evaluate whether a story is true or factual but rather how it constitutes the parties to the conflict as enemies.[3] A narrative approach to mediation is deeply imbedded in an understanding of individual and collective identity as constructed over space and time. Different from conflict settlement and conflict resolution approaches, it is profoundly cultural in orientation for it assumes that different people perceive reality – and thus conflicts – in different ways and that every resolution has to take this into account.[4] In this sense, in narrative mediation the mediators seek to open up a space among the tightly woven stories of the opponents in order to allow for different, less totalising, descriptions of events.[5] From the perspective of the mediator, understanding stories requires a set of theoretical assumptions, including (a) that social processes (negotiation) are both dynamic and interactive – stories emerge in interaction; (b) that problematic stories are transformed in interaction; (c) that the transformation of stories requires reflection and inquiry with others, over time; and (d) that fostering inquiry (in self and others) is facilitated by appreciative and legitimising moves in interaction, rather than negative and delegitimizing moves.[6] Hence, according to this narrative perspective, mediation processes change both story and (the perception of) reality.

In this sense, while contributions to the field of mediation are often limited in scope by only focusing on workshops and third party intervention, in this book the term 'mediation' covers a much broader and complex notion.[7] Mediation is used synonymously with Gadamer's notion of *fusing horizons* and includes, similar to narrative mediation, aspects of social transformation and change. As argued in Chapter 2, in a war-torn society the parties to the conflict have to develop new ways of relating to each other, without the tensions of the past. Therefore, the process of mediation – or fusion of horizons – requires a degree of creativity to invent new identities and to re-member the society. Mediation is hence a poetic process of creating something new out of what has been.[8] In this sense, mediation happens always and everywhere, it is ontological in character and a core feature of life. Thus, in the words of Gilles Deleuze:

> Mediators are fundamental. Creation is all about mediators. Without them nothing happens. They can be people ... but things too. Whether they're real or imaginary, animated or inanimate, you have to form your mediators. It's a series. If you're not in some series, even a completely imaginary one, you're lost. I need my mediators to express myself, and they'd never express themselves without me: you are always working within a group, even when you seem to be working on your own.[9]

Deleuze draws our attention to the perennial influences and impulses we are exposed to and which lead us to mediate and change our identity. We thus constantly change who we are and what we aspire to. In analogy, communities are also in constant transformation. As argued by Vattimo, rather than being closed and isolated they move with their horizons.[10] In the odd time in-between war and peace, the poetic character of mediation provides the possibility for fundamentally changing the boundaries which the violent conflict sought to challenge. In the following, I therefore analyse whether the traditional mediation efforts in Teso have encouraged the emergence of alternative narratives about the insurgency.

Mediation in Teso

The Teso insurgency was mediated by a number of different actors who were all indigenous to Uganda or even to the region itself. This contributed significantly to their success since traditional mediation is most likely to be effective between people whose various residential and kinship ties require them to deal with one another in the future. For 'when social relationships are enduring, disputants need to find a settlement to continue to live together amicably'.[11] In the following, I describe the actions taken by the government, the army, the Presidential Commission for Teso (PCT), churches, women and elders. Of these agents, only the Presidential Commission qualifies as a third-party mediator in the classical sense. Nevertheless, even though the impact of the other actors was much less formal and organised they played a significant role in changing the perception held by the Iteso and Kumam of the government.

Even though the mediation process was conducted by Ugandans it was not entirely without external influence. Based in the UK, a group of people who had formerly worked in the region and who had maintained very close ties with their Iteso colleagues and friends learned about the strikes against Teso and launched a publicity campaign. The former director of Ngora hospital, John Maitland, criticised the Ugandan government in a letter published in *The Independent* newspaper and in a BBC interview for the NRA atrocities. In his newspaper letter Maitland wrote:

> [I]n Teso, where the military crackdown took place, promises will not convince a population embittered by years of military confrontation. The 'cordon and search' operations... combined with the visitations by rebel militia and raiders from the north, have devastated a once economically self-sufficient area. One and a half million people from Teso are suffering from severe poverty, malnutrition and disease. They have lost everything – homes, crops, schools, cattle, clinics and social structures.[12]

Maitland's BBC interview was heard all over Uganda and the Ugandan media picked up the story. Museveni's response in an interview was rather confident:

> This morning there was an interview with somebody who said he was a chairman of Teso relief committee and he alleged that NRA was carrying out a scorched earth policy. I wonder what your comment on this is?
>
> [Museveni] But you know those fellows are just talking stories. Our work is to crush the bandits, which we have done in the whole of the north; and this small area of Kumi, where they will remain, you are going to crush them. So, the sympathisers of the bandits will have to talk on BBC since the BBC is available to them. But for us, we shall do our work.
>
> These are our people. You know how many chairmen we lost, the RCs? But you have been hearing the chairman, you see what has been happening when the people elect a chairman, the bandits come and kill him. They elect another bandit [as heard], they come and kill him. So they (?are wanting) to destroy our democratic institutions. And we can't allow that to happen. We are also going to crush them.

Once you kill people, and that is what we have done in the north, that is why you hear the north is now peaceful. Now this small area of Kumi which was remaining, we are also going to crush them. Now, if they go to BBC and BBC sympathises with them, we have also got our own radio here. So, our radio doesn't go very far. It just ends here around the lake [presumably Lake Victoria]. But that is good enough, eh, it is good enough.[13]

In addition, the British Foreign and Commonwealth Office (FCO) became aware of the violence in north-east Uganda. At the time of the insurgency, Grace Akello, a politician from Teso, was resident in the UK where she, together with her British friends from the Teso Relief Committee, organised a demonstration against Museveni in Whitehall.[14] The adverse publicity in the UK was very inconvenient for Uganda since Museveni, who had just seized power, relied heavily on the support of international donors. The UK was, and still is, one of the country's biggest donors and a pronounced advocate of Museveni's government, so that a public demonstration in London had the potential to harm this relationship. As a result, Museveni contacted Grace Akello in London and sent a small delegation of senior government members to discuss the insurgency.[15] He invited Akello to return to her country and to take up the position of the secretary of the PCT which was launched to mediate between the government and the Iteso and the Kumam. Akello accepted, albeit reluctantly.[16]

With both the beginning and the end of the insurgency being very local processes it is important to wonder whether Museveni would have offered his gesture of mediation through the Teso Commission had it not been for the international pressure. In many cases, local uprisings and violent dissent remain unnoticed, and thus often futile, as long as the government's military can keep the insurgency at bay. International recognition, however, lends a voice to the insurgents and is therefore a very important mechanism.

The government

All in all, the government launched a number of different initiatives to end the conflict in Teso. Twice it sent mediators, first in the form of three ministers and then in the form of the Teso Commission, as illustrated below. Crucially, the mediators did not represent independent external facilitators but they were closely tied to the Teso community where they assumed the role of persons of integrity usually reserved for elders. This provided them with a powerful role and it carried the expectation that they would have the interests of the Teso community at heart. Today it is difficult to assess why Museveni sought to establish peace in Teso. One possible explanation is that the NRA was already preoccupied with fighting Alice Lakwena and the Holy Spirit Movement in the north of Uganda and that it did not have sufficient means to fight two insurgencies at the same time. In addition, it has been suggested that Museveni severely underestimated the size of the insurgency in Teso and that he did not consider it as a serious threat.[17] Museveni's advisors at the time downplayed its importance by telling him that he should not think of Teso in terms of 'a rebellion', but rather mere anarchy, for the rebels had no motivation to topple the government.[18] There was never an ideological struggle and the UPC, as the strongest regional party, did not offer an alternative political programme to the NRM on how to govern Uganda. In the eyes of the government, the cause was local, and so were the targets.[19] Although the rebels in Teso would have resented this explanation and denigration of their violent struggle, it might have helped to prevent the augmenting of the NRA's actions against Teso. The conception of the insurgency as insignificant might have aided the fact that the government was willing to reach out to the people in Teso and to offer a cease-fire.

Nonetheless, some efforts were made to build basic trust between the Iteso and the Kumam on one hand and the new government on the other, such as a general amnesty for all rebels. The Amnesty Statute included the following elements:[20]

– amnesty for all persons within or without Uganda who were fighting as combatants or aiding the prosecution of war in any other way.
– amnesty for all members of former armies, fighting groups, former police forces, prison services and state securities.
– report and surrender of all weapons of these groups.
– resettlement of 'reporters'.

Today, many ex-rebels refer to the Amnesty Statute as an important incentive for their surrender since it provided them with a safety net and gave them an opportunity to admit that their going to the bush had become a failure. Thanks to the Amnesty Statute they could make this step reversible without being harmed and punished. Moreover, for many young rebels the lack of employment opportunities and future perspectives had been a driving force to join the insurgency. Yet after a few years in the bush they realised the danger and hardship of being a combatant. The financial rewards promised when joining the rebels never materialised, leading to a feeling of disillusion and deception. When the government reached out to them through offering financial rewards and employment in the NRA if they only surrendered, the youth suddenly had a new and positive outlook on the future. Consequently, they surrendered in large numbers and many were absorbed into the army or police forces. It was particularly the work of the Teso Commission that encouraged this so-called reporting, as illustrated below.[21]

The 1st peace initiative

The first initiative undertaken by the government in late 1987 – under the guidance of Ministers of State Ateker Ejalu and Paul Etjan, the former Kumam and the latter Etesot – was comprised of three Iteso ministers: Minister of Labour S. K. Okurut, Deputy Minister of Animal Industry Dr Okol Aporu and Minister Ekino.[22] However, the initiative soon encountered difficulties. Despite worries about their safety, in 1988 the three ministers travelled to Soroti town where they were met by the Anglican Bishop Illukor to discuss the insurgency. Since the meeting went well, the three ministers continued their journey to Kumi town where they received a surprising message that they were expected to meet with members of the Rebel High Command at a location in Ngora. The ministers went, accompanied by two priests. At their arrival they were immediately brought to the Serere Research Station where they realised that they had walked into a trap and had been taken hostage by the rebels. They remained in captivity for two years. In the end, Ekino died in the course of the liberation under mysterious circumstances; Apuro passed away shortly after his release which has aroused suspicions of poisoning,[23] while Okurut has failed to have a successful political career ever since.

According to the report of a rebel eyewitness to the detention of the hostages in Ngora, the ministers' attitude towards the rebels was characterised by arrogance and superiority.[24] Before the meeting, Okurut, a former prominent UPC politician, had allegedly called the rebels 'thugs and thieves without any political agenda' on the national radio station. The group of ministers thus received little respect, and a great deal of resentment, from the rebels. There was a general feeling that, even though they were of Iteso decent, the ministers were little concerned about the cause of the insurgency and the suffering and plight of the people of Teso, but rather only interested in their personal political careers and the good-life in Kampala.[25] Hence, what contributed significantly to the failure of the mission was that the ministers had no integrity as mediators in the eyes of the Rebel High Command.

The 2nd peace initiative: The Teso commission

The most successful initiative to end the Teso insurgency was the Presidential Commission for Teso. Comprised only of local people, it crossed a bridge between the two adversaries: the people from Teso and the Museveni government. Again hand-picked by the Minister of State Ateker Ejalu in 1990, the Teso Commission consisted of a number of respected Iteso.[26] Apart from Grace Akello as the Secretary it included Prof. Opio-Epelu as Chairperson, later Deputy Vice Chancellor of Makerere University, James Eceret, an economist, Mzee Oguli, who later managed the PCT office in Soroti, as well as secretaries, drivers and local assistants.

While the first initiative lacked credibility, the composition of the Teso Commission immediately earned a reputation for its integrity and credibility, even though it was clearly operating on behalf of the government. As Akello noted:

> Most of the people in Teso saw the Commission as an organ to stop the bleeding, and to find a niche for them in the political order of Uganda. It was seen as independent. They knew that I was working for Museveni, but they knew that I was working under protest. So they knew that I was critical.[27]

In this sense, it has been argued that PCT was 'probably the best catalyst for change' for Teso.[28] What contributed to its acceptance was that the Commission sought advice from a wide range of public figures including politicians, activists, rebels, local leaders and clerics. The mandate of the Teso Commission was split into two phases: in the first phase in 1991–1992, the overall priority was to establish security in Teso and it was assumed that this could only be achieved and preserved by local people while the government could only supplement the process.[29] Peace and security were considered to be vital for economic development and social progress. The second phase, 1993–1994 until early 2000s, addressed more practical issues such as re-stocking and the re-integration of ex-combatants. The Commission's stated strategies to achieve peace and security were as follows:[30]

- the sensitisation of people about the correlation between peace and development;
- the strategic reduction of army presence (and restoration of police services);
- the acceleration of recruitment and training of Local Defence Units (LDUs) so that local people could defend their property against

cattle rustlers and anti-social behaviour (this mainly related to the Karamojong rustling);
- the reinstatement of former security personnel (after screening) or alternatively resettlement of former rebels.

In order to encourage the rebels to abandon their struggle, the Teso Commission set up a series of seminars in villages and trading centres, which resembled traditional conflict management meetings and were held in public places to allow all members of the community to witness the proceedings and to increase their stake in the matter. Convened by the Commissioners, they were informative and well attended and they encouraged a close proximity between Commissioners and the local people so that individual matters could be raised and personal problems solved. To this end, the Commission always started their sessions by dedicating the first day to asking people what was most important to them, permitting people to state their grievances and to vent their anger.[31] The main complaints of the Iteso and Kumam were related to cattle rustling, abject poverty and the general lack of support for the region. Political concerns were hardly ever voiced.[32] This strong emphasis on economic development was however only on the surface and served as a metaphor for the general sensation of not being welcome in Museveni's new Uganda.

The Teso Commission responded to this problem by addressing the pronounced allegations – and by implication the underlying subtext – through immediately responding to the complaints raised by the Kumam and Iteso. If they demanded development aid, the Teso Commission provided it. If they asked for oxen, the Teso Commission delivered the animals. If they demanded ploughs, the Teso Commission organised the supply. If they complained about the misbehaviour of NRA soldiers, the Teso Commission guaranteed that the army took care of their prosecution. For the people in Teso this experience of asking the representatives of the President for assistance and receiving it with little delay very much contradicted their perception of the government being hostile towards them as a people. As a consequence, they began to adjust their image of Museveni.

Significant for their success was also that, as mentioned above, the Teso Commissioners selected a disputing mode which was informed by their ongoing, long-term relationships and that they were all local mediators with strong social and family bonds to the region. When visiting a new area they met with friends or family members, sat down with them over supper and discussed the political situation. Apart from economic development, women, youth and leaders from various levels were given special consideration. The rationale of focusing on women was to reach their husbands or sons. The Teso Commission was well aware that the people at large supported the 'boys', emotionally as well as practically, and that the women were in frequent contact with their male family members. By appealing to a sense of responsibility towards their family the Teso Commission encouraged the women to influence their husbands and sons at any given opportunity, successfully undermining the support of the insurgency in the non-combatant community. According to Mzee Oguli, a conversation would run as follows:

> Every time there was a concentration of rebels we held meetings surrounding their place. The idea was that these people would send some people to ask them to listen to us. Or some rebels came and listen to us. The majority of the people who came to our meetings were women, men were not there. One day when we went to Gweri. There were many women, men were also there. A woman sat in front with a baby of about four months. And as I was speaking I picked on her and I said: 'Where is your husband?'
> And she said: 'My husband went to the bush two years ago.'
> I said 'Is that your baby?'
> 'Yes!'
> 'But how old is your baby?'
> '3–4 months.'
> 'But how did you get that baby when your husband is not there? Or he sneaks in? Do you usually have that child sick?'
> 'Oh, many times!'
> 'Do you have a problem of food?'
> 'Oh yes!'
> So we started to have a conversation there. 'Why don't you tell him that "it is peaceful now? Why can't you come back and help me?" Go and cry! When he sneaks in you cry and say: "Please you come. Nobody will kill you." And we have assured you that whoever gives in is not going to be killed. Why don't you tell him to come?'
> From there we were beginning to break through.[33]

This example illustrates how, in their seminars, the Teso Commission succeeded in shifting the intentions of the women and elderly, who stayed at home, from strengthening 'the boys' to appealing to the rebels' reason and responsibility to care for the well-being of their families. The strategy of the Teso Commission was to convince people that a peaceful way of dealing with their problems was much more beneficial for them as individuals and the region as a whole. This was of major importance since it led the civilian community, over time, to withdraw its support for the fighting.

Taking care of surrendering combatants, referred to as 'reporters', was another major assignment of the PCT. As soon as a rebel came out of the bush, the Teso Commission took him to a place outside of Teso for a few months to prevent his return. Thereafter, the ex-combatant attended the PCT's seminars in his home area to assure his family, but more importantly other potential reporters, that he was safe and taken care of. In doing so the commission successfully established trust and confidence among those insurgents who were still considering surrendering.

Despite these efforts, today many people suggest that the Teso Commission was only successful because it entered the process of mediation when the violent conflict was already fading out and that – because of frustration and destitution – many rebels had already surrendered before the PCT took up its tasks. Yet, even if this was the case the Commission still had an important role to play. Peace processes are always reversible, many peace initiatives reach the stage of apparent breakthrough only to collapse, while about half of all accords fail within five years. In Teso, this was prevented by the Commission which was seen as a guarantor for the government's commitment to the people. Through the PCT, the government promised that the Teso economy would start prospering again and that it would compensate for the loss of cattle. As a consequence, the task of the Teso Commission was to rehabilitate the Iteso's mind through restocking.[34] Building trust and confidence in the NRM government was of salient importance. In this sense, the government's strategy proved to be successful. The combination of the Amnesty Statute and the development assistance led to a feeling of appreciation among the Kumam and Iteso. The fear of prosecution due to the former Obote alliance was dissolved through the Statute, and the hardship and suffering of Teso recognised through aid and relief, and later restocking.

To return to the discussion of mediation at the outset of this chapter, the question arises whether the government's actions contributed to changing the discursive structures which gave rise to the conflict in the first place. Despite its successful impact on terminating the fighting, did it merely solve immediate concerns or did it also contribute to the creation of a new relationship between the Museveni government and Teso? In order to be effective, as discussed in Chapter 1, traditional conflict management builds on three aspects: relationship, restitution and identity.[35] Relationship implies that a mediation process needs to preserve the quality of the relationship between the parties to the conflict so that the objective of the mediators is less to find a solution to the problem than to manufacture some form of consensus. This was apparent in the mediation by the Teso Commission which did not set out to actually solve the problem of the people from Teso – whatever this would have implied – but rather to amend the relationship between the parties, at least from the Teso side. This was achieved through restitution in form of development assistance, which was supposed to re-establish the balance between the opponents. In particular, the pledge of compensation in the form of economic re-construction encouraged the Iteso and Kumam to believe that they were increasingly included into the wider Uganda, and that they would move from neglect to prosperous integration. Their image of Museveni changed from enemy to patron – or benevolent dictator. The people in Teso, over time, ceased conceiving of themselves as enemies and put hope and trust in the care of their president. In this sense, the traditional approach by the mediators was successful in reducing opposites and dichotomies, such as good/evil, strong/weak, right/wrong, where one always excluded the other, and turned them into a more holistic worldview, as discussed in Chapter 2. This had the effect of preserving the identity of the people of Teso, as well as that of the overarching nation of Uganda.

Strategically, in the course of the mediation, the PCT changed the narrative about the opponent from 'Museveni being the enemy' to 'Museveni being the care-taker and provider'. By avoiding political confrontation, the discourse about the insurgency was turned into a struggle for material commodities, which were deliberately depoliticised. And through providing the commodities which had come to occupy a central place in the discourse of the insurgency, the PCT solved the conflict. What the Teso Commission thus achieved was to transform an irreconcilable binary, of 'us' vs. 'them' into a more fluid distinction. The sharp boundaries were eroded and the structural exclusion transformed. With reference to Jabri's requirement of reducing the prevailing structural properties of exclusion, the Teso Commission can hence be considered a success. Today, though, this view has changed considerably, and the Teso Commission is no longer thought of so highly. I will turn to this in the following chapter.

The army

The insurgency was characterised by a large number of severe human rights abuses against both combatants and non-combatants, most notably the suffocation of 47 Iteso in a railway wagon in Mukura, Kumi district in 1987.[36] In general, the NRA soldiers became notorious for raping, looting and indiscriminate killing. In order to safeguard the reputation of the NRA, attempts were made to prosecute and punish so-called out-of-service atrocities by soldiers such as rape, defilement and murder, including the public execution of offenders. Today, many ex-combatants, especially those who were in the Rebel High Command, refer to personal relationships with high-ranking NRA officers as being crucial for their surrender. For instance, Sam Otai, 2nd Rebel Commander, was communicating with a senior military officer, Charles Agina, through letters delivered by his wife, while Musa Echweru, responsible for arms supply, refers to Brigadier Chefe Ali as a key figure in the trust-building process between the rebels and the army.[37] Importantly, when coming out of the bush the Rebel High Command were received respectfully by their former enemies, and they discussed the matters of the insurgency frankly and openly, so that some rebels even learned to appreciate the government's political philosophy.[38] In the words of Musa Echweru,

> [t]he Movement [NRM] has continued to be pragmatic. There was a message of reconciliation. Those who came out were actually treated well. This kind of flexibility was initially there. This flexibility was seen and needed. Even if you had disagreement, you were still seen to be acceptable. You could sit down and discuss issues.[39]

The NRA/M policy of welcoming, or even rewarding, former rebels had a significant impact. Echweru soon became RDC of Nebbi district, while Omax Omeda, former rebel leader, was appointed Minister for Works, Housing and Communication. In Teso, more cynical observers therefore suggested that the rebels were 'bought' by the government.

Hence, while at the beginning of the insurgency the behaviour of the NRA strongly fuelled the violent conflict, after a change in army personnel there was also a 'change from NRA combatants to agents of peace'.[40] The personalities of individuals had a great impact. Through showing respect for the Iteso and Kumam rebels, and even offering them lucrative army or civil positions, the rebels felt they were equal to the NRA officers. While the insurgency was fought on the grounds of exclusion and neglect, the attitude of the NRA towards the rebels built a bridge for co-operation and potential reconciliation.

Churches

Parallel to the government, the Teso clerical community had a major impact on the termination of the insurgency. More generally, in Africa, faith groups play a significant role in the social and political sector. This situation dates back to the late 19th century when missionary organisations established mission schools, hospitals and dispensaries.[41] In today's Africa, churches and mosques have gained an ever more prominent role as advocates for human rights, social injustice and poverty reduction and it has been argued that they have an obligation to 'struggle for societal transformation in the effort to build an equitable society where no one is oppressed'.[42] What is unique about the position of churches or mosques is that they simultaneously reach the grass-roots of a society and the political elites of a country. They are thus in an exclusive position to negotiate local needs and national politics. Nevertheless, due to their political role churches and mosques themselves often become involved in national politics and conflicts and turn into opponents of the state.

The largest Christian churches in Uganda are the Anglican Church of Uganda, the Catholic Church, the Uganda Orthodox Church, the Pentecostal Church and the Seventh Day Adventist Church. Since the political parties and internal conflicts prior to Museveni's victory in 1986 had been, *inter alia*, fought on religious terms, churches in Uganda are highly politicised.[43] Nevertheless, it has been suggested that in the 1990s they played an important role in national reconstruction: their views were considered while drafting the national constitution and they carried out civic education programmes prior to the Constituent Assembly as well as Presidential and Parliamentarian elections, which they also monitored.[44]

However, even though their general political impact cannot be disputed, not all churches were interested in building-up Museveni's Uganda. For instance, in Teso during the initial stages of the insurgency, leaders of the Anglican Church of Uganda were particularly supportive of the insurgency. The political power of senior clerics such as, for example, the now retired Anglican Bishop Illukor is not dissimilar to that of a regional king – a parallel often made in Teso – and they have strong potential to influence their congregation.[45] Many of the rebels as well as rebel leaders were faithful Christians and thus receptive to the discourse encouraged by the churches.[46] In the words of the priest Richard Okiria '[t]he rebels were very religious. They would come to church and sing in the choirs. On Sundays. And then the other days they were killing'.[47]

And yet, over the course of time, and with the increasing suffering in Teso, the churches changed their opinion and started 'preaching the message of peace and reconciliation'.[48] Their efforts benefited from the very close ties between Bishop Illukor, Grace Akello and the UK-based Teso Relief Committee which financially supported the Anglican Church and its development projects. Moreover, two priests, Father Michael Corcoran and Father Richard Okiria, undertook the personal initiative to intervene in the conflict. In 1991, Okiria, priest in the parish in which the High Command was based, made contact with the rebels who persecuted innocent local civilians.[49] Similarly, Corcoran was in frequent contact with the rebels. Together they convinced the Catholic and the Anglican Bishops of Teso to propose to facilitate between the parties to the conflict. After long negotiations in 1991/1992, the churches convinced Hitler Eregu, 1st Rebel Commander, to accept their offer to mediate between the High Command and Museveni. The rebels appreciated the recognition they received from the churches, especially when they invited international journalists to cover the insurgency, and even though the government was initially reluctant to enter the talks they eventually conceded.[50] Moreover, due to the interaction between the churches and 'the boys' a number of high-ranking rebels such as Sam Otai, 2nd Rebel Commander, surrendered with large groups. Others used the churches as places to capitulate or to find refuge from their former fellow rebels as well as NRA soldiers.[51] By maintaining close links with the rebels, the churches provided the necessary safe havens for surrendering soldiers and thus contributed significantly to the resolution of the violent conflict.

Today, the contributions of the churches to end the insurgency in Teso are rated highly in the region. Since the churches were first critical of Museveni and then turned around to 'preach a message of non-violence and reconciliation' they earned the reputation of acting in the best interests of Teso. Nevertheless, their strategy was less to advocate collaboration with Museveni, and thus to alter the structural properties of friend/enemy, but rather to appeal to the Iteso and Kumam to recognise the futility of killing and suffering. In doing so, while the churches had an impact on the reduction of violence, they did not improve the relations between the parties to the conflict. Until today, these relations remain antagonistic.[52]

Women

Despite an increase in the number of female combatants world-wide, the most prominent role for women in war remains that of the victim.[53] In this context, it has become increasingly popular to argue that women suffer most from violent conflict.[54] It is however difficult to uphold this argument in the light of the direct exposure to fighting and death faced by combatants. In Burundi, for instance, it has been estimated that boys are two to four times more likely to be killed than girls.[55] Nevertheless, to acknowledge the plight of women in times of insecurity is essential, for rape and violation, assault and attack are not merely side effects of conflicts – and which are in and of themselves bad enough – but also increasingly strategic tools of warfare. This does not only hold true for female combatants but also for civilians, and in the light of AIDS (systematic) rape by both rebels as well as soldiers has become a lethal weapon.[56] In addition, women suffer heavily from the absence of men in households and on farms, as well as from the economic deprivation that accompanies violent conflict, in particular, in cases where the government practises a scorched earth policy or introduces sanctioning mechanisms. Moreover, in many African cultures, widowed women have no right to land and property which leads to an inescapable spiral of poverty, displacement and dislocation as well as the permanent disruption of family bonds.

This resonated in the experience of Teso during the insurgency where almost only women remained in the villages while their husbands and sons joined the rebels – either voluntarily or through forceful recruitment – or they left for safer regions of Uganda. At the time, men in Teso had no choice but to either partake in the insurgency or to abandon their families, while women, left to their own devices, had to accomplish all the tasks of every day life.[57] In addition to this burden, they faced poverty and famine, and their children suffered from diseases and lack of medical care. Many women lost their sons and husbands in the insurgency and they themselves became targets of NRA offensives. Rape and (sexual) abuse by soldiers was frequent, sometimes with the rationale of punishing their rebel husbands in the bush, yet the Teso women were also victims of sexual violence committed by their own 'boys'.

The heightened awareness of the suffering of women in wartime has led to an increasing focus on women as peace-builders, leading to the promotion of women's influence 'from the village council to the negotiating table'.[58] The UN Resolution 1325 which specifically addresses their role in conflict and peacebuilding is one important step into the right direction. On a general note, as the 'gentle sex', women are often ascribed peaceful attitudes such as non-violence and co-operation, rather than aggression. By way of justification, biological arguments are frequently rehearsed, 'for no mother would want her children to be killed in combat'. Nevertheless, across different cultures some mothers seem less anxious about their sons, such as the wives of Karamojong warriors, who, rightly or wrongly, have a reputation of inciting their husbands to cattle raid.[59] Moreover, the former British Prime Minister and mother

Margaret Thatcher showed no hesitation when leading her country into the Falklands War against Argentina in 1982, while in Rwanda during the 1994 genocide some of the most atrocious crimes – including against women – were committed by women.[60] The simple stereotype of women being peaceful and men being aggressive does not hold if tested against history.

In Uganda, too, the significance of women as peace agents is often explained with reference to the 'gentle sex'. And indeed, at first sight, women seem by far gentler than men. Nevertheless, if one looks at the social constitution of women in Uganda it becomes apparent that many characteristics are deeply enshrined in traditional roles and forms of up-bringing. Anthropological studies about women and war argue that if there is, in fact, an apparent difference between men's and women's predisposition to violence, this is less founded in fixed drives and material determinants of behaviour, but rather in culture and ideology, as well as social values and socialisation.[61]

Conditioned by their cultural environment, in Teso the influence of women on their husbands and sons was mainly informal yet it proved to be effective. Since the insurgency in Teso was mostly fought on the grounds of economic deprivation and a policy of neglect by the new government, which manifested itself in poverty and famine, the women realised that the violence only worsened their situation. Consequently, in informal and casual meetings while collecting water from the wells or during agricultural work, or while mourning about lost family members, the women exchanged their worries and fears and collaborated in sending messages to related rebels in the bush to encourage their return. They used emotional pressure to appeal to their husbands' and sons' responsibility to care for them and their children instead of making their conditions even more difficult.[62] Some women even went as far as refusing their partners their 'marital duties' in order to exercise pressure on them.[63] The informal role women played is apparent in the words of an ex-rebel.

> Women played a very big role. Especially here in Teso, the women helped us so much. The morale they give to you. You can be in the bush for as long as seven days, that means you have not taken care of yourself, and she still hugs you and tells you: 'You are nice.' So you can see what it means. Then in terms of pacification they can say: 'Here, the children, they need you! So I think the best is whatever happens out there – let's go. You may lose what happens out there, but you save your life for my sake and for the children.'[64]

However, even though the engagement of women appears to be a collaborative effort with a clear objective, according to most of my interviewees, it was mostly the deployment of their pitiful situation. Women used their distress to emotionally appeal to their husbands and sons, but they had very little influence on political decision-making. Due to their poor education paired with the traditionally patriarchal culture, women were not able to organise themselves formally and to take measures against their fighting men. Rather, their influence was successful in contributing to the end of the insurgence because it revealed a paradox in the struggle. Since one of the rebels' motives was to alleviate poverty and economic exclusion, they had to acknowledge that the insurgency was counter-productive. Had the rebels been stronger it is questionable whether they would have listened to their wives, and maybe their wives would not have objected to the insurgency in the first place.

Elders

Traditionally, elders are the most highly respected mediators in African cultures. As we have seen in the first chapter, most African societies are based on a hierarchical system which provides elders with a reputation of wisdom and ultimately social and political power. Their social status provides the respect necessary to act as facilitators or judges. Even though the increase of Western influence and its supposedly egalitarian culture of modernity increasingly undermine this tradition, until today the role of a *Mzee*, the Swahili world for elder, is of major significance. In Teso, many elders objected to the insurgency since they realised that it would only bring suffering to the region. Although they agreed that the fighting was justified they, nevertheless, emphasised that the rebels had no chance against the government troops and that a violent conflict would hinder development progress. Even though most elders advised against the fighting, the rebels did not listen. Occasionally, when an elder spoke out, he was killed. Despite the limited influence of Teso elders, one major initiative to mediate in the insurgency was undertaken by Haji Okodel from Kumi district in 1992. He chaired a meeting between a selected team of Iteso elders and the Brigadier Command in Mbale which led to their jointly promotion of a strategy of persuasion, rather than force, to end the fighting. Apart from this, it appears that no public clan meetings or debates facilitated by elders occurred. On a domestic and family level, though, elders consulted and advised their rebel sons and called for an end to the fighting so that, in a way similar to the rebels' wives, they had an informal impact on the promotion of peace in Teso. Due to the minor role elders played in the termination of the insurgency, it remains difficult to assess their impact on changing the prevailing power asymmetries of inclusion and exclusion.

Mediation and the end of the insurgency

The insurgency in Teso did not conclude officially via a truce or a peace accord. Hitler Eregu, the 1st Commander of the Rebel High Command and one of the last 'boys in the bush', left Uganda in May 1992 which, according to most people, constituted the end. However, smaller groups of insurgents continued fighting until 1994 when they either surrendered or where captured by the NRA.[65] One insight gleaned from analysing the role played by different actors that contributed to the end of the insurgency is that third party intervention has to happen on different levels and at different stages of a conflict. The various agents influenced and mutually conditioned the constituency from different angles, leading to a greater impact.[66] For instance, on a leadership level, the Teso Commission and the churches addressed a similar group of people: the local population on one hand, and the Rebel High Command on the other. They communicated about their ventures and supported each other on a small scale. Okiria helped Akello to meet with the 2nd Commander Otai, while Bishop Illukor participated in seminars and conferences organised by the Teso Commission. Together they were successful in convincing the remaining rebels to come out of the 'bush' and to surrender their guns. On a more informal, domestic level, the influence of women and elders led to a shift in the attitudes of the rebels and to their giving up the struggle.

As central to this book, the question emerges whether the mediation efforts in Teso were successful in terminating the fighting and whether it laid the foundations for a wider process of conflict transformation and social change? In Chapter 2, we established that the transformation of a conflict requires the challenging and changing of the structural properties which gave rise to the conflict in the first place. The invention of peace has to be situated in discursive practices which, rather than reifying exclusion, incorporate difference.[67] I argued that this discursive process resembles what Gadamer calls *a fusion of horizons* in which both parties no longer remain who they are. In the following, I return to this concern, link it to the process of hermeneutics and evaluate whether the mediation in Teso has led to social change.

An initial assessment of the different mediation efforts – by different agents – indicates that they did indeed lead to changes in Teso. With reference to Giddens's structuration theory it can be argued that they constituted a form of agency which challenged and changed the structural properties prevailing in Teso at the beginning of the insurgency. For at the outset, from the Iteso and Kumam perspective, people felt economically, politically and culturally marginalised in Museveni's Uganda. Their self-understanding was informed by an 'us' vs. 'them' dichotomy; the prevailing structural properties were defined in terms of Teso vs. Museveni. In the course of the meditation – through the agency of the various mediators, that is, first and foremost the Teso Commission – this strict binary was challenged and changed into a more holistic and less exclusive view. The Commissioners used their authority as respected community members to create a harmonious imagery, replacing the one based on division and accomplishing to re-establish social and moral order as central to traditional conflict management strategies.[68] This was done by fostering the belief that the people of Teso were respected in Uganda. In this sense, the mediation by the PCT led to opening up a space among the tightly woven narratives of the Teso people and enabled a less totalising view of the Museveni government.

In particular, the promise of development, at a time where famine was looming in the region, assured people that the government would assume an authoritative yet caring stance towards them. As mentioned above, the language used in the process of the PCT mediation was mainly with reference to development and food security. One of its strategies was the 'sensitisation of people about the correlation between peace and development'.[69] In the words of the Commissioner Akello

Then PCT realised that there were some people who wanted to listen to what we wanted to say, that was to support them economically. Some kind of hope that they have to start all over again. We wanted them to feel that they had a stake in the economical future of Teso. Instead of fighting, they now concentrated on development.[70]

In their meetings, to refer to development ordered the mediation discourse in a way that made it possible for the Commissioners to respond positively by pledging funds. As a consequence, although development was not the cause it turned into part of the solution to the violent conflict. The promise of development was understood as a form of restitution or compensation – which is of significant importance in traditional conflict management. As explored in Chapter 1, traditional approaches do not understand a dispute to exist between two parties but maintains that the harm has been done to the whole group. As a consequence, its objective is to restore social relationships, for instance, through restitution.[71]

This restoration of the relationship may occur following the compensation of the harm incurred, such as, for instance, through economic development. In Teso, this strategy proved to be successful.

Regarding Gadamer's notion of fusing horizons we can therefore ask whether in Teso, in the early 1990s, a process of fusion did indeed take place. To repeat, in the encounter with an other, Gadamer argues, we refer to our own preconceptions and prejudices which result from our own historical situatedness. Only through these are we able to understand the issue at stake. Stimulated by the other, in the hermeneutic process we question our historical situatedness, that is, our *Vor-urteile* (prejudices and prejudgement), potentially leading to amending or even discarding them. In Teso, the work of the Commission, in particular, did indeed encourage the civilian population to challenge their prejudices and prejudgements about the Museveni government. Since development had turned into the central issue, they re-evaluated their critique of the NRM and changed the prevailing narrative from Museveni being their enemy to being their provider or patron. In doing so, the people of Teso altered the specific past they recalled and which defined their present. In their recollection, the motivation which drove the insurgency was no longer defined in political terms, but on the basis of struggling for development. Changing the past, however, was only possible in light of anticipating a particular future, that is, the future of prosperity and peace in a wider Uganda. As noted by Akello in the above quote, they had found a 'niche ... in the political order of Uganda'.[72] Consequently, they no longer needed to make their 'true identity' reliant upon scapegoating (false) difference.[73] Both, the NRM government and the Teso community, through a process of dialogue, entered into a 'communion in which they remained not who they were'.[74] Their identity changed from aggressor to patron, in the case of Museveni, and from excluded to stakeholder, in the case of the people of Teso. In this sense, remembering the past in mainly economic terms led to a re-membering of the society which was no longer defined in opposition to Museveni. The mediation was poetic, in Deleuze's sense, since it encouraged a process of creating something new out of what had been. Still, as we see in the following chapter, this form of re-membering was not to be long-lived.

5
Narrating the Cause of the Teso Insurgency

As we have seen in the previous chapter, the Teso insurgency was mediated and terminated in 1992 through the combined effort of local initiatives, indigenous mediators, churches and the Presidential Commission for Teso (PCT). At the time, the different mediation efforts were successful in re-membering the Teso society which no longer defined itself in opposition to Museveni. Today, however, despite this initial achievement, and even though the people of Teso have no intention to return to fighting, peace in Teso remains shallow. As one of the poorest regions in Uganda, people still feel politically and economically neglected and they still harbour resentment against the government.

How can this be explained? Throughout this book I argued that changing identities is central to the hermeneutic process of evaluating past and future. This ontological moment always takes place in the present milieu, so that the encounter with the other has a significant impact on it. In this chapter, I therefore begin with describing the economic and political situation in Teso. Since development has played such a significant role in the mediation process I start by showing how little it has improved and how impoverished people still are. Significantly, the lack of development constitutes the present milieu from which the Iteso and Kumam evaluate their horizons. Moreover, it represents the other, the government of Uganda, which has failed to live up to its promise. As a consequence, in the second step I argue that the way people in Teso retrieve their past, for example, how they remember what caused the insurgence, perpetuates their anger against the government. Through drawing on discourse and language, the performative power of narratives shall be illustrated and the benefits and politics behind privileging one story over another revealed. From an inward looking perspective, people have chosen an interpretation of the past which allows for constructing a collective Teso identity which provides some comfort after the violent conflict. From an outward looking perspective, their choice of interpretation of the past has been provoked by their negative experience of their other – to return to the hermeneutic encounter – in form of the Ugandan government by which they still feel neglected.

Poverty, disillusion and anger

Shortly after the insurgency, famine was looming in Teso and until today the sub-region remains one of the poorest regions of Uganda.[1] Not much economic progress has been made since the insurgency, leaving people disillusioned about the promise of development by the government. As illustrated in the previous chapter, part of the mandate of the PCT was to sensitise the people about the correlation between peace and development and to promote economic prosperity and one major task was the restocking of cattle lost during the insurgency.[2] In the formerly cattle herding society, only 7 per cent of cattle remained.[3] In a culture where cattle means not only food but also political power and social welfare, this was a considerable shock. However, the restocking of cattle in Teso was of little success and has left the population, once more, with the bitter feeling of neglect. As a result, the good reputation of the Teso Commission has suffered significantly, and individual members are sometimes accused of 'eating money', or at least of using their positions as Commissioners as spring-boards for their personal careers. Today, when asked about the Teso Commission the response of most Kumam and Iteso is thus rather negative. The degree of frustration is apparent in this remark by an interviewee: 'Akello delivered Teso to NRM, and NRM to Teso. The NRM has gained more than the Iteso: the conflict ended but there were few economic improvements'.[4] Today, it is impossible to evaluate in detail how much money was spent on restocking cattle in Teso. The Commission received generous funds from the Danish International Development Agency (DANIDA), as well as from other international donors.[5] Simultaneously, a number of international NGOs financed the reconstruction process outside of the PCT framework. Yet, like in other areas of Uganda, corruption reduced the budget drastically,[6] and difficult demands and monitoring systems established by international donors proved to further consume large amounts of funding.[7]

On a more positive note E.A. Brett argues that in a post-conflict environment

> [c]ivil wars are best ended through a process of reconciliation and reconstruction designed to restore faith in the representativeness and equity of the political and economic system. Several countries are now attempting to do this in Africa, but there is little doubt that Uganda has now produced the most successful record of sustained progress.[8]

The background to Uganda's success-story, Brett suggests, is based on Museveni systematically attempting to overcome mistrust by incorporating opponents into a 'broad-based' government, through constitutional and administrative reforms as well as a programme of economic liberalisation and reconstruction, which aims at addressing the needs of marginalised regions of the country.[9] As for Teso, though, none of the strategies identified by Brett can be labelled successful. Firstly, the Kumam and Iteso feel that there is little space for them in the 'broad-based' government. Although the Iteso later provided two ministers, Grace Akello and Max Omeda, people maintain that they are merely ministers of state and not cabinet ministers and that their influence is limited. The real decisions, people say, are made by people close to Museveni. Secondly, people in Teso argue that the economic changes introduced by Museveni's government might have been beneficial for some areas of the country, yet not for Teso, where, according to the UNDP figures, development actually declined.[10] Uganda's decentralisation was encouraged by the World Bank's liberal market politics through its Structural Adjustment Programme (SAP), which had devastating effects on many African communities, including in Teso where many people lament the disappearance of state organised market structures and guaranteed crop prices, such as during the Obote years.[11] Most farmers in Teso cannot afford to transport their goods to the large markets of Kampala where they could achieve higher prices, and so farming has become less lucrative, reducing wealth in the sub-region.

On a more general note, the experience of exclusion is always subjective. As a result, in Teso, it is difficult to draw a line between the collective feeling of being disfavoured by the government and the actual neglect based on a deliberate, unequal distribution of government resources.

The number of Iteso and Kumam in public offices and private enter-
prises suggests that there is no general, national policy of discrimination
against people from Teso. Yet some people are concerned, as expressed
by Richard Okiria:

> The people think that the present government is mainly pro-west
> [Uganda] and that we have been economically discriminated. Could
> it [the insurgency] happen again? I am worried.[12]

Significantly, it does not matter what the 'reality' is – that is, whether
the Teso region is in fact discriminated against by the Ugandan government – but how the people interpret the situation. If they subjectively
feel deprived of what they think are their rights as citizens of Uganda
then steps need to be taken to gain their trust and confidence and to convince them of the opposite. Importantly, though, the interpretation and
experience of the present milieu informs how they remember their past.
In the following I analyse how this negative interpretation manifests
itself regarding Teso's identity.

Narratives, identity and memory

Narrative approaches to conflict studies have become increasingly
popular in recent years. They suggest that stories are not simply representations of a reality but that they involve selectivity, rearranging,
rediscription and simplification.[13] In other words, 'narratives mediate
between the self and the world'.[14] Narrative approaches are based on
the argument that '[t]he event is not what happens' but rather 'that
which can be narrated'.[15] In this sense, events are properties of the past
while narratives are properties of the present. For Mikhail Bakhtin, these
narrated and the narrative events 'take place in different times and in
different places, but at the same time these two events are indissolubly
united'.[16] Narrated and narrative events are characterised by the interplay of available resources and patterns of narrative performance, on the
one hand, as well as by the emerging functions and outcomes of the performance, on the other.[17] In a post-war environment such as Teso, one
function of narratives is to form the social fabric which permits people
to create meaning and make sense of their existence. They thus provide
a framework by which to reconstruct the fractured, collective identity,
a necessity for any war-torn society, as argued in Chapter 1. Antze and
Lambek thus suggest that

[t]here is a dialectic relationship between experience and narrative, between the narrating self and the narrated self. As humans, we draw on our experience to shape narratives about our lives, but equally, our identity and character are shaped by our narratives. People emerge from and as the products of their stories about themselves as much as their stories emerge from their lives. Through the act of memory they strive to render their lives in meaningful terms. This entails connecting the parts into a more or less unified narrative in which they identify with various narrative types – heroes, survivors, victim, guilty perpetrator, etc.[18]

Remembering the past is, therefore, reflected in the particular narratives on which people draw to make sense of their lives. They do so not as individuals, rather their memory is determined by their social environment.[19] It is thus produced by, as well as productive of, a collective identity in the present. Importantly, though, our discussion of hermeneutics in Chapter 2 argued that the choice of a particular narrative does not only serve the function of rendering life more meaningful but it is also conditioned by the present circumstances such as the encounter with one another. As I illustrate in this chapter, the present identity is situated in the hermeneutic process of retrieving past and future *and* the encounter with the former enemy, in our case the Museveni government.

This suggests that a sequence of events can be emplotted in various ways by various people, as illustrated below through a selection of different narratives on what caused the Teso insurgency. Recognising this undermines narratives which claim to be the only representation of reality and it calls for interrogating their authenticity.[20] The privileging of one particular story leads to 'narrative closure' understood as the 'process through which narratives seal off alternative interpretations to themselves'.[21] While a sense of closure might be an important requirement to provide meaning in a post-war environment, as argued in Chapter 2, it also obstructs alternative, less exclusive interpretations of friend and foe. As such, closure can stand in the way of future reconciliation.

Competing narratives in Teso

The history of the Teso insurgency has so far remained undocumented and only oral accounts are available. What follows outlines three different narratives about the causes of the insurgency which are however neither exclusive nor exhaustive. They were obtained in response to my question: 'What caused the Teso insurgency?' For foreigners who arrive in the Teso region only the first version is on offer. People refer almost exclusively to the Karamojong cattle raiding as the cause for taking up armed struggle, to the exclusion of all other accounts. When listening to, for instance, senior school students it becomes apparent that this is also the version passed on to the younger generation, a group which has no personal memory of the time of the insurgency.[22] As a collective memory, it turns into local history. However, in the course of my research, alternative voices began to emerge, as reproduced in the following.

Karamojong warriors' raiding

As we saw in Chapter 3 on Teso's effective history, shortly after his inauguration Museveni disbanded the militia which protected the border between Karamoja and Teso. The Karamojong warriors used the power vacuum to raid their neighbours with an intensity previously unknown, even exceeding the extent experienced under the Okellos in 1985–1986.[23] Within a few months after the NRM came to power, the Karamojong warriors had overrun the whole of Teso, then comprised of Soroti and Kumi districts and it is estimated that the number of livestock shrunk by 93 per cent.[24] According to an OXFAM report the number of cattle in Soroti district diminished from 317,563 in 1980 to 20,000 in 1989 and in Kumi from 135,000 to 15,000.[25] The report estimates that the cattle stock in Kumi went down to 3–4000 after renewed raiding in 1990–1991. When the raiding of Teso began in late 1986, people had no means to protect themselves against the armed Karamojong warriors who advanced as far as Lake Kyoga, harassing and killing people indiscriminately. Witnesses affirm that they were accompanied by their wives and children who collected clothing and household goods while the warriors took the animals.

As early as April 1987 diplomatic attempts were made to stop the rustling. In a meeting at the Conference Centre in Kampala the government was urged to stamp out the raids, to disarm the Karamojong, to establish an emergency relief programme and to implement development projects in Karamoja in order to provide sufficient water and pasture for the Karamojong cattle. From the Karamojong side, elders promised peace and pleaded with the government to advance economic growth in their districts. The appeals remained unsuccessful and the government remained inactive. The failure to secure stability in Kumi and Soroti was explained by a lack of military resources, for the new government had to fight against violent opposition in the north and west of the country. In Museveni's words: 'We did not have enough forces to deal simultaneously with the cattle raiding. As a result the Karamojong cattle raiding intensified, especially in Teso'.[26]

Nevertheless, the inactivity of the NRM was interpreted by many people in Teso as a deliberate policy of intimidation aimed at depriving Iteso and Kumam of their main source of livelihood. At the time, cattle were the major economic commodities in the region. People called their cows their 'bank', for they provided them with the means to pay tuition fees, dowries, day-to-day necessities and food.[27] Moreover, cattle were also of social and cultural significance since they served as symbols for wealth and prosperity and thus provided power. Large herds of cattle were often invested in the acquisition of new wives and dependants. The loss of cattle due to raiding and the insurgency not only deprived the Iteso and Kumam of their economic, but also of their social livelihood.[28]

With the beginning of rustling, the first rumours spread that the NRA actively supported the assaults in order to undermine the economic and social foundation of Teso. People reported lorries loaded with cows leaving for Kampala, and that they went 'as far as Museveni's house in western Uganda'. Even though the allegations were never verified mistrust remained. In order to change the perception, towards the end of the insurgency, Museveni invited a group of Iteso to western Uganda to prove that he had not 'stolen' Teso cattle. The delegation's report was negative, yet its findings were not accepted by most people in Teso.

Although the Kumam and Iteso always admit that the NRM/A-Karamojong co-operation is only alleged it is nevertheless a shared belief and as such legitimates the collective resentment against the NRM/A and Museveni. The cattle rustling narrative is invoked whenever the cause of the Teso insurgency is explained. It symbolises the perceived deprivation and punishment for their support of Obote and legitimates taking up arms. Against this backdrop, the insurgency was seen as just.

Harassment of former Special Forces and military

Parallel to the cattle rustling, the NRM local administration started a policy of harassing the Iteso and Kumam.[29] Former political leaders and military personnel were arrested without explanation, but also less prominent Kumam and Iteso suffered intimidation.[30] Torture in custody was frequent. One narrative, alternative to the cattle rustling, is therefore that the insurgency was caused by the harassment of the former Luwero combatants, in particular, as well as the Kumam and Iteso in general. There was widespread fear of being punished for the atrocities committed in Luwero, where allegedly up to 300,000 people were killed by the Special Forces, and from where the NRA soldiers and the soldiers from Teso already had a six-year history of fighting each other. Rumours spread rapidly that Museveni's NRA, while fighting Obote's troops in Luwero, had threatened punishment once they came to power.[31] A further rumour spread at the time was of the cruelty and violence of Museveni's troops. The Teso rebels

> told heart-chilling stories of hideous crimes that the NRA allegedly committed on innocent civilians. Such crimes, according to the rebels, included cutting open pregnant women's tummies, bashing babies' heads on trees, burying people alive and cutting off people's ears. Those in the know, however, said that those were some of the crimes that the [Teso] rebels themselves used to mete out to innocent people in Luwero Triangle, during their war with Museveni.[32]

For the former Kumam and Iteso combatants, in response to the harassment, self-defence seemed necessary. In the words of a former rebel leader and later member of government:

> The truth about the insurgency is very clear. We were forced to go into the bush. The administrators who came to Soroti first, or to Teso as a region, had their own problems. They really mishandled the situation. For when the arrests of prominent politicians started, when they started prosecuting former Special Forces and police understandably people ran away. We were not organised that we wanted to fight government – people just run to the bush for fear of being harassed. Then, after some time, we saw the thing continued, and we thought that the only way to handle this situation was to group ourselves. Maybe where we went wrong was that we did not contact the authority, but we did not have the opportunity to reach the President. So the only way we thought we had was to take up our arms and to defend ourselves.[33]

The new government legitimised the arrest and intimidation of Iteso and Kumam by arguing that it was hunting for dissidents, especially from a political organisation called Force Obote Back Again (FOBA). The hunt for FOBA members was intense and affected the whole of Teso. FOBA was discussed in the press at large, and funds were allocated to the army to conduct an operation to clear Teso of FOBA members. Apparently, though, FOBA never existed but was invented as a joke by former UPC politicians in a bar in Kampala. Today, it is difficult to find out if the

NRM/A genuinely believed in the existence of FOBA or if they only needed a pretext to legitimise the strong actions against the Kumam and Iteso. Regardless of the 'FOBA-joke', the concern of the NRM/A that violent opposition might flare up in Teso was not unwarranted. When withdrawing from Luwero the thought of revenge was already playing on the mind of a number of Kumam and Iteso soldiers and Special Forces, as we see in the following.

Political motives

The third narrative to explain the causes of the insurgency suggests that there were political ambitions to topple Museveni. Some UPC politicians, most notably Peter Otai, former Minister for Defence in Obote's government, realised the degree of resentment against Museveni in Teso and used the situation for their own political objectives. Based in Kenya and London they promised arms and military support, yet failed to deliver. The frustration at the time is apparent in the remarks of a former rebel-leader:

> For us at home [in Uganda] we wanted government to recognise our existence. To say: 'These are people of Uganda, what has been done to them'. But the politicians [abroad] wanted to use us as mercenaries to fight for them. Which was very unfair. And we never got any assistance from them.[34]

Much of the political ambitions had their roots in Uganda's history. As described in Chapter 3, Teso had always been a UPC stronghold and had supported Obote since independence. During his presidency, Teso was prosperous and peaceful, employment rates were high and people were generally content. After having been privileged by Obote, the policy of Museveni was perceived as strong neglect. The good-life the Iteso and Kumam had appreciated for so long suddenly came to a halt. Moreover, the political motivations behind the insurgency are closely related to the ethnic divisions that run through the Ugandan polity. Ethnicity is an often-cited cause for violent conflict in Africa and, despite wide recognition that ethnic differences are constructed rather than given, ethnicity is not imaginary.[35] Firstly, because it is a subjective reality, and secondly, because it has historically developed and consolidated over time. For people in Uganda ethnicity is, therefore, plausible and meaningful. In this sense, according to a now-discredited tradition of colonial anthropology, the African continent is divided into Hamitic and Nilotic tribes in the North, and Bantu in the South.[36] The separation runs right through Uganda, splitting East and West into two different camps. According to this framework, Museveni belongs to the Banyankole, a Bantu group, while the Iteso are Nilo-Hamites, a Nilotics sub-group.[37] Colonialism, throughout Africa, invented categories to define not only who people were but also which qualities their 'tribe' possessed.

> Terms like the Bantu, the Nilotics, the Nilo-Hamites, the Sudanics, and all that, began to crop up in school classrooms, so that a child who was a 'Nilotic' was now made to learn in his Primary 3 or 4 that he was, while another child in another class was similarly now made to know that he was from the 'Bantu' group.[38]

According to Museveni, in agreement with many historians and as discussed in Chapter 3, ethnic separation in Uganda is a result of the colonial legacy where cash crops and economic development were introduced to the central and western region of the country, whereas the north and the north-east served as a reserve for labour and army recruitment.[39] Inequalities in wealth were created, generating conflicts between the different ethnic groups. In Museveni's words '[t]he rivalry over access to opportunities and resources gave rise to the formation of attitudes of superiority and inferiority complexes'.[40] Significantly, due to the legacy of colonialism and subsequent party politics, at the time of the insurgency, the Ugandan polity was radically split along ethnic lines, leading to a rejection of Museveni by the Iteso as the 'right' president to govern the country and provoking politicians to topple his government.

Eventually, the combination of the cattle rustling, the hunt for former Special Forces combatants, the indiscriminate arrests of Iteso and Kumam as well as political objectives led to the creation of the Rebel High Command. Their first attacks were simultaneously on the Soroti Flying School, Soroti Barracks and Soroti Hotel. Although largely unsuccessful, the rebels managed to free their detained comrades from Soroti prison and increased their manpower. Significantly, today, it is very difficult to establish whether the insurgency preceded the cattle rustling, or whether it was a consequence. As mentioned above, in the locally narrated history the violent uprising is referred to as a response to the Karamojong warriors' raiding and the government's inactivity, which was interpreted exclusively by the Iteso and Kumam as neglect and punishment for their former allegiance with Obote. However, it is also possible that the rebels had already planned the insurgency before the cattle rustling began. In Teso today, nobody is prepared to answer this question.

Challenged Teso identity

The above provides an account of some of the different narratives on what caused the Teso insurgency. One feature that runs through all stories is that the reality of the Kumam's and Iteso's existence in Uganda had changed. To repeat, during Obote's presidency the people from Teso had been relatively privileged. To this day, they draw attention to the fact that, before the insurgency, they were educated, affluent and westernised, and that they had good relations with the colonial rulers. All of this was lost due to Museveni's seizure of power and the subsequent violent conflict. Manifested in politics such as the removal of the militia along the border to Karamoja, as well as the disbanding of the security service personnel and the Special Forces, the people of Teso realised that their position in Uganda had changed. Moreover, a vast number of Iteso and Kumam lost their employment, leading to severe economic difficulties. People had to return to farming in an environment where land was scarce and already a source of conflict and where the cattle livestock had been reduced dramatically. While some regions of Uganda, particularly Museveni's home area, began to prosper, the people in Teso felt that their status was declining. The Kumam and Iteso had to give up what had historically constituted their identity, that is, being relatively privileged compared to other ethnic groups in Uganda. They had to re-adjust themselves in light of a changing nation and find a new niche for their existence.

The government's version of the causes of the insurgency is that a number of Kumam and Iteso politicians, with the intention to regain power, manipulated and misled the Teso population and that, by drawing on the issue of cattle rustling, vast support was mobilised. The NRA, however, admitted to having made a mistake by not responding to the cattle rustling by the Karamojong directly but instead attacking the Iteso and Kumam rebels. They nevertheless justified their strategy by saying that 'cattle rustling is a criminal offence but rebellion against an established government is not only criminal but also treasonable'.[41] In the military rhetoric at the time, described in the widely read NRA journal and mouthpiece *Tarehe Sita*, the insurgency was explained as follows:[42]

The conflict in Teso is essentially a problem of armed criminals who sometimes collude with misguided rebels. In addition, there are other criminal gangs (esp. in Soroti district) of former UNLA soldiers comprised mostly of elements who have committed crimes while serving in the army and who now fear facing law. They did not surrender their guns when they were demobilised during and after the Okello regime. Karamojong mainly raid for cattle and fight those who try to prevent them. Rebels, on the other hand, steal everything and indiscriminately harass, rape and regularly murder civilians. Karamojong and rebels are not organised. After sharing their loot, their unity rarely goes beyond collective defence against other gangs and the NRA. Efforts by UPDA rebels to join forces with Karamojong have failed because Karamojong are only interested in cattle rustling. FOBA has not been successful in unifying different forces in Soroti. FOBA is still handicapped by internal power struggles. In Teso the NRA's integrity is tarnished to alienate it from popular support.

What is apparent in the above quote is that the Teso insurgency was not given any status by the NRA/M, it was not recognised as an insurgency, but rather degraded to thuggery or criminal offence. The deliberate downplaying had important implications for both political and military responses. Militarily the NRA/M started a strong offensive against the Teso rebels,[43] and a scorched earth policy against civilians.[44] Paired with the inability to prevent the Karamojong cattle rustling this also served a strategic purpose. At the beginning of the insurgency in Teso, rebels in the northern Ugandan region Acholi (today Kitgum and Gulu) were already fighting against Museveni and the government was concerned that the Acholi and the Teso rebels would join their struggles and become too powerful. And indeed, the Teso Rebel High Command had meetings with Alice Lakwena, and later Joseph Kony, to contemplate potential co-operation.[45] Against this backdrop, for the government to sustain the assaults by the Karamojong warriors along the Acholi and Teso border guaranteed a buffer zone and prevented the two insurgencies from fusing.

From a political perspective, not to recognise the insurgency undermined its national impact. The rebels were not given any legitimacy and thus their cause remained unrecognised. This policy of deliberate ignorance meant not having to address the political claims made by the Teso people, while at the same time undermining the insurgency militarily. As we saw in the previous chapter, to recognise an insurgency is important for it legitimises the struggle, as the Iteso and Kumam experienced through the support from 'friends' in the UK. Simultaneously, however, the fact that Museveni suppressed rather than promoted bipolar enemy structures between his government and Teso made it easier for him to then, at a later point, reach out in a gesture of mediation.

Narratives and the remaking of unmade worlds after violent conflicts

In the first instance, for a new visitor to Teso to encounter different narratives on the cause of the insurgency – and the exclusive preference of one in particular – leaves one at best puzzled. The competing stories raise questions about the truthfulness of the prevailing account. However, what looks like deception at first sight is far more an ontological phenomenon and a common feature of every community. Above, we argued that people select the narratives on which they draw to make up their lives. Stories are always told in a certain situation or milieu and with a certain audience in mind.[46] The interpretation and recollection of the past, expressed in the choice of a particular explanation and narrated in a particular way, is always performed as a response to the encounter with the other and with view to a particular future. As discussed above, the experience of the other, that is, the former enemy, remains negative since Museveni has not kept his promise to improve the development of the region. Consequently, the prospects for the future are negative, too.

In addition to these external stimuli, from an inward looking perspective the insurgency 'unmade' people's worlds, requiring the creation of a new, collective identity in the future. This resonates in Carolyn Nordstrom's argument that '[w]ars unmake worlds, both real and conceptual'.[47] As a result of violent conflict, people lose their houses, friends and family members, jobs, wealth and material goods. In addition, they might be permanently disabled, HIV positive as a result of rape or suffer from post-traumatic symptoms. Ex-soldiers and ex-rebels are difficult to re-integrate into the community, their future is often marked by severe poverty leading to even more severe frustration. Family and neighbourhood support structures are eroded, institutions such as churches or schools have lost credibility. Migration and refugee movements unsettle local notions of belonging and what constitutes a home so that most of the material past is gone forever.

In Teso, too, at the end of the insurgency people had lost a lot. Many had been killed during the fighting and during insurgency-related crimes. While many died in combat it is assumed that even more fatalities occurred among civilians caught in the crossfire between the NRA and the rebels.[48] Furthermore, there was a high mortality rate in the settlement camps where malnutrition and diseases were rampant. Even though there are no numbers for all insurgency-related deaths the loss of life is expressed in the fact that the Teso districts Kumi and Soroti were the only two in the whole of Uganda to experience a negative annual growth rate between 1980 and 1991.[49]

Moreover, at the community level trust in each other and faith in the future was very low, while tensions remained high. An aggressiveness previously unknown prevailed among the Teso people. But not only were these 'real worlds' unmade by the insurgency – concepts were eroded, too, and apparently fixed notions of good and bad, right and wrong, friend and enemy were shaken beyond repair. In Teso, atrocities were committed by the NRA, but also by the rebels and the Iteso and Kumam; cattle were stolen by the Karamojong, but also by the local people; rebels fought in the bush, yet surrendered and joined the NRA the same day; neighbours supported each other, but they also committed crimes against each other; the church preached reconciliation, and incited the people to support the armed struggle; the cause was just, yet was it really justified? This list of eroded concepts could be easily extended. It reveals that during violent conflict previously established meaning is lost. And the loss of certainty and faith, in combination with poverty and destruction, are heavy burdens to carry.

To re-make a world and to re-gain lost certainties is a difficult task. In this context, to remember the past in a particular way carries the promise of narrating a community whole again. As suggested at the outset of this chapter, people emerge as products of the stories they tell. Thus, remembering the past is produced by, as well as productive of, a collective identity, it re-members a society. In Teso, to tell the local history about the insurgency with reference to cattle rustling has the advantage of producing a new, coherent Teso identity. In this context, it has been argued that '[i]f winners write history, losers dwell on it more'.[50] In order to explain this phenomenon, the term 'chosen trauma' has been suggested, which refers to an event

> that causes the group to feel helpless and victimized by another group .... The group draws the mental representations or emotional meanings of the traumatic event into its very identity, and then it passes on the emotional and symbolic meaning from generation to generation. For each generation the description of the actual event is modified; what remains is its role in ... the group identity.[51]

Hence, a true narrative is not only produced by, but at the same time productive of a collective identity. The repetition of tales about the own identity – as well as the identity of the enemy – becomes a social reality for those who participate in this discourse. A common identity, a 'we-feeling', is shared among people who apply the same concepts and their social interaction becomes meaningful for, and indicative of, their belonging together. As for Teso, to narrate the causes of the insurgency with reference to cattle rustling by the Karamojong provides exactly this 'we-feeling'. From today's perspective, everybody who lived in the region at the time fell prey to either the Karamojong or/and the NRA atrocities. In this interpretation, the perpetrators (the Karamojong and the NRA/M) and victims (the Iteso and Kumam) are clearly defined so that shared experience has the potential to unite people under the guise of 'victimhood'.

And yet, what is wiped out in the production of a collective Teso identity is the difference between people who were only victims, on one hand, and people who had political motivations to go into the bush, on the other. Discussions about their reasons to participate in the insurgency have disappeared from the public discourse and been submerged in the guise of collective victimhood. This is particularly interesting since, as stated above, during the insurgency, crimes were also committed by Iteso and Kumam against each other. I was given many accounts indicating that atrocities and violence also occurred inside the community. While this is not uncommon during violent conflict, to accept it is highly unsettling for any post-conflict society and a 'true' identity has to be established as a means of coming to terms with the disruptive experience. As argued above, societies torn by violent conflict need to establish new certainties and coherence to come to terms with the past and to re-make unmade worlds. In light of internal mistrust and suspicion, in particular, a collective identity carries the promise of consolidation.

Importantly, the constitution of a collective Teso identity based on victimhood has a significant impact on the potential for reconciliation. As argued in Chapter 1, identities are established in relation to difference, and in the case of Teso the former enemy, the Museveni government, was the obvious other in opposition to whom a new identity could be created. However, to repeat 'the multiple drives to stamp truth upon ... identities function to convert difference into otherness, and otherness into scapegoats created and maintained to secure the appearance of a true identity'.[52] Thus, the way the past is remembered does not only constitute a coherent identity internally, it simultaneously defines outside relations. In the process of narrating their identity 'true', people in Teso (again) turned the former enemy into a 'scapegoat'. To portray Museveni as the perpetrator who caused the insurgency produces and re-produces a solid 'us' vs. 'them' dichotomy. An apparently authentic discourse defines who is friend and who is foe, it introduces a sense of narrative closure which does not allow for alternative interpretations. As argued above, to practice closure is an essential requirement to define social relationships which have been destroyed by a violent conflict and it allows for re-making eroded concepts. Still, in Teso, remembering the past in this particular way has led to an exclusive interpretation of self and other. It has introduced an authentic truth – and identity – which stands in the way of future reconciliation. For, as we have seen in Chapter 2, even though closure and the establishment of new meaning might be important, it should not be static, but as Vattimo argues, it should remain contingent.

Moreover, the promotion of the cattle-raiding story serves a political function. Regarding Ugandan national politics, if indeed innocent the Iteso and Kumam have the negotiating power of a victim. The Museveni government, solely responsible for the violent conflict, owes the people what they have lost: development, education, political participation and the like. There is thus an important political dimension in the selection of one narrative over another: to be constituted in a certain way entitles to certain demands.

To conclude, in hindsight a number of different narratives are on offer to explain the motivation behind 'going into the bush'. The one which has turned into the true story about the cause of the insurgency – and which is today remembered – re-members the people of Teso as victims and the Museveni government as perpetrator, enabling the constitution of a coherent collective identity. While this is helpful for the process of dealing with the past it obstructs future reconciliation, and maintains a shallow peace in Teso. Nevertheless, as argued throughout this book, remembering is always conditioned by the present milieu and the experience of the other. And it is this other – the Museveni government and its unfulfilled promise of development – that provokes the particular memory in Teso.

6
Facing Past and Future after the Teso Insurgency

While the previous chapter focused on the performative function of narratives about the cause of the insurgency we now turn to a different aspect of assessing the long-term impact of the mediation efforts in Teso. Considering the particular account of the Teso insurgency today, the question poses itself whether the Kumam and Iteso have to some extent be managed to dissent from the hierarchical relations that tied them to the Museveni government and which they sought to challenge with the insurgency. Has challenging led to long-term changing?

In order to understand the presence or absence of long-term social change, as well as how remembering the insurgency re-members the Teso community, I first sketch the responses to the only war memorial to commemorate the insurgency – a mausoleum close to the trading centre of Mukura in Kumi district – to then, second, explore the significance of the invention of the new cultural leader of the Iteso *Papa Emorimor* to highlight an innovative way of trying to change the role of the Iteso in the wider Uganda. These two examples represent certain aspects of the hermeneutic process of retrieving the past and casting oneself forward into the future. Albeit different in scope, they both serve to illustrate how the people of Teso are dealing with their past today, and how this shapes their prospects for the future.

The Mukura memorial

On 11 June 1989, 47 people suffocated in a railway wagon in Mukura, Kumi district. In the preceding days, about 300 Kumam and Iteso civilians had been rounded up by NRA soldiers on the suspicion of being rebels. After being kept under terrible conditions, including torture and abuse, they were incarcerated in a railway wagon where many of them died from the lack of oxygen. According to an eyewitness:

> That was Tuesday, the 11th. These people were locked up there [in the railway wagon]. Over 100 according to my estimate, they were over 100. Commotion broke out, inside the coach. They stayed there for almost one and a half hours. Then commotion was fading, fading, fading, fading, till eventually everything cooled down. Then I was again picked, that 'okay, you come'. They were by then making porridge. The soldiers were making porridge. They told me to come out. They opened the coach and I found bodies doing what?, lying there . . . inside the coach.
>
> Then they asked me to go and pick . . . to pick some more people to come and carry out the what?, carry outside the bodies. Some had not died in fact. Some were apparently dead. Those who were found apparently dead . . . as they were trying to recover they could be trampled upon, at the necks here. They just step on you [making a snap with the fingers].
>
> And they died. More than half. Only some few, I don't know how lucky they were, I picked some and helped them to enter the what?, the goods shed now. Very late . . . it was already dark now even, I am sure that some recovered during the night, but then they were finished by the soldiers.
>
> . . . those who were apparently dead, when they recovered they were finished.[1]

Among the abuses committed by the NRA during the insurgency the Mukura railway incident stands out not only as a manifestation of brutal violence against a group of potentially innocent civilians, but also as the only case where the Ugandan government acknowledged responsibility for what happened and apologised to the people. Still, government and army insist that the incident had not been planned, but that it was an accident, or a misjudgement, on behalf of the local NRA officers.[2] The explanation commonly referred to is that the local NRA officers misjudged the danger of suffocation in the wagon, they were simply unaware of the implications of locking a large group of people into a railway wagon. As such the incident becomes an accident which disperses responsibility. Nevertheless, in order to compensate for the loss of human life, Museveni promised the people of Mukura financial support and free education for the orphans, as well as a memorial for the victims.[3]

Reparation and compensation, as offered by the Museveni government, are potentially strong symbolic acts for they recognise individual and collective suffering.[4] From the viewpoint of restorative justice, restitution payment by the perpetrator can also symbolise the perpetrator's commitment to apologising and taking responsibility. Due to the strong symbolic value, disputes over reparations are therefore particularly revealing of the social and political current, as well as the attitudes the former parties to the conflict have towards one another at present. The Mukura memorial thus provides valuable insights into how the people from Mukura relate to the Museveni government today. Crucially, the promise of free education, which eventually turned into the promise to build a secondary school, had not been fulfilled when I visited the site in April 2000, 11 years after the incident. The resentment of the people in Mukura was high and led to the threat by local politicians not to support the Referendum 2000 about the future of the no-party (or Movement) system.[5] Subsequently, Museveni reasserted his pledge.[6] Still, local people believe that much of the financial compensation allocated for reparations was 'eaten' by politicians.

The memorial promised by Museveni was nonetheless built. It has the shape of a small house with windows on each side while inside a plaque lists the names of the 47 people who suffocated in the wagon. Apparently, though, the list is incorrect and some of the people are still living in Mukura trading centre, only a few yards away. In addition, it is important to recognise that the use and style of memorials is not beyond cultural contestation.[7] Many cultures, and I would suggest that this is also true for the Iteso and Kumam, have no tradition of erecting and visiting sites of remembrance and commemoration. And yet, in the specific case of Teso, a highly Christianised society, the dead are mourned over at graves so that a custom of using graves as symbols for loss and bridges to the hereafter is practised. The mausoleum, erected by the Museveni government, resembles a grave and as such has hence some general legitimacy as a symbol. Still, even though, in a Christianian context, mourning and commemoration is practised over graves, to have relatives and family members buried in a public mass grave offends cultural norms. In Teso, as well as in most of Uganda, family members are buried at home in the homestead. According to local custom, their souls – and by proxy their family – do not find rest until they have returned home to their ancestors' ground where they can be commemorated and mourned over. Here, the deceased remain alive by continued participation in the social structure of the home. Barbara Harell-Bond refers to similar remarks made by Ugandan refugees based in Sudan according to whose custom the failure to perform burial rites is subject to supernatural sanctions.[8] Hence, '[a] proper burial is the most important act of respect which can be paid to the deceased. There is probably no greater disgrace to a family than to have failed to observe funeral customs'.[9] This failure to pay respect was also expressed by my interviewees in Mukura who missed the reconciling experience of bringing the dead home, of making the physical and communal bodies whole again. In Mukura, people therefore told me that 'their grave was missing'. Significantly, when they wanted to take their loved-ones home they were not allowed. This perpetuates their resentment against the government, standing in the way of future reconciliation.

Commemoration and memorials

When one walks from Mukura trading centre towards the site of the incident one first sees two abandoned railway wagons and assumes that this is the scene of crime.[10] Emotional reactions are stirred; the massacre is pictured in the mind of the onlooker. Only when coming closer does one notice the new white mausoleum which is the actual memorial. Asked what the memorial signifies as a symbol, my interviewees replied that it testifies to the atrocities committed and even if people start forgetting, the memorial will remind them of the incident. In this sense, it marks the 'presence of the absent'.[11] Local residents interpret its installation as a sign of the government feeling ashamed of its actions. Yet the memorial has provoked strong, albeit subdued, controversy since local people wish the mausoleum did not have the shape of a house but that of the railway wagons that were left behind. What the Iteso and Kumam want to be reminded of is not the private pain of losing a loved-one, but rather the public crime of the killings committed by NRA officers and soldiers. This experience runs counter to the argument that '[c]ommemoration silences the contrary interpretations of the past',[12] and that it introduces a sense of closure which does not allow for re-interpreting an event. For in Mukura, the past of the insurgency is still very alive and vibrant for it is the subject of constant debates over the interpretation of the events as well as its representation in form of the memorial.[13] The tension between constant contestation and closure is well expressed in the contradictory comment by one informant that people dislike the memorial yet at the same time they do appreciate it. But only because they have learned to do so. My interviewees told me that the place was not frequently visited by relatives.

Despite the government and the people of Mukura having different intentions regarding the memory of the mass killings, as manifested in the disagreement over how to symbolise the incident in form of a memorial, it can be argued that

> [s]ymbols [here: memorials as symbols for the past] are effective less because they communicate meaning (though this is also important) than because, through performance, meanings are formulated in a social rather than cognitive space, and the participants are engaged with the symbols in the interactional creation of a performance reality, rather than merely being informed by them as knowers.[14]

The formulation of meaning is closely tight to the way a past is remembered, here mediated by a memorial, and it has a cohesive force on group relations. In other words, the way the Kumam and Iteso interpret the memorial is produced by, and productive of, their collective identity – the way they remember re-members their community. What is significant in the case of Mukura, however, is that the collective identity arises *in opposition* to the memorial. The interpretation of the mausoleum does not lead to shared commemoration for the deceased, as envisaged by the Museveni government, but rather to shared anger against the perpetrators of the crime. People define themselves in opposition, yet nevertheless in relation, to the memorial and in doing so they produce and reproduce their identity in opposition to the government.

At this point I would like to suggest a hermeneutic reading of the interpretation of the Mukura memorial in order to establish what insights it provides into potential changes in the antagonistic relationship between Iteso and Kumam on one hand and the government on the other. As for the notion of interpretation in general, it is important to recognise that despite potentially different interpretations, events are not entirely free of meaning and thus cannot lead to any interpretation.[15] Not 'anything goes' in the act of remembrance, for actual events frame what is possible.[16] What is true for the interpretation of events is equally true for their representation in form of monuments. As for the mausoleum in Mukura, both parties understand it as a place to commemorate the victims, yet they differ widely in their opinion whether it is an adequate representation of the massacre, or whether leaving the actual railway wagons behind would have been more appropriate. In their selective interpretation of the past, the people of Mukura and the Museveni government choose to remember some things while forgetting others. The Mukura example thus illustrates what has been argued in Chapter 2: with reference to collective memory the process of forgetting is not to sink into oblivion but rather 'to remember differently'. In the process of remembering, communities are re-membered, are re-shaped, according to the preferred interpretation of the past.

So, the Mukura incidence is interpreted differently by different communities. As discussed previously, interpreting the past takes place in anticipation of a particular future. Past, present and future are not linear sequences, rather the present is determined by both the way we understand our past as well as how we cast ourselves forward into the future. In Gadamer's words: '*Zukunft ist Herkunft*' (Future is origin).[17] For the Museveni government, the future aspired to is that of keeping Teso calm. With an ongoing insurgency war in northern Uganda, keeping the Iteso and Kumam inactive seems to be a reasonable strategy, even though one could question the benign intention behind this move. For the Iteso and Kumam, on the other hand, peaceful co-existence is much more contested. Their interpretation of the past, like the Mukura killings, does not allow much room for envisaging a positive future. As shown in Chapter 5, they very much see themselves as innocent victims who were violated by Museveni. The memorial in Mukura, instead of leading to social healing through commemoration, produces and reproduces anger and resentment against the government. In this sense, the memorial gives testimony to how much both the Museveni government and the Iteso and Kumam are still enclosed in their different positions in an asymmetric relationship, which bears strong traces of inequality and domination. The way the Iteso remember the Mukura killings prohibits them from dissenting from the power asymmetries which gave rise to the violent conflict in the first place. Through the performance of memory, people produce and reproduce their position of feeling neglected, victimised and at the mercy of Museveni's politics. The Museveni government apparently altered its position to some extent through the promise of compensation, it established the monument and pledged financial assistance. Yet since the funds have so far not been allocated, the government's action lost momentum and credibility.

In conclusion, the memorial in Mukura is today interpreted in a fashion which is indicative of the Iteso and Kumam attitude to the Ugandan government. Despite the intention of Museveni to contribute to a rapprochement between the former parties to the conflict, albeit not necessarily in a genuine way, the memorial produces and re-produces antagonistic feelings among the people of the region and keeps the binary between 'us' vs. 'them' in place. It highlights the failure of the long-term impact of the mediation efforts to re-member the community for it keeps the structural properties of inclusion and exclusion between Teso and the wider Uganda in place.

Inventing *Papa Emorimor*

While the discussion of the Mukura memorial helped to illustrate how people in Teso remember their past, we now turn to assessing the regions prospects for the future. This is done by analysing efforts to construct a new, collective Teso identity with the aid of the first cultural leader of the Iteso, *Papa Emorimor*, who was inaugurated in 2000. In what follows, I first introduce the institution of the cultural leader and discuss it against the backdrop of Eric Hobsbawm and Terence Ranger's concept of 'invented traditions', in order to then question whether the invention of *Papa Emorimor* is a sign of a changing Teso identity.

In contrast to Teso, other regions of Uganda look back at a substantial history and culture of kingship – the five existing traditional Ugandan monarchies are located in the regions Buganda, Bunyoro, Ankole, Toro and Busoga – even though their influence was disrupted in the course of the history. As described in Chapter 3, in 1966, as a result of political turmoil and power struggles, the Obote I regime dissolved all kingdoms. Almost two decades later, while fighting against the Obote II government in the Luwero Triangle, in order to increase his support among the people Museveni promised that he would reinstall the kingdoms when he became President of Uganda. In 1993, seven years after his victory, he eventually kept his promise and passed a law to annul Obote's enactment that abrogated the kingdoms and reinstalled the kings as cultural representatives, albeit without political power. The Traditional Rulers Statute of 1993 legislated the return of 14 items to the Buganda kingdom, including assets and properties.[18]

The idea of having a cultural leader for Teso as an equivalent to the other kings of Uganda had been circulating for decades, yet only after the experience of the insurgency were concrete steps taken. Even though Museveni had reinstated the other kings, he did not welcome the Iteso initiative to create a cultural leader at first. As a result in 1999, following a series of controversies between Museveni and the Iteso Cultural Union (ICU) responsible for the creation of the *Emorimor*, the police disbanded a meeting which was supposed to appoint a candidate for the *Emorimor* election.[19] In protest, the Iteso went to the public Independence Square in Soroti, spontaneously chose one person out of their midst, lifted him up and called him '*Emorimor*', successfully resisting Museveni's constraints. The random nomination was later withdrawn and the initially selected person appointed. Eventually, on 30 April 2000, the first *Papa Emorimor* was inaugurated in Soroti town.

As the figurehead of the ICU the *Emorimor* is elected for five years, with a maximum of two terms in succession. The first *Papa Emorimor*, Augustin Osuban Lemukol, studied in the UK and served as a civil servant under Obote and as commissioner of agriculture under Museveni. The institutions *raison d'être* is to fill the void of non-representation in the wider Uganda. To this end the duty and mandate of the *Emorimor* is to:[20]

- promote the unity of Teso,
- preserve and promote culture, music, dance and poetry of the Iteso,
- promote and develop the Ateso language,
- promote and research into the history of the Iteso and to publish the findings of any such research,
- set up or support cultural centres or museums for the promotion and preservation of Iteso culture and history,
- encourage the Iteso clans to organise themselves and to appoint or elect their clan leaders,
- establish and support the office of the *Emorimor*, as a symbol of Unity in Teso, and to
- encourage and promote socio-economic development in Teso.

Museveni was the guest of honour at the *Emorimor*'s inauguration in Soroti on 30 April 2000.[21] In the course of the ceremony, the president donated a car (in his own words: 'My office is very poor at the moment but in three or four months' time, it will be rich. I will then avail the *Emorimor* the shoes which fits modern times so that he can tour his kingdom'[22]), and even danced with ICU representatives and traditional dancers.[23] And yet, the celebration ceremony ultimately turned into a campaign for the June 2000 Referendum about the future of the political system of Uganda. Speakers such as the former Teso Commission secretary Grace Akello seized the occasion to promote the Movement system. In his own speech, Museveni drew on the existence of the different ethnic groups in Russia and the importance of a superior person to hold them together. He accounted for the necessity to have a strong leader to guide the country out of underdevelopment and 'backwardness'. Implicit in his analogy was a warning towards the Iteso not to separate themselves from the nation at large, and him as the president. As quoted in a newspaper

'Women who carry babies on their backs should not engage in throwing stones. If you do so, you risk your child being hit with a stone.' He [Museveni] said he had given the message in a joking way but was serious. 'For me I have already placed my baby down, so if you are interested, let us start throwing stones,' Museveni said.[24]

The impression I gained during fieldwork suggests that people in Teso will not engage in throwing stones again. For them, the inauguration of the *Emorimor* does not signify an act of aggression, but the opening of possibilities to have their identity represented, guarded and asserted in the wider Uganda.

Invented traditions

Many people agree that the Iteso need a strong figurehead to culturally represent and unite them, in particular after the insurgency which had a destructive impact on local confidence, certainty and cultural values. Some supporters of the *Emorimor* go as far as suggesting that if he had already been in place in 1986/1987 he would have prevented the insurgency through disciplining the youth and communicating the plight of the Iteso people to the President of Uganda. The basic concept of an *Emorimor* is inherent in the Iteso clan system. Traditionally, every individual clan appoints a representative who reconciles internal conflicts and holds his people together. However, in particular, since the insurgency, Iteso cultural attributes have been steadily declining. In response to the diminishing cultural practices, the tradition was hence altered from one *Emorimor* per clan to one *Emorimor* for all clans so that the new, elected *Emorimor* has become a modern 'super-*Emorimor*' for all Iteso in Uganda and abroad: he embodies a tension between modern progress – for he is democratically elected – and the conservatism of returning to traditional customs. His main function is to unite the Iteso – his title translates as 'Father of Unity' – and to represent the people towards the outside world. The ICU invented a sophisticated election process, which marries modern notions of democracy with traditions of kingship. As such, it provides an example of Eric Hobsbawm's term invented traditions, which signifies

> a set of practices, normally governed by overtly or tacitly accepted rules and of a ritual or symbolic nature, which seek to inculcate certain values and norms of behaviour by repetition, which automatically implies continuity with the past. In fact, where possible, they normally attempt to establish continuity with a suitable historic past.[25]

At first glance, in many aspects, in particular, regarding the historically prevailing egalitarian structure of Teso, the invention of *Papa Emorimor* provides a break with the past. Nevertheless, since on a much more local clan level the concept of *Emorimor* has a longstanding tradition the elevation of this tradition to a super level can be interpreted as a historical continuation. In this sense,

> insofar as there is such reference to a historic past, the peculiarity of 'invented traditions' is that the continuity with it is largely factious.... [T]hey are responses to novel situations which take the form of references to old situations, or which establish their own past by quasi-obligatory repetition.[26]

According to Terence Ranger, when invented traditions become realities they distort the past through making reference and harking back to what was not there.[27] Once taken for granted, their existence is legitimated through narratives about an immemorial time, affecting the constitution of the present identity. In this sense, the invention of a tradition is indicative of the spatio-temporal predicament of a society, which spurs the necessity to fill a void. As already argued in the previous chapter, in post-conflict Teso, there was a strong call for unity and representation towards the rest of Uganda since the Iteso felt excluded by national politics and longed for a figurehead to speak on their behalf. Hence, despite the explicit obligation of the institution of the *Emorimor* being merely cultural, it serves the political function of promoting the needs and aspiration of the Iteso in the wider Uganda. As apparent in the following extract from a newspaper article:

> The Iteso cultural leader, *Emorimor* Augustin Lemukol Osuban, has urged the Iteso to uphold their culture and language. He said some Iteso had abandoned their mother tongue. 'We have reached a point, whereby if you find two or three people in Teso speaking in English, then you know that they are Iteso,' he said. Speaking after his installation on Sunday, Osuban said the human and material resources the Iteso have been blessed with could make them realise tremendous development. 'I am sure that if the over 2.5 million Iteso within Uganda and outside come together, we would do something remarkable,' he said.[28]

It will take some time for the *Papa Emorimor* institution to be 'naturalised' in Teso. To date, the invention is still too new and many Iteso have difficulties in identifying themselves with the concept. Some Iteso suggest that the artificial installation of a super-*Emorimor* is redundant and that people should return to the cultural traits that are already inherent in the traditions. Moreover, some of the rural youth feel excluded from the election process and not represented by the 'old, traditional men who want to drink blood and wear hides'.[29] They have little sympathy with what they see as anachronism and conservatism and favour progress in terms of better agricultural development. Furthermore, the Iteso are not the only residents of the Teso sub-region but in addition to various ethnic groups from other areas of Uganda, the indigenous Kumam form a considerably large section of the population. There have always been tensions between the Kumam and the Iteso, which were enforced by the insurgency where inter-ethnic assaults occurred on occasion. With the Iteso having a cultural leader, and thus gaining strength inside and outside of Teso, the potential for conflict with the Kumam increases. *Papa Emorimor* thus faces many challenges. In addition, in contrast to the other kings of Uganda he has no assets and his financial backing has not yet been secured. The institution will rely on income-generating projects, fundraising and membership subscription. As an artificially invented attribute of Iteso culture it will take some time for the *Emorimor* to become widely accepted and to gain the support of his people. Only then will his primary role, to be the Father of Unity, be feasible.

To return to the question set out at the beginning of this chapter, it remains to be seen whether the institution of the *Emorimor* has the potential to challenge the structural continuities of domination and exclusion between the people of Teso (particularly the Iteso) and the Museveni government. Will it change the way the government and Teso relate to each other? Despite the difficulties of predicting the future, I would like to suggest that the *Emorimor* does indeed hold the possibility of transforming the way the people from Teso relate to the Museveni government. In line with Giddens's structuration theory, it seems possible to argue that the agency of the institution potentially *challenges and changes* the prevailing structural continuities of inclusion and exclusion. This, however, will require time and patience. Nevertheless, the invention marks a proactive step towards future transformations and the enlargement of the space for the Iteso to act.

Teso in-between war and peace

The Iteso are looking forward to the future. We tried to make the Iteso see life as just a matter of changes and seasons. One of the favourite quotes that they now use is that you should go with the wind, you should blow as the wind blows. Have you ever seen grass in the storm?

When there is a really, really heavy storm with huge winds the grass blows on one side and it falls downs. You see it almost completely down. It just lies peacefully on itself. When the storm goes, one or two or three days later it stands up again. But look at the trees, some of the big, great trees. Because they are out there they are standing in the storm and they think they are big and strong and so on. Many of them, when the storm comes, you find them down on the ground. So why don't you go as the grass and come up again. Other people say this is an imagery of cowardliness.[30]

More than a decade after the end of the insurgency, Teso still has not reconciled with the Museveni government. In this chapter, I illustrated two different ways of coming to terms with the past: while the first example, the collective memory of the Mukura killings, seems to produce and reproduce the antagonistic relations between the Iteso and the government, the second example bears the potential for transforming the structural properties that gave rise to the violence in 1986. The two perspectives thus reflect two tendencies in Teso today: anger about the past and preparation for a more empowered future.

Despite the current discontent in Teso, people generally agree that they will not 'go back to the bush'. After having endured widespread suffering and distress, a new insurgency war seems to offer no solution. Moreover, as stated above, the Museveni government might be arrogant and ignorant towards the Kumam and Iteso, yet there are no explicit, institutionalised policies of exclusion, discrimination and prosecution. On the basis of rather vague and ambiguous reasons to take up arms, as illustrated in Chapter 5, the costs of fighting are too high compared with the potential success. Peace in Teso might be shallow, but it will remain peace – and this in itself is some achievement considering the violence in many regions in Africa.

While Chapter 4 closed with a rather positive outlook on the future of Teso in a wider Uganda, the above analysis of the long-term impact of the mediation efforts on conflict transformation and social change is less encouraging. From what can be interpreted in hindsight, at the end of the insurgency people had high hopes that they would start living in prosperity and security again. Yet the developments in the years since the termination of the violent conflict strongly contradict these aspirations. So why did the mediation process fail to change the prevailing structures of inclusion and exclusion, that ran through the Ugandan society? I will turn to this in the following chapter.

7
Conflict Termination and the Absence of Transformation in Teso

According to John Paul Lederach, the cessation of fighting is often considered to be the cumulating point of a peace process, even though this moment only marks a beginning. 'In reality . . . [the endings of violent conflicts] are nothing more than opening a door into a whole labyrinth of rooms that invite us to continue in the process of redefining our relationships.'[1] To analyse this opening, this odd time in-between war and peace, has been at the centre of this book. I argued that the termination of a violent conflict and the possibility of its long-term transformation have to be situated into the wider social and historical context of the parties to the conflict. This transformation requires changing the exclusive boundaries that demarcate 'us' from 'them', as well as changing the composition of the own identity group in relation to the enemy. Central to this process is the way the past is remembered and the future anticipated. Remembering after violence constructs a collective identity which may or may not render future reconciliation possible.

Regarding the ending of the Teso insurgency I showed how one of the parties, the people of Teso, refers to particular memories of the past and turns them into narratives about the insurgency. Their choice of narratives is conditioned by the way the insurgency was terminated, and how their relationship with the enemy, the government of Uganda, has developed since. In the same vein, the interpretation of the only war memorial in Mukura maintains their antagonistic relationship towards their former enemy. More than a decade after the end of the fighting, these particular memories perpetuate the antagonistic relationship between the parties to the conflict, standing in the way of sustainable peace. This negative attitude is surprising considering the initial success of the mediation efforts in Teso. So what went wrong?

Identities, remembering, closure and power

In order to respond to this question, in this chapter I return to the hermeneutic framework of analysis for the transition from conflict to peace, as introduced in Chapter 2, and consider each of its four inter-related points in turn: change of identities, remembering, closure and power. Regarding the first aspect, hermeneutics suggests that a process of conflict transformation leads to changing the identities of the parties involved. Through altering the way the parties see themselves as well as the former enemy the exclusive structures which gave rise to the conflict are re-negotiated. In Teso, while there was some initial change in the collective identity away from antagonism as a result of the mediation process, it was neither sustained nor consolidated. When Museveni came to power in 1986, the people of Teso took up their arms to fight his government. Even though today, as illustrated in Chapter 5, it is almost impossible to establish the causes of the insurgency, it is apparent that, at the time, the relationship was marked by severe antagonism, eventually leading to aggression and violence. Historically and socially, this dates back to the region's particular experiences during colonialism, which produced and consolidated cleavages that still run through the Ugandan society. Initially, the various mediation efforts by the government, most notably the Teso Commission, altered this conflicting relationship to the point that the people of Teso gave up their struggle and 'came out of the bush'. In the cause of the mediation, as illustrated in Chapter 4, the Iteso and Kumam adjusted their image of Museveni from being their opponent to being their patron, providing development and security for the region. At this point in time, they no longer defined their identity in opposition to the government, but the hermeneutic process of assessing and discarding their *Vorurteile* led to a communion in which they did not remain who there were, that is, they started seeing themselves less as a marginalised but as an appreciated part of Uganda. Here, then, the mediation efforts by the government proved successful in changing the Teso identity.

And yet, as we have seen in the Chapters 5 and 6, shortly after the end of the insurgency the people of Teso returned to their negative interpretation of and antagonistic attitude towards the Ugandan government. Two aspects are of significance here: internally, the community felt the need to create a coherent identity after their world was un-made by the experience of the insurgency, and externally, their view of their other, the government, was marked by the latter's failure to live up to its promises of compensation, that is, providing development assistance, on the grounds of which the outcome of the mediation was based. In other words, the way the Iteso and Kumam saw themselves, as well as their former enemy, led them to return to the drawing of fixed boundaries between 'us' and 'them'.

Crucial for this return to an antagonistic relationship was that the initial change was never sustained and consolidated. Identity shifts are based on routinised practice, which render them 'normal' and thus require consolidation through repetition.[2] Only through repeating what provoked the change in the first place does this new 'reality' become normalised and a permanent feature. The NRM government's promise of development and care for the people of Teso, despite being convincing during the mediation process, failed eventually to consolidate the amicable relationship, because it was only sustained for the period of the mediation process and not beyond. The government failed to repeat it according to the expectations of the people from Teso and thus to sustain the identity changes.

To turn to the second aspect, processes of identity change are subject to how communities remember their past (and hence re-member their community), as well as how they anticipate their future. In the Chapters 5 and 6 we saw that the way the past is remembered today reinforces the antagonism of the people of Teso towards the government. The narratives on the causes of the insurgency, as well as the interpretation of the Mukura memorial, illustrate just how deep the resentment lies. They furthermore provide an example for the dialectic aspect of narrating the past since, as discussed in Chapter 5, '[p]eople emerge from and as the products of their stories about themselves as much as their stories emerge from their lives'.[3] In other words, remembrance has a significant impact on the constitution of the Teso identity, as much as it is conditioned by the experience of the government of Uganda not promoting the development of the region. Hence, the way the past is remembered re-members the community in opposition to the government.

Against the backdrop of such a pessimistic account, the invention of the new cultural leader *Papa Emorimor* stands out as a potentially positive development for the future. As a spokesperson for the Iteso (yet not for the Kumam), the cultural leader, if successful, can communicate the Teso concerns to the government and advocate for the region's needs. If accepted in his community, the institution of the *Emorimor* can serve as a positive outlook to the future, providing Teso with greater confidence that the region will play a more significant role in Uganda. Eventually this might open the possibility for the people to render their so far clear demarcations of 'us' vs. 'them' more permeable.

Thirdly, I argued in Chapter 2 that in order not to provoke a renewed outbreak of violence, a transition from conflict to peace must not introduce a new sense of closure, but remain contingent and contestable. This was, however, not the case in Teso. Although the shared meaning accomplished in the process of mediation terminated the conflict between the Museveni government and the Iteso and Kumam, it remained static. Despite the fusion of horizons in the hermeneutic encounter during, for example, the PCT session, horizons were not progressively opened up towards a 'better' future, but rather they introduced a sense of closure among the parties involved. The end of the mediation efforts marked the end of the engagement of the government and even though agreements on terms such as restocking were reached they have not been open to a public debate ever since. In other words, in Teso, the hermeneutic process led to a degree of closure and authenticity. In Chapter 2, we suggested that in order to avoid the pitfalls of authenticity, hermeneutics has to be understood as both – the finding of shared meaning and the opening up of this meaning. As stated by Vattimo, it implies 'an interpretative belonging which involves both *consensus and the possibility of critical activity*'.[4] In Teso, the challenging of exclusive boundaries did not lead to their constant contestation or to any critical activity, but the government remained in its powerful position. This leads us to the fourth and final, and in the context of Teso most important, aspect of the hermeneutic framework of analysis: power.

As argued throughout this book, the way we remember and what we anticipate for the future is always conditioned by the encounter with an other, and it is at this latter aspect where the conflict transformation process failed in Teso. The Kumam and Iteso's experience of the government of Uganda was coloured by its inactivity regarding advancing development in the region. Crucially, since the mediation was based on traditional conflict management it did not provide any checks and balances to guarantee the implementation of its outcome in form of compensation so that the people of Teso had no possibility to hold the government accountable to its promise. What is critical for the analysis of conflict transformation in this book is that the relationship between the people of Teso and the government of Uganda was marked by a power asymmetry, which was already prevalent towards the end of the insurgency and which manifested itself in the course of the mediation process. Due to the eroding support among the population, coupled with their weak military position, the insurgents had little bargaining power. In the meetings and seminars held by the Presidential Commission this imbalance of power relations revealed itself in the outcome of the process which was more to the benefit of the government than the people of Teso. As quoted before, it 'delivered Teso to NRM, and NRM to Teso. The NRM has gained more than the Iteso: the conflict ended but there were few economic improvements'.[5] Since power takes such a central role, the following explores its impact in greater detail.

On a general note, the role of power and coercion in mediation is a widely studied subject.[6] In order to escape the impact of power asymmetries, Joseph A. Folgner and Robert Bush introduce the concept of 'transformative mediation' to refer to attempts to challenge prevailing structural cleavages and to stress the empowerment of the parties in conflict. Folgner and Bush suggest that a party is empowered when

- it reaches a clear realisation of what issues matter and why, coupled with a realisation that their importance is legitimate;
- it realises more clearly what goals and interests are aspired to, why they are pursued, and that they are important and in need of consideration;
- it becomes aware of the range of options available to secure these goals;
- it realises that it can choose as to how to pursue these goals;
- it has a mandate to make conscious decisions about what actions to take.[7]

It is therefore anticipated that the realisation of these points provides the party with a greater sense of self-worth, security, self-determination and autonomy necessary for finding an equitable, long-term resolution to the conflict.[8]

This strategy does however not hold when related to the experience in Teso. For considered against the backdrop Folgner and Bush's requirements, it appears that the Iteso and Kumam in 1991–1992 were indeed to a large extent empowered. In the workshops and seminars organised by the Teso Commission, they had the opportunity to reflect upon their goals and interests, why they were important and how they could be pursued. As a consequence, they opted for economic and personal security as their priorities and for the government of Uganda, through the Teso Commission, to attend to their demands. It was this immediate objective that people were pursuing; it informed how they framed their arguments and aspirations. And this although, as we have seen in Chapter 5, the causes of the conflict were more complex than the mere lack of development.

Yet, how has their perception of the situation come about? In essence, in the course of the mediation, the Kumam and Iteso perception and interpretation of their situation was very much informed by the mediators of the Teso Commission who set the agenda. As central to the notion of narrative mediation, a mediation process potentially re-defines the stories people chose when they refer to a violent conflict.[9] Influenced by the setting, mediation processes change both story and (the perception of) reality. For 'the production of discourse is at once controlled, selected, organized, and redistributed according to a certain number of procedures whose role it is to avert its powers and dangers, to cope with chance events, to evade its ponderous, awesome materiality'.[10] In other words, in the seminars of the Teso Commission – and elsewhere – discourses ordered the realities. Some interpretations of the reality were organised *into* the discourse, while others were organised *out*. In the workshops, the government exercised control, and thus power, over what could and what could not be debated. Their use of a particular language to represent the 'reality' – that is, the lack of development as the driving force behind the insurgence – influenced the meaning and interpretation of the situation 'in order to impose a particular perspective from which events are expected to be perceived by the targeted audience'.[11] To discuss the appeasement merely in terms of economic and personal security created a particular discourse according to which the Teso struggle was mainly fought along these lines. And it permitted the government of Uganda to offer development as a bargaining chip in the course of the mediation process and thus not only to create but also to fulfil the expectations of the Iteso and Kumam. Eventually, this was successful in leading to the termination of the conflict and to an end of the fighting. Even though against the backdrop of Folgner and Bush's list of requirements the people of Teso seemed empowered at first, the course of the mediation process was profoundly influenced by the government, which determined its outcome to its advantage.

As a consequence, due to prevailing asymmetric power relations, which manifested themselves in the mediation process, the peace achieved in Teso remained shallow, leaving the people of Teso with resentment and bitterness towards the Museveni government. Today, through drawing on a particular interpretation of the past, which narrates the Museveni government as perpetrator and the people of Teso as victims, the Teso horizon is interpreted in a way which obstructs future reconciliation. The hermeneutic process of retrieving the past in light of an anticipated future has led to a writing of local Teso history which stands as a solid monument and a sense of closure limits what is possible in the future. This does, however, not suggest that this closure has to be permanent. In the case of Teso, one could think of *Papa Emorimor* as an institution to provide a new channel for Iteso (and

Kumam) representation towards the Ugandan government. In addition, non-governmental institutions such as peace initiatives, churches and youth clubs could provide frameworks through which the relation to the former enemy can be redefined.[12]

Hermeneutics as a framework of analysis

Hermeneutics, it has been argued in this book, is a valuable framework through which to analyse the transition from conflict to peace. The recognition of the backwards and forwards movement in the encounter with the other, the enemy, enables us to assess how shared meaning is produced or obstructed, how boundaries are opened or closed and if and how power asymmetries are challenged. In this sense, this book analysed the *challenging and changing* of structures that give way to violent conflicts. It is a first attempt to link hermeneutics and peace and conflict studies, marking the beginning of a wider research agenda. As such it responds to recent, post-positivist contributions to conflict analysis which – among other objectives – use deconstruction as a framework to draw attention to excluded voices. Despite being in broad agreement with these approaches, I argued that the challenging of boundaries as suggested by scholars such as Campbell is not sufficient to interpret the time after a violent conflict in which new meaning needs to be established and peace invented. In order to push current debates forward the book therefore moves from the discursive analysis of the invention of war to the discursive analysis of the invention of peace. In other words, while the work Campbell and others discusses how enemies are constructed in discourse and language, this book has turned the argument around to analyse how peace is invented in discourse. This is given expression through the framework of hermeneutics which, through its notion of fusing horizons, at the same time provides a metaphor for the ontology of peace. Importantly, however, peace in this book is not understood as a *telos*, but as an interactive process of fusing horizons – a fusion which is, and should be, challenged in the very moment of its existence.

Regarding the ethical implications of hermeneutics – since it has famously been argued that theory is always for somebody and for some purpose[13] – the preference of hermeneutics over, for example, deconstruction suggests a particular ethical attitude towards otherness.[14] In contrast to deconstruction, which seeks to liberate difference, hermeneutics (especially in Gadamer's tradition) calls for an engagement with difference. Gadamer contends that the other is most appreciated when engaged with in conversation (in the widest sense). In other words, for

Gadamer's hermeneutics it is a sign of respect for otherness to expose oneself to the new and unfamiliar, and to learn to understand her or him in all her or his manifold difference. However, similar to deconstruction, this call for engagement is not derived from a normative framework but rather from the recognition of an always already present process which occurs when people engage with each other. However, different from deconstruction, hermeneutics emphasises not what is unrepresented, that is what is 'other' and in need of liberating, but rather it recognises the other yet stresses the process of the production of shared meaning. In Gadamer's words: 'Whoever wants me to take deconstruction to heart and insists on difference stands at the beginning of a conversation, not its end'.[15] Gadamer thus sees hermeneutics as being complementary to deconstruction. The important difference is the perspective, which ultimately leads to different ethical attitudes: liberating difference or engaging with it. This book thus argues that hermeneutics allows for conceptualising peace, as in the end of a conversation, and not simply the opening up of a space for the other.

And yet, it is important to remember that introducing hermeneutics to conflict studies does not create a new 'method' to bring about peace and co-existence. Hermeneutics is simply a way of seeing and interpreting the world, not an action-plan to change it. All attempts to reduce hermeneutics to a praxeological impulse would run the risk of turning it into a method, which would destroy its openness and emphasis on contingency. However, the insights gleaned through a hermeneutic interpretation might allow for discussing politics in a particular light. With reference to efforts to reduce the occurrence of violent conflicts these politics would include a participatory approach (based on the notion of conversation and dialogue), a respect for difference (based on the acknowledgement that meaning is produced in the evaluation of the own as well as the other's horizon), an open, process orientated structure (based on the fusion of horizons being a process), as well as an appreciation of, and a willingness to, change. Hence, even though the approach taken in this book is to focus on the local level and traditional conflict management in Africa, its implications are much wider. With peace-building in war-torn societies being a burgeoning industry hermeneutics allows us to assess approaches and instruments which seek to contribute to social change and the consolidation of a sustainable peace after violent conflict. This may include, *inter alia*, reconciliation initiatives, transitional justice projects, memory work, nation-building and unification policies, as discussed in the following chapter.

Limits of traditional conflict management

To return to the discussion of different approaches to terminating violent conflicts at the beginning of the book, the analysis of the Teso mediation enables us to assess the strengths and weaknesses of traditional conflict management approaches and their modern hybrids such as the Teso Commission. I argued that in comparison to conflict settlement and conflict resolution traditional approaches promise to hold a number of benefits, including a high degree of local ownership and cultural appropriateness. In particular, through the use of mediation they strive for reaching consensus, restoring relationships and order, as well as for contributing to the reconciliation of the parties to the conflict. Crucially, in traditional conflict management, conflicts are not treated as isolated events but they are situated into the social context of the communities.

The case of Teso reveals, however, that these valuable strengths are marred by a number of weaknesses. First of all, traditional conflict management has the tendency to maintain the *status quo* rather than to introduce changes. Through being based on consensus and through seeking to restore relationships, harmony and order, it is inherently conservative, because wider structural inequalities remain ignored and social contexts unchanged. The Teso mediation serves as a stark reminder of how much underlying power asymmetries determine their outcomes. Traditional approaches, therefore, limit their contribution to the wider transformation of the antagonistic relationship between the parties to the conflict and to long-term social change.

In the same vein, the acceptance of an authority – in form of elders or, in our case, the Commissioners – opens the possibility for the abuse of their powerful role, as illustrated in this book. In contrast to conflict settlement and resolution approaches, mediators are not simply looked upon as facilitators but as leaders who can actually end the conflict. As a consequence, despite being situated in, rather than separated from, the relevant communities traditional efforts do not simply de-politicise conflicts by ignoring the particular backgrounds of the parties, but they turn the backgrounds of the parties into parts of the solutions. In other words, they are essentially built on asymmetries and inequality and perpetuate them in the process. Consequently, they do not adhere to what we from a Western perspective consider to be just.[16]

A further problem arises regarding the sustainability of traditional conflict management. Since there are no checks and balances it cannot be guaranteed that agreements and promises are in fact being kept. This is particularly important if compensation was part of the consensus reached in the mediation process, but if it is not kept in the aftermath. The promise of economic development by the government of Uganda serves as a stark reminder of how easily such a consensus can deteriorate if the parties do not adhere to their word.

The above criticism is particularly relevant if the mediation process was between different communities rather than within one community which shares the same values and norms. For,

> [w]hen there is no sense of collective responsibility, there is no point in thinking in terms of reintegration and no social regulation can operate. When a conflict crops up at a macro level, such as intertribally or between states, there are no more superordinate values that can be emphasized to trigger the resolution mechanism. The social fabric produced by the culture is insufficiently dense and resistant to be able to serve as a referent for the purpose of reinserting the deviant member.[17]

As a consequence, it is important to note that traditional conflict resolution has only a limited application for conflicts between communities, or as in our case, between a community and the state. Even though, similar to communal conflicts, many external conflicts centre on struggles over power, 'the wide range of actors and forces, including external ones, as well as the national and sometimes regional scope the conflicts, render expedient traditional strategies inadequate'.[18] In the absence of community relations to bind the parties to the conflict together, new values need to be build before, during and the conflict management process.[19] How this can be encouraged after the violence is the subject of the final chapter.

8
Dealing with the Past of Violent Conflicts

This book has sought to tell 'a different kind of peace story'.[1] It began with a discussion of different approaches to terminating violent conflicts and concludes that, as the example of Teso illustrates, mere termination is not enough since it may leave the antagonistic relationship between the parties to the conflict in place. With about half of all settlements relapsing into violence within five years, dealing with the past of a violent conflict is paramount. In lieu of a conclusion, and in the light of the achievements and failures of the Teso mediation, this final chapter therefore opens up the scope of the book to explore what means and mechanisms exist to tackle the legacy of a violent past. In other words, it seeks to illustrate what types of peace can be envisaged and pursued.[2] As argued in Chapter 2, after a violent conflict it is of major importance to develop a new, peaceful future which does not reproduce the tensions of the past which led to the fighting. In the following, I therefore investigate how a conflict transformation process can be encouraged by outsiders to these communities, such as national or international organisations. Since war-torn societies are gaining in interest of academics and practitioners alike the instruments transitional justice, reconciliation initiatives and unification policies are being developed as ways of dealing with the past of a violent conflict. What impact they have on the transformation of conflicts is the subject of the following chapter.

Transitional justice

Despite its relative novelty, the notion of transitional justice is rapidly gaining prominence as a field of investigation into processes of post-conflict transformation and peacebuilding. While some scholars prefer a limited, exclusively punitive and retributive understanding, the term is generally used more widely to incorporate compensatory, distributive and restorative justice.[3] By and large, the aim of transitional justice is to uncover the truth of human rights crimes, to publicly acknowledge the suffering of victims, to identify and punish the responsible individuals and groups, to establish the rule of law and to contribute to reconciliation as well as political and economic development.[4]

Historically, the evolution of the concept of transitional justice, and its academic reflection, has moved through various stages.[5] After World War II the objective was to prevent the repetition of crimes such as the Holocaust and war crimes through retribution, in particular, through the Nürnberg Trials and Tokyo Tribunals. Subsequently, during the Cold War, regime stabilisation became a central concern, leading to a policy of pardon and oblivion, as, for instance, apparent in the ample amnesty law in Brazil in 1979, the Naval Club agreement in Uruguay in 1984 and the 'due obedience' and 'Final Stop' degrees in Argentina in 1986 and 1987.[6] This phase was followed by an approach to transitional justice which focused heavily on truth commissions, in particular in Latin America. Presently, with the establishment of the International Criminal Court (ICC) the prosecution component of transitional justice has gained new prominence turning criminal justice into a central component of transitional justice. At the same time, while students of transitional justice were initially concerned mainly with macro-level instruments such as judicial (e.g., tribunals), non-judicial (e.g., truth commissions), and national or international tribunals (e.g., the International Crime Tribunals for Rwanda and Yugoslavia, ICTR and ICTY) as well as a focus on perpetrators, the attention has recently been broadened to include micro levels, such as victims and their concerns.[7]

The political space opened up by the end of the East–West antagonism and the ensuing proliferation of violent conflicts, in particular, have turned conflict transformation through transitional justice into a possibility. In the eyes of international donors '[p]rosecution of perpetrators of grave human rights violations is not only an obligation under international law, but also a key element of activities to address the past'.[8] Nevertheless, so far only a few studies are available to assess the impact of transitional justice instruments on conflict transformation.[9] In this context, parallel to the increased interest in transitional justice its criticism is growing. It is for instance argued that the top-down approach of transitional justice often only addresses the most prominent conflict lines – for instance, 'black' and 'white' in the case of the South African TRC – while other cleavages, such as the relationship between black security forces and members of their home communities where they committed crimes, remain unaddressed.[10] Moreover, Fletcher and Weinstein suggest that a predominantly judicial view on war-torn societies (even though this is based on a rather narrow definition of transitional justice) misses the serious social impact of violence on the community level, and in particular gender-based violence.

> To date, truth and justice have been the rallying cries for efforts to assist communities in (re)building in the aftermath of mass atrocities. These employ a paradigm that focuses on individuals who have been wronged (victims) and those who inflicted their wounds (perpetrators). Missing is an appreciation for the damage mass violence causes at the level of communities.[11]

Others add that social, economic and distributive justice are equally important for transforming in post-conflict societies.[12] This is particularly pertinent in cases where the violent conflict was sparked by a sense of inequality and structural violence.

As indicated above, historically the most common way of rendering justice post-conflict has been through criminal courts with punitive capacities. In addition to domestic courts, international crime tribunals, such as the ICTR and ICTY, as well as the newly established ICC, have recently gained momentum. It has been suggested that trials in the aftermath of violence contribute to conflict transformation by 'putting past wrongs right', restoring the victims' dignity, reducing the desire for revenge, providing accountability, retribution and deterrence as well as an acknowledgement of the harm done.[13] They individualise guilt and draw a clear line between the victims and perpetrators – even though this is not always possible – which renders the rest of the people innocent, enabling them to improve their relationships.[14] An alternative view suggests that justice is less about the punishment of perpetrators than the vindication of victims through recognising their injury, which constitutes a necessary step for the healing process.[15] In this sense, while punishment remains the prime objective, some courts – most notably the ICTR – make wider claims such as contributing to national reconciliation.

So far, there is, however, no empirical evidence that criminal trials have contributed to influencing the relationship between the parties to the conflict and to transforming violent conflicts.[16] Rather, international tribunals, in particular, potentially obstruct national reconciliation processes for they deprive the society of the opportunity to prosecute criminals themselves, often leading to conflict between the tribunal and the new government, such as in the case of Rwanda. Or else, they may encourage the perception among the parties to the conflict of being unjustly held responsible for war crimes, as manifest in the bitterness of Croats and Serbs – and to a lesser extent Bosniaks – towards the ICTY, again reproducing conflict lines. In individual cases, such as the ICTY has repeatedly shown, tribunals can turn war criminals into national heroes and martyrs, perpetuating anger and resentment among the victims. Even though they might still the initial impulse of the victims for revenge, the impact of trials on reducing divisions between parties to a conflict is therefore questionable. Rather, they potentially perpetuate the conflict through maintaining an 'us' vs. 'them' dichotomy. One of the main dividing lines among academics and practitioner is thus the tension between justice and reconciliation. While some argue that the two aspects are mutually constitutive, others suggest that justice can also lead to friction and deepen the already existing cleavages in post-conflict societies.[17] Moreover, there is disagreement over whether there is a duty to punish, regardless of the political context, or whether political constraints on justice are legitimate.[18] It is furthermore important to ask: 'Who is actually guilty?' With reference to the Holocaust, Karl Jaspers identifies four categories of guilt: the criminal guilt of those who committed the actual crimes, the political guilt of those who helped them to get to power, the moral guilt of by-standers and the metaphysical guilt of those who survived while others were killed and who thus failed to do everything possible to prevent the massacres.[19] The challenge for transitional justice is how these various levels of guilt can be addressed?

In addition, many – in particular, local – people affected by violent conflict are often far removed from the processes and politics of courts and tribunals – as in the case of Rwanda – so that their decisions (or even existence) are often not known and thus have no impact on the relations between the parties to the conflict. At the local community level, day-to-day matters (such as in poor countries mere survival) and relatively peaceful co-existence with former enemies are more pressing issues than pursuing justice, even though this might remain a remote wish of those who have been wronged.[20]

One further point of contention about post-conflict justice is the question whose justice is exercised, and for whom. Julie Mertus differentiates various interest groups in post-conflict environments – for example, the international community, local power brokers, victims, perpetrators and by-standers – who have different objectives and motivations regarding naming crimes, prosecuting perpetrators, developing legal frameworks or recording history.[21] For instance, for the new post-conflict government, the objective of transitional justice is often to introduce a new political order. Through the break with the past, a new government absolves all responsibilities of former crimes and thus legitimates the new state. In contrast, victims are more concerned with revenge and vindication while the international community is motivated by upholding and refining its standards and institutions. The importance of Mertus's differentiation lies in the acknowledgement that there is not simply one form of justice, but that different groups have different interests and ensuing strategies, rendering justice a political project.

In addition to trials and tribunals, the interest in truth commissions is growing rapidly. In many cases, they are promoted as alternative ways of dealing with past injustices and as an instrument for addressing the relationship between the parties to the conflict.[22] Through the testimonies of victims and perpetrators, they reveal the abuses of a particular regime or violent conflict in order to establish a comprehensive record of the crimes. In this sense, individual testimonies serve as alternative sources of 'memory' for events that had been wiped out from official 'memory'.[23] The introduction of closure with a painful past through an official record of the atrocities is intended to consolidate new democracies by fostering a national consensus. Even though some truth commissions have a rather limited mandate of simply creating a record of past wrongs (which might later be used for prosecution such as in Chile and Argentina), their role is increasingly shifting to incorporate elements of restorative justice and reconciliation.[24] For instance, based on the dictum 'revealing is healing' the South African TRC attempted to promote a national healing and reconciliation process through encouraging a cathartic moment.[25] And yet, research shows that healing in South Africa seems far-fetched considering that two-thirds of South Africans believe that the TRC's investigations led to a deterioration of race relations.[26]

Despite their increasing popularity – reflected in the establishment of truth commissions in many post-conflict contexts – critics reject their often profoundly Christian character, which situates them firmly in a Western cultural horizon and potentially renders them blind to culturally situated aspects of truth, justice and reconciliation.[27] Truth commissions have furthermore been accused of seeking to establish a single, uniform national memory of the past, which reduces the complexity of individual experiences and minimises the importance of dealing with particular issues on a local level.[28]

Moreover, truth commissions are essentially political tools and thus subjected to political will.[29] When lacking the independence of the government – as well as the ownership of the population – they potentially fail, as in the case of Serbia, where the commission was set up due to US pressure and turned into an instrument by the power holders to deny responsibility for war crimes through exclusively blaming the other side. It has thus been argued that it is important not to overestimate the impact of truth commissions on post-conflict environments.[30] Even though they often conclude with policy recommendations to prevent future violence their advice remains ineffective in the absence of political will. As illustrated in Guatemala, for instance, despite the initial presidential support, the recording of crimes by the commission failed to provoke political action, and its recommendations – for example, to promote the role of indigenous people – were ignored after a change in government, leaving the main conflict lines in place.

A further point of contention is the possibility of establishing the truth about past human rights abuses *per se*. In this context, it has been suggested to broaden the understanding of truth from a merely positivist perspective to a more interpretative approach.[31] With similar intentions, the TRC differentiates between four notions of truth ranging from factual truth via narrative and social truth to restorative truth.[32] First, forensic or factual truth is based on collected evidence. On an individual level, this includes what happened to whom, where, when and how, and who was involved while, on a more general level, it incorporates the contexts, causes and patterns of human rights violations. Second, the Commission refers to personal and narrative truth signifying the meaning victims and perpetrators give to the multi-layered experience of the crimes. This story-telling supposedly has healing potential. Third, social truth signifies the dialogic process of sharing experiences with the aim of transcending the divisions of the past by carefully listening to the contexts and motives of all involved. It is here where truth borders reconciliation. Healing and restorative truth, lastly, places facts into the context of human relationships since the establishment of a truth about the past, it is argued, prevents the recurrence of violence in the future. Importantly, though, even with a broad understanding of the notion of truth there is so far little evidence that truth telling does in fact promote conflict transformation for agreement about its content is highly unlikely in a post-conflict scenario, in particular, over who is responsible for what crimes.[33]

Reconciliation

Parallel to transitional justice, the academic and practical interest in reconciliation initiatives has gained in prominence since the end of the Cold War. The meaning of the term reconciliation – as well as its practise – remain, however, highly contested. In its most basic sense reconciliation refers to 'the process of developing a mutual conciliatory accommodation between antagonistic or formerly antagonistic persons or groups'[34] or to 'render no longer opposed'.[35] Against this backdrop, approaches to reconciliation span from a profoundly moral – and often Christian – understanding, on one side of the spectrum, to a rather pragmatic view based on co-existence, on the other. Inherent in a Christian interpretation of the term is the idea that the restitution of the victim's dignity goes hand in hand with the redemption of the perpetrators and their sins.[36] In contrast, a pragmatic view considers reconciliation to be essential for addressing the relationship level of violent conflicts in order to prevent a relapse into violence. In this sense, reconciliation initiatives examine and address the relationship between the parties to the conflict and their violent past, leading to some degree of social transformation, if successful. One central characteristic is thus that reconciliation goes beyond resolution and political arrangements to resolve differences and hostile actions through leading to a change in antagonistic attitudes. Crucially, thus, it differs from a rights-based approach such as transitional justice since it seeks to reduce the dichotomous relationship between the parties to the conflict in order to permit peaceful co-existence and sustainable peace.

Even though reconciliation is often equated with producing harmony[37] – and criticised for eradicating difference[38] – it can also be interpreted as a profoundly political tool. For Jean Bethke Elshtain, it implies 'bringing matters into the framework within which conflict can be adjudicated short of bloodshed'.[39] This renders possible a future where 'one no longer begins with the deadly a priori assumption that the majority or a sizable proportion of one's fellow countrymen or women are outsiders or enemies'.[40] Instead, Elshtain suggests, everybody is enclosed within a single socio-political frame. In this sense, while reducing antagonism, reconciliation does not seek to eliminate difference.

Despite different interpretations, historically reconciliation remains a Western-centric notion. Revealingly, neither the term nor the context can easily be translated into many other languages, even though other cultures and religions may have somewhat similar concepts such as *pomirenja* in Serbo-Croatian, *nahe biti* in Timorees or *musalaha* in Arabic. In order to pay tribute to non-Western approaches of dealing with the past it has thus been suggested to treat the term reconciliation as a container concept without defined meaning, which nevertheless allows for discussing politics and processes related to social and political transformation after violent conflicts.[41] This can lead to a cross-cultural agreement about various aspects significant for establishing a peaceful future. They may include that reconciliation does not equal forgetting or forgiving, that it is a long process which cannot be formalised since it depends on the local context, that it has to derive from within society and cannot be imposed from outside, that individual reconciliation cannot be presumed and that therefore the focus should be on national reconciliation, and, lastly, that social reconciliation should be a collective process which requires significant social and political change.

Reconciliation initiatives can be placed at the national or individual level. Regarding the former, it 'can allow opposing parties to debate and govern together without latent conflict and bitterness over past lies'.[42] In this sense, national reconciliation initiatives are part of the wider agenda of political change in post-conflict situations, often with the intention of enhancing the credibility of new regimes. Consequently, democratisation and reconciliation are intertwined; in fact, they depend on each other. 'While democratic compromise produces the solutions regarding the *issues* in conflict, . . . reconciliation addresses the *relationships* between those who will have to implement those solutions'.[43] In most approaches, however, this political dimension of reconciliation projects is missed or deliberately de-emphasised. In contrast, from an individual perspective, reconciliation is much more complex and thus more difficult to achieve since each person's needs are different. Some people, survivors in particular, might even resist any suggestion to reconcile since they refuse to settle with the murders of their loved-ones. And yet, what speaks against differentiating national and individual levels is that the violence of the past is highly personalised in people's memories. Despite high levels of political awareness and a general understanding of the broader political dynamics of the past, people approach reconciliation in personal terms, that is, they hold individuals accountable.[44]

Key players in post-conflict reconciliation processes are often governments or non-governmental organisations. Since the strategy of the former is mainly to create a unified nation through memory and a collective identity, it shall be addressed separately in the next section on unification policies. Regarding non-governmental agents, the central aspect of many, in particular Western, reconciliation initiatives is to address – or 'solve' – the causes of the conflict. This requires the establishment of confidence and trust as well as an agenda of 'working through' the differences and antagonisms. In many cases, the most prominent agents to set up reconciliation initiatives are churches and mosques, such as, for example, the Inter-Religious Council in Sierra Leone or the Mozambican Christian Council who are addressing the legacy of two of Africa's most violent conflicts.

Moreover, local leaders and traditional healers play a prominent role in reducing the antagonism between the parties to the conflict. These traditional resources are however not available to all societies. In the countries of former Yugoslavia, for instance, traditional reconciliation mechanisms either do not exist or cannot be used due to the religious divide. Importantly, in contrast to Western approaches, many traditional reconciliation initiatives follow an approach based less a problem-solving than on closure, that is, a 'burying the past and moving on'. This is often based on symbolic gestures such as 'bending spears' or killing oxen, or on rituals of cleansing or re-initiation. For instance, in Sierra Leone 'bush wives' (female sexual slaves) spend several days with traditional healers who rub chalk on their bodies, give them new cloths and jewellery and include them in dancing and drumming in order to render them 'clean' again.[45] While hybrids between modern and traditional approaches are increasing in popularity, it is however important not to fall prey to a romanticisation of past or of 'nativism'.

Unification

The last body of approaches to dealing with the past of violent conflicts focuses on what I call unification policies. Unification policies are top-down efforts to influence the relationship aspect of conflicts through turning a war-torn society into one collective identity. For instance, creating a national identity – in particular, via the notion of an all inclusive political identity, that is, citizenship – can be a vehicle for overcoming cleavages which have led to violent conflict in the past. This is predominantly done by re-shaping the identity of the parties to the conflict through referring to a common past and future. As argued throughout the book, collective identities are produced through memory discourses since remembrance has a coercive force which creates a sense of belonging. This view is complemented by Renan, as quoted in Chapter 2, who reminds us that collective identities are also produced by forgetting.[46] Whole societies may choose to forget uncomfortable knowledge and turn it into 'open secrets', which are known by all, and knowingly not known. In this context, Stanley Cohen introduces the term 'social amnesia', which refers to a mode of forgetting by which a whole society separates

itself from its discreditable past record.[47] This might happen at an organised, official and conscious level – the deliberate cover-up, the rewriting
of history – or through the type of cultural slippage that occurs when
information disappears. Instead of ethnic division it may lead to a 'fictive
ethnicity', a community instituted by a nation-state. 'Fictive ethnicity'
does, however, not signify an illusion but rather a fabrication, since

> [n]o nation possesses an ethnic base naturally, but as social formations
> are nationalised, the populations included within them, divided up
> amongst them or dominated by them are ethnicised – that is, repre-
> sented in the past or in the future as if they form a natural community,
> possessing of itself of origins, culture and interests which transcends
> individuals and social conditions.[48]

Through this discourse on fictive ethnicity, group identities are subor-
dinated to the unity of all as citizens. In this context, current writing
about the politics of memory has been strongly influenced by the work
of Benedict Anderson and Eric Hobsbawm. Hobsbawm, as discussed in
Chapter 6, is predominantly concerned with how authorities invent
traditions – and their seeming continuity with the past – in order to
maintain their authority, forge social cohesion and create a common
culture.[49] For him, politics resembles a project of social engineering. Hobsbawm's notion of the nation is similar to Anderson's view of a nation as
collectivity defined by its own manner of imagining itself.[50] The significance of both lies in their illustration of how political power shapes what
is remembered and what is forgotten, and how this constitutes collective
identities in the present. In this sense, '[m]emory is a struggle over power
and who gets to decide the future'.[51] Remembrance remains a profoundly
political endeavour since it is central to present day conflicts over forms
of the state, social relations and subjectivity. The political aspect is rooted
in the practice which binds up rituals of national identification to fab-
ricate a collective identity.[52] This takes place, *inter alia*, at the level of
national commemorations, the re-writing of history and its teaching as
well as through museums and memorials. As argued throughout this
book, the way a violent past is remembered is central to every conflict
transformation effort. As a consequence, if our identity is always rooted
in the past, the question is not whether one should remember, but how.[53]

Compared to transitional justice, which seeks to put wrongs right,
and reconciliation, which seeks to address and/or solve the causes of the
conflict or terminate it through symbolic gestures, unification policies
attempt to create one collective identity and to unify the parties to

the conflict. This carries the risk that, in spite of their peace-promoting appearance, unification policies potentially serve as a means to eradicate difference and to cover up power politics by new leaders. In its extreme, this can contribute to silencing critical voices and stifling dissent from unity.[54]

The impact of transitional justice, reconciliation and unification on transforming violent conflicts

Against the backdrop of the objective of this book, the question arises how transitional justice, reconciliation initiatives and unification policies impact on processes of conflict transformation and social change. Albeit pursuing the same aim – dealing with the past of a violent conflict – instruments and policies based on these notions pursue different strategies, use different instruments and rely on different agents. In this sense, transitional justice seeks to put past wrongs right, restore the victims' dignity and punish the offenders. It is built on individual and not collective guilt. Through using instruments such as trails and tribunals or truth commissions it can pursue both, punitive and restorative justice yet it remains a top-down instrument targeting individual victims and perpetrators. In contrast, reconciliation initiatives seek to address the causes of a conflict or to symbolically terminate them. Their strategy is thus to change the relationship between the parties with the aid of, *inter alia*, community dialogues and exchanges, either through top-down national projects or bottom-up community initiatives. Importantly, though, they tend to focus on the communities, rather than on individuals, and emphasise the collective. Unification policies, finally, attempt to create a collective identity, for instance, on the basis of citizenship, and apply instruments such as nation-building, public memory work, history telling and social engineering. In most cases, they are initiated by the government, that is, they operate top-down and address individuals who share some common traits which might unite them into one collective identity.

Important for the context of this book on conflict transformation is that the three instruments of dealing with the past differ in their approach to difference. Transitional justice, through its focus on individual perpetrators and victims as well as its confrontational character, maintains the difference between the parties to the conflict – and potentially also the antagonism. As discussed above, trials and tribunals, in particular, may lead to a sense of injustice, self-victimisation and resentment. This perpetuates rather than reduces the antagonistic relationship between the parties to a conflict. In contrast, reconciliation initiatives

maintain difference yet, if successful, they reduce the level of antagonism between the parties. This, so it is often criticised, might happen at
the expense of justice. Unification policies, lastly, seek to dissolve the difference between the parties to the conflict, turning them into one unit.
This bears the risk of ignoring their antagonistic relationship which may
continue to simmer in the background and collapse if the society comes
under new duress.

Since the example of Teso has shown that after the termination of
a violent conflict dealing with the past is crucial, the question poses
itself whether there is a way to judge which of these instruments – or
which combination thereof – is best suited for a post-conflict society?
While this is, of course, dependent of the actual context of the war-torn
society it is important to bear in mind 'that wars ... only really end when
they are *transcended*, when they ... [go] beyond the traditional currency
of victory and defeat'.[55] As argued in Chapter 3, the transcending of a
war does not simply re-distribute power but challenges *and changes* these
very structures. At first sight, this is most likely when following the path
of reconciliation, even though this might be difficult for people who
consider themselves to be victims of war and violence. In this case, it
might be helpful to introduce different instruments at different points
in time.

Nevertheless, after being exposed to a violent conflict, the social structures that had previously made up the world and provided meaning to
its inhabitants lie in shambles. This book has argued that these worlds
cannot be simply recreated, they have to be created anew, for recreation
would simply reproduce the tensions that led to the violent conflict.
Between the old and the new worlds lies a discontinuity which calls for
bridging. To avoid setbacks and to promote a peaceful future in the odd-
time in-between war and peace requires an act of creative imagination
or a poetic process. The post-conflict society, together with the former
enemy, has to establish new ways of relating to each other, ways that do
not re-create the tensions of the past.

Admittedly, this is not an easy task. To return to Uganda, albeit not
to Teso, in the northern region of the Acholi the Lord's Resistance Army
(LRA) has been tyrannising the residents for almost two decades. Still,
despite the experience of violence and hardship, the tendency among the
local population after the recent ceasefire agreement between the LRA
and the Ugandan government is to say 'peace now, justice later'. This
stands in contrast to the efforts of the international community to try
Joseph Kony and his key leaders in front of the ICC, as initially requested
by the Ugandan government. At present, the search warrant against

Kony and his people stands in the way of a long-overdue peace accord since the LRA refuses to surrender as long as it faces criminal prosecution. The situation in northern Uganda hence highlights the dilemmas and challenges when faced with the legacy of violence. While this book does not provide any simple answers it has sought to highlight the importance of looking at the social and historical contexts of conflicts and how they influence the invention of peace. This requires, first and foremost, paying attention to the local, often neglected voices of those who were affected by the violence and who have to live with the kind of peace that will prevail in the future. What lies in-between war and peace is central to this analysis.

Notes

Introduction

1. This inverts the title of a book by Carolyn Nordstrom. Carolyn Nordstrom, *A Different Kind of War Story*, Philadelphia: University of Pennsylvania Press, 1997.
2. From a different, often more institutional and political angle this is also the subject of peacebuilding literature. See, for instance, Edward Newman and Oliver P. Richmond, eds, *Challenges to Peacebuilding: Managing Spoilers During Conflict Resolution*, New York/Tokyo: United Nations University Press, 2006; Roland Paris, *At War's End. Building Peace after Civil Conflict*, Cambridge: Cambridge University Press, 2005; John Stephen Stedman et al., *Ending Civil War: The Implementation of Peace Agreements*, Boulder: Lynne Reiner, 2002.
3. Post-positivism is used as an umbrella term for interpretative approaches to social science including post-structuralism, post-modernism, post-Marxism, phenomenology, deconstruction and critical theory. See, for instance, Richard Ashley and R.B.J. Walker, Reading Dissidence/Writing the Discipline: Crisis and the Question of Sovereignty in International Studies, *International Studies Quarterly*, Vol. 34, No. 3, 1990; James Der Derian, ed. *International Theory. Critical Investigations*, London/Basingstoke: Palgrave Macmillan, 1995; James Der Derian and Michael J. Shapiro, eds, *International/Intertextual Relations. Postmodern Reading of World Politics*, New York: Lexington Books, 1989; R.B.J. Walker, *Inside/Outside: International Relations as Political Theory*, Cambridge: Cambridge University Press, 1993.
4. David Campbell, *National Deconstruction. Violence, Identity, and Justice in Bosnia*, Minnesota: University Press, 1998; David Campbell, Why Fight: Humanitarianism, Principles, and Post-Structuralism, *Millennium*, Vol. 27, No. 3, 1998; Vivienne Jabri, *Discourses on Violence. Conflict Analysis Reconsidered*, Manchester: Manchester University Press, 1996; Oliver P. Richmond, *Maintaining Order, Making Peace*, Basingstoke: Palgrave Macmillan, 2002; Michael J. Shapiro, *Violent Cartographies. Mapping Cultures of War*, Minneapolis: University of Minnesota Press, 1997; Hidemi Suganami, *On the Causes of War*, Oxford: Clarendon, 1996; Franke Wilmer, The Social Construction of Conflict and Reconciliation in the Former Yugoslavia, *Social Justice*, Vol. 25, No. 4, 1998.
5. David Campbell, *Writing Security: United States Foreign Policy and the Politics of Identity*, Manchester: Manchester University Press, 1992.
6. John A. Vasquez, War Endings: What Science and Constructivism Can Tell Us, *Millennium*, Vol. 26, No. 3, 1997, p. 672.
7. Jacob Torfing, *New Theories of Discourse. Laclau, Mouffe and Zizek*, Oxford: Blackwell, 1999, p. 300.
8. David Howarth, 'Discourse Theory and Political Analysis', in David Howarth, et al., eds, *Discourse Theory and Political Analysis. Identities, Hegemonies and Social Change*, Manchester: Manchester University Press, 2000, p. 3.

9. Thomas Speckmann, Frieden schaffen nur mit Waffen. Vom Wiederaufbau gescheiterter Staaten, *Merkur*, Vol. 59, No. 5, 2005.

10. Jabri, *Discourses on Violence*. Esp. Chapter 6.

11. Ibid., p. 157.

12. For a brief excursion in this direction, also prompted by Vivienne Jabri, see Hugh Miall et al., *Contemporary Conflict Resolution*, Cambridge: Polity Press, 1999, pp. 293–5.

13. Gianni Vattimo, *Beyond Interpretation. The Meaning of Hermeneutics for Philosophy*, Translated by D. Webb, Cambridge/Oxford: Polity Press, 1997, p. 10.

14. Maurice Halbwachs, *On Collective Memory*, Chicago/London: University of Chicago Press, 1992, p. 43. For a seminal study on the impact of different context on remembering see Liisa H. Malkki, *Purity and Exile. Violence, Memory, and National Cosmology among Hutu Refugees in Tanzania*, Chicago: University of Chicago Press, 1995.

15. Milan Kundera, *Testaments Betrayed*, London: Faber and Faber, 1995, p. 128.

16. Although the fusion of horizons involves at least two parties, it is not the objective of this book to portray both sides equally. The main focus is on the people of Teso, while the Government of Uganda's position is only infrequently articulated through speeches by Museveni, government publications or the reports of the Teso Commission. Two reasons are significant for this one-sided portrayal: one hermeneutic, one practical. Firstly, from a hermeneutic perspective, one of my central arguments is that in the hermeneutic process of understanding we always bring ourselves in. It is through our horizons that we interpret the other, and it is our horizon that changes in the process of understanding. The subject of this book is to illustrate how the horizon of the people of Teso changed in the process of understanding the Museveni government. Any interpretation of the government, therefore, has to be considered through their lens, and not through that of an external analysts, as much as this is possible. Hence, in this book the Museveni government is equally absent and present. It is absent because its horizons are not discussed explicitly, yet it is present by proxy through the way it constitutes the people of Teso in opposition to it. Through discussing the Teso identity, which in its antagonism is established through difference, the government always remains central to the analysis. The interpretation of the mediation process by the Iteso and Kumam is highly dependent on this disposition. In this sense, it does not matter what the government itself did or does but how the Iteso and Kumam interpret it. Secondly, from a practical perspective, the book could only be a time and space restricted project and to add an in-depth analysis of the Ugandan government would have exhausted its limits. In addition, an analysis of a government comes with obstacles such as limited access to information and resources. This book therefore does not tell the story of Uganda but only of Teso.

17. Patrick Chabal and Jean-Pascal Daloz, *Culture Troubles. Politics and the Interpretation of Meaning*, London: Hurst, 2006, p. 21.

18. Michel Foucault, 'Two Lectures', in Michael Kelly, ed. *Critique and Power. Recasting the Foucault/Habermas Debate*, Cambridge, MA/London: MIT Press, 1994, p. 22. The focus on the local shall, however, not be to the exclusion of

regional, or even global, aspects but rather acknowledge their interaction, or the lack thereof.

19. For a more detailed discussion see Tim Holmes, *A Participatory Approach in Practice: Understanding Fieldworkers' Use of Participatory Rural Appraisal in Action Aid the Gambia*, Brighton: Institute of Development Studies, 2001; Jay Rothman, Action Evaluation and Conflict Resolution: Theory and Practice, *Mediation Quarterly*, Vol. 15, No. 2, 1997; Patricia Spittal, '"We are Dying. It is Finished". Linking an Ethnographic Research Design to an HIV/AIDS Participatory Approach in Uganda', in Susan E. Smith et al., eds, *Nurtured by Knowledge. Learning to Do Participatory Action Research*, Ottawa: International Development Research Centre, 1997.

1 Violent conflicts and their termination

1. HSR Group, 'Human Security Report', HSR Group, 2006.
2. Egohosa E. Osaghae, 'Applying Traditional Methods to Modern Conflict: Possibilities and Limits', in William I. Zartman, ed. *Traditional Cures for Modern Conflicts. African Continent 'Medicine'*, Boulder: Lynne Rienner, 2000, p. 208.
3. Robin Luckham, Ismail Ahmed, Robert Muggah and Sarah White, *Conflict and Poverty in Sub-Sahara Africa: An Assessment of the Issues and Evidence*, Brighton: Institute of Development Studies, 2001, p. 4.
4. Alex de Waal, *Sudan: What Kind of State? What Kind of Crisis?* London: LSE Crisis States Research Centre, 2007, p. 16.
5. Elisabeth Porter, Gillian Robinson, Marie Smyth, Albrecht Schnabel and Eghosa Osaghe, *Researching Conflict in Africa. Insights and Experiences*, Tokyo/New York: United Nations University Press, 2005, p. 2.
6. Mats Berdal and David Malone, eds, *Greed and Grievance: Economic Agendas in Civil Wars*, New York: International Peace Academy, 2000; Mark Duffield, *Global Governance and the New Wars: The Merging of Development and Security*, London: Zed Books, 2001; Mary Kaldor, *New and Old Wars: Organized Violence in a Global Era*, Cambridge: Polity Press, 1999.
7. Paul Collier and Anke Hoeffer, On the Incidences of Civil War in Africa, *Journal of Conflict Resolution*, Vol. 46, No. 1, 2002; Chris Cramer, Homo Economicus Goes to War: Methodological Individualism, Rational Choice and the Political Economy of War, *World Development*, Vol. 30, No. 11, 2002.
8. Cramer, Homo Economicus Goes to War.
9. Mary Kaldor, *Global Insecurity: Vol. III of Restructuring the Global Military Sector*, Cassell: Pinter, 2000, p. 7.
10. See, for example, Mats Berdal, How 'New' Are 'New Wars'? Global Economic Change and the Study of Civil War, *Global Governance*, Vol. 9, No. 4, 2003; Paul Richards, *Fighting for the Rain Forests. War, Youth and Resources in Sierra Leone*, London: James Currey: African Issues, 1996.
11. Paul Richards, *No Peace, No War. An Anthropology of Contemporary Armed Conflict*, Oxford: James Currey, 2005, p. 15.
12. Jabri, *Discourses on Violence*, p. 3.
13. Richards, *No Peace, No War*, p. 4.
14. Richmond, *Maintaining Order, Making Peace*, p. 9.

15. Mark Howard Ross, Creating Conditions for Peacemaking: Theories of Practice in Ethnic Conflict Resolution, *Ethnic and Racial Studies*, Vol. 23, No. 6, 2000, p. 1023. See also Miall, Ramsbotham and Woodhouse, *Contemporary Conflict Resolution*. Esp. Chapter 7.
16. Roger Fisher, William Ury and Bruce Patton, *Getting to Yes: Negotiating Agreement without Giving In*, New York: Penguin Books, 1983; Cordula Reimann, *Assessing the State of the Art in Conflict Transformation*, Berlin: Berghof Research Center for Constructive Conflict Management, 2001, p. 8; Ross, Creating Conditions for Peacemaking, p. 1022.
17. Reimann, *Conflict Transformation*, p. 9.
18. Fisher, Ury and Patton, *Getting to Yes*. As also described in Ross, Creating Conditions for Peacemaking.
19. Ross, Creating Conditions for Peacemaking, p. 1011. See also Roger Fisher, Elisabeth Kopelman and Andres Schneider, *Beyond Machiavelli: Tools for Coping with Conflict*, Cambridge: Harvard University Press, 1994; Ronald Fisher, *Interactive Conflict Resolution*, Syracuse: Syracuse University Press, 1997.
20. Fisher, Kopelman and Schneider, *Beyond Machiavelli*.
21. Ross, Creating Conditions for Peacemaking, p. 1022.
22. John Burton, *Conflict: Resolution and Provention*, New York: St. Martin's Press, 1990; Fisher, *Interactive Conflict Resolution*.
23. Reimann, *Conflict Transformation*, p. 9.
24. Burton, *Conflict: Resolution and Provention*, p. 23.
25. Ibid., p. 36.
26. Ibid., p. 242.
27. Ross, Creating Conditions for Peacemaking, p. 1022.
28. Burton, *Conflict: Resolution and Provention*, p. 205.
29. Jeffrey Rubin, 'Western Perspectives on Conflict Resolution', in Paul E. Salem, ed. *Conflict Resolution in the Arab World: Selected Essays*, Beirut: American University of Beirut, 1997, p. 6.
30. Richmond, *Maintaining Order, Making Peace*, p. 132.
31. Vivienne Jabri, 'Revisiting Change and Conflict: On Underlying Assumptions and the De-Politicisation of Conflict Resolution', in David Bloomfield and Beatrix Schmelzle, eds, *Conflict Transformation and Social Change*, Berlin: Berghof Center for Constructive Conflict Management, 2006, p. 3.
32. The role of women is particularly worth mentioning here. Like all members of a society they are greatly affected by violent conflicts yet due to their often-inferior role they are rarely party to conflict settlement or resolution efforts. In recognition of this deficit, in October 2000, the United Nations Security Council unanimously passed Resolution 1325, the first resolution ever that specifically addresses the impact of war on women as well as the contribution of women to ending violent conflicts. While this is an important step forward it remains to be seen whether the Resolution will lead to actual changes.
33. Jabri, 'Revisiting Change and Conflict'.
34. Oliver P. Richmond, 'A Genealogy of Peacemaking: The Creation and Re-Creation of Order', *Alternatives*, Vol. 26, No. 3, 2001, p. 322.
35. Norbert Ropers, *Roles and Functions of Third Parties in the Constructive Management of Ethnopolitical Conflicts*, Berlin: Berghof Research Centre for Constructive Conflict Management, 1997, p. 8.

36. Susanne Buckley-Zistel, Development Assistance and Conflict Assessment Methodology, *Journal for Conflict, Security and Development*, Vol. 3, No. 1, 2003, p. 121.
37. Ropers, *Roles and Functions of Third Parties*, p. 8.
38. Mark Duffield quoted in Oliver Richmond, *Maintaining Order, Making Peace*, p. 126.
39. Paul E. Salem, 'A Critique of Western Conflict Resolution from a Non-Western Perspective: Selected Essays', in Paul E. Salem, ed. *Conflict Resolution in the Arab World*, Beirut: American University of Beirut, 1997, p. 13.
40. George E. Irani and Nathan C. Funk, Rituals of Reconciliation: Arab-Islamic Perspectives, *Arab Studies Quarterly*, Vol. 20, No. 4, 1998, p. 58.
41. Ibid., p. 61.
42. Salem, 'A Critique of Western Conflict Resolution', p. 22.
43. This argument is central to Jabri, *Discourses on Violence*; Richmond, *Maintaining Order, Making Peace*.
44. Marc Howard Ross and Jay Rothman, 'Issues of Theory and Practice in Ethnic Conflict Resolution', in Marc Ross and Jay Rothman, eds, *Theory and Practice in Ethnic Conflict Resolution. Theorizing Success and Failure*, Basingstoke/London: Macmillan, 1999; Ross, Creating Conditions for Peacemaking, p. 1022.
45. Reimann, *Conflict Transformation*, p. 13.
46. Adam Curle, *Making Peace*, London: Tavistock, 1971; Johan Galtung, *Peace by Peaceful Means: Peace and Conflict, Development and Civilisation*, London: Sage, 1996; John Paul Lederach, *Building Peace. Sustainable Reconciliation in Divided Societies*, Washington: United States Institute of Peace, 1997.
47. Raimo Vayrynen, 'To Settle or to Transform. Perspectives on the Resolution of National and International Conflicts', in Raimo Vayrynrn, ed. *New Directions in Conflict Theory. Conflict Resolution and Conflict Transformation*, London/Newbury Park/New Delhi: Sage, 1991.
48. Hugh Miall, *Conflict Transformation: A Multi-Dimensional Task*, Berlin: Berghof Centre for Constructive Conflict Management, 2004, p. 10.
49. Ed Garcia, 'Addressing Social Change in Situations of Violent Conflict: A Practitioner's Perspective', in David Bloomfield and Beatrix Schmelzle, eds, *Social Change and Conflict Transformation*, Berlin: Berghof Center for Constructive Conflict Management, 2006.
50. This aim inverts Jabri's argument that 'violent conflicts are social phenomena emerging through, and constitutive of, social practices which have, through time and across space, rendered war an institutional form that is largely seen as an inevitable and at times acceptable form of human conduct'. Jabri, *Discourses on Violence*, p. 3.
51. See also Susanne Buckley-Zistel, In-Between War and Peace. Identities, Boundaries and Change after Violent Conflict, *Millennium*, Vol. 35, No. 1, 2006.
52. Ledearch, *Building Peace*, p. 39.
53. Ross, Creating Conditions for Peacemaking, p. 1022.
54. Ibid., p. 1021.
55. Kevin Avruch, Type I and Type II Errors in Culturally Sensitive Conflict Resolution Practice, *Conflict Resolution Quarterly*, Vol. 20, No. 3, 2003, p. 354.

56. For an overview see, for instance, Tim Murithi, *Final Report of the All-African Conference on African Principles of Conflict Resolution and Reconciliation*, Addis Ababa: UNITAR, 1999; Paul van Tongeren, Malin Brenk, Marte Hellema and Juliette Verhoeven, eds, *People Building Peace II: Successful Stories of Civil Society*, Boulder: Lynne Rienner, 2005; Stef Vandeginste and Filip Reijntjens, 'Traditional Approaches to Negotiation and Mediation. Burundi, Rwanda, and Congo', in Luc Reychler and Thania Paffenholz, eds, *Peacebuilding. A Field Guide*, London: Lynne Rienner, 2001.

57. William I. Zartman, 'Introduction', in William I. Zartman, ed. *Traditional Cures for Modern Conflict: African Conflict 'Medicine'*, Boulder: Lynne Rienner, 2000, p. 7.

58. Tim Murithi, African Approaches to Building Peace and Social Solidarity, *African Journal for Conflict Resolution*, Vol. 6, No. 2, 2006, p. 14.

59. Volker Böge, *Traditional Approaches to Conflict Transformation – Potential and Challenges*, Berlin: Berghof Center for Constructive Conflict Management, 2006, p. 6.

60. Osaghae, 'Applying Traditional Methods', p. 204.

61. Murithi, African Approaches, p. 14.

62. Jannie Malan, 'Traditional and Local Conflict Resolution', in Paul van Tongeren, et al., eds, *People Building Peace II: Successful Stories of Civil Society*, Boulder: Lynne Rienner, 2005.

63. Susanne Buckley-Zistel, '"The Truth Heals"? – Gacaca Jurisdiction and the Consolidation of Peace in Rwanda', *Die Friedens Warte*, Vol. 80, No. 1–2, 2005.

64. Osaghae, 'Applying Traditional Methods', p. 204.

65. Ernest E. Uwazie, 'Social Relations and Peacekeeping among the Igbo', in William I. Zartman, ed. *Traditional Cures for Modern Conflict: African Conflict 'Medicine'*, Boulder: Lynne Rienner, 2000, p. 15.

66. Ben K. Fred-Mensah, 'Conflict Management Practices in Buem-Kator', in William I. Zartman, ed. *Traditional Cures for Modern Conflicts: African Conflict 'Medicine'*, Boulder: Lynne Rienner, 2000, p. 35.

67. William I. Zartman, 'Changes in the New Order and the Place for the Old', in William I. Zartman, ed. *Traditional Cures for Modern Conflicts. African Conflict 'Medicine'*, Boulder: Lynne Rienner, 2000, p. 228.

68. Guy Oliver Faure, 'Traditional Conflict Management in Africa and China', in William I. Zartman, ed. *Traditional Cures for Modern Conflicts. African Conflict 'Medicine'*, Boulder: Lynne Rienner, 2000, p. 158.

69. Volker Böge, *Neue Kriege und traditionelle Konfliktbearbeitung*, Duisburg: INEF, 2004, p. 53.

70. Faure, 'Traditional Conflict Management', p. 158.

71. Zartman, 'Changes in the New Order', p. 222.

72. Faure, 'Traditional Conflict Management', p. 153.

73. Birgit Brock-Utne, 'Indigenous Conflict Resolution in Africa', Paper presented at the Indigenous Solutions to Conflicts, University of Oslo, Institute for Educational Research 2001.

74. Faure, 'Traditional Conflict Management', p. 155.

75. Ibid., p. 156.

76. Uwazie, 'Social Relations and Peacekeeping', p. 29.

77. Faure, 'Traditional Conflict Management', p. 157.

78. Uwazie, 'Social Relations and Peacekeeping', p. 19.
79. This argument is central to Max Gluckman, *Custom and Conflict in Africa*, Oxford: Blackwell, 1955.
80. Fred-Mensah, 'Conflict Management Practises', p. 31.
81. Buckley-Zistel, 'The Truth Heals'? p. 119.
82. Susanne Buckley-Zistel, Remembering to Forget. Chosen Amnesia as a Strategy for Local Coexistence in Post-Genocide Rwanda, *Africa*, Vol. 76, No. 2, 2006, p. 144.
83. Uwazie, 'Social Relations and Peacekeeping', p. 19.
84. As argued in Volker Böge, *Traditional Approaches*.
85. Mark Hoffman, Defining and Evaluating Success: Facilitative Problem-Solving Workshops in an Interconnected Context, *Paradigms*, Vol. 9, No. 2, 1995; Ross and Rothman, 'Issues of Theory and Practice in Ethnic Conflict Resolution', p. 5.

2 Inventing war and peace

1. Vasquez, War Endings: What Science and Constructivism Can Tell Us, p. 25.
2. Jabri, *Discourses on Violence*, p. 131.
3. Ibid.
4. Anthony Giddens, *The Constitution of Society. Outline of the Theory of Structuration*, Cambridge: Polity Press, 1984, p. 25.
5. Ibid., p. 17.
6. Ibid., p. 25.
7. Ira J. Cohen, *Structuration Theory. Anthony Giddens and the Structuration of Social Life*, Basingstoke/London: Macmillan, 1989, p. 2.
8. Giddens, *The Constitution of Society*, p. 25.
9. Ibid., p. 26.
10. We shall see the importance of repetition illustrated in Chapter 7.
11. David Campbell, The Politics of Radical Interdependence: A Rejoinder to Daniel Warner, *Millennium*, Vol. 25, No. 1, 1996, p. 139.
12. William E. Connolly, *Identity/Difference. Democratic Negotiations of Political Space*, Ithaca/London: Cornell University Press, 1991, p. 64.
13. Campbell, *Writing Security*, p. 8.
14. Andrew Linklater, *The Transformation of Political Community. Ethical Foundations of the Post-Westphalian Era*, Cambridge/Oxford: Polity Press, 1998, p. 114.
15. Eric Ringmar, *Identity, Interest, Action. A Cultural Explanation of Sweden's Intervention in the Thirty Years War*, Cambridge: Cambridge University Press, 1996, p. 78.
16. Ibid.
17. Jabri, *Discourses on Violence*, p. 134.
18. Ibid., p. 130.
19. Campbell, *Writing Security*, p. 8.
20. Connolly, *Identity/Difference*, p. 66.
21. Ibid., p. 64.
22. Ibid., p. 67.

23. For a case-study using this mode of reasoning see David Campbell, *Politics without Principles. Sovereignty, Ethics and the Narrative of the Gulf War*, Boulder/London: Lynne Rienner, 1993.
24. Jabri, *Discourses on Violence*, p. 134.
25. Ibid., p. 132.
26. Ibid., p. 173.
27. Mats Berdal and David Keen, Violence and Economic Agendas in Civil Wars: Some Policy Implications, *Millennium*, Vol. 26, No. 3, 1997, p. 801.
28. Ibid.
29. Ibid., p. 802.
30. Richards, *No Peace, No War*, p. 4.
31. Campbell, *Writing Security*, p. 6. For a more detailed argument see Buckley-Zistel, In-Between War and Peace.
32. Here I am following Simon Critchley's discussion. Simon Critchley, *The Ethics of Deconstruction. Derrida and Levinas*, Edinburgh: Edinburgh University Press, 1999, pp. 21–2.
33. Rodolphe Gasche, *The Tain of the Mirror: Derrida and the Philosophy of Reflection*, Cambridge, MA/London: Harvard University Press, 1986, p. 123. I am grateful to Arletta Norvall for this point.
34. Critchley, *The Ethics of Deconstruction*, p. 35.
35. Campbell, *National Deconstruction*, p. 23.
36. Campbell, *Why Fight*, p. 514.
37. Ibid.
38. Campbell, *Writing Security*, p. 5.
39. Campbell, *Why Fight*, p. 520.
40. Understanding among people is central to Ludwig Wittgenstein's *language games*. According to Wittgenstein we can make sense of the world only through agreeing on shared concepts. These linguistic concepts resemble games in which the participants have agreed upon one particular meaning for one particular object, or rather its representation in the form of a word. Ludwig Wittgenstein, *Philosophical Investigation*, Translated by G.E.M. Ancombe, Oxford: Basil Blackwell, 1993. Section 65.
41. Carolyn Nordstrom and Antonius C.G.M. Robben, 'Anthropology and Ethnography of Violence and Sociopolitical Conflict', in Carolyn Nordstrom and Antonius C.G.M. Robben, eds, *Fieldwork Under Fire. Contemporary Studies of Violence and Survival*, Berkley/Los Angeles/London: University of California Press, 1995, p. 14.
42. Nordstrom, *A Different Kind of War Story*, p. 190.
43. Michael Ignatieff, *The Warrior's Honour. Ethnic War and the Modern Conscience*, London: Chatto & Windus, 1998, p. 178.
44. Vakim Volkan and Norman Itzkowitz, 'Modern Greek and Turkish Identities and the Psychodynamics of Greek-Turkish Relations', in Antonius C.G.M. Robben and Marcelo M. Suárez-Orozco, eds, *Cultures under Siege. Collective Violence and Trauma*, Cambridge: Cambridge University Press, 2000, pp. 232–3.
45. For illustration see Buckley-Zistel, Remembering to Forget.
46. John Paul Lederach, 'Just Peace – The Challenge of the 21st Century', in European Platform for Conflict Prevention, ed. *People Building Peace*, Utrecht: European Platform for Conflict Prevention, 1999, p. 33.

47. Chris Coker, How Wars End, *Millennium*, Vol. 26, No. 3, 1997, p. 621.
48. Jabri, *Discourses on Violence*, p. 157.
49. Ibid., p. 146.
50. Throughout this book, I, however, use the term 'hermeneutics' only when referring to Heidegger's and Gadamer's notion.
51. Although Gadamer repeatedly draws attention to the fact that *Truth and Method* is not about truths and methods his readers seem to be reluctant to consider his work from a different perspective, as we shall see below. For an explicit rejection of the connection between title and content see, for instance, Hans-Georg Gadamer, Practical Philosophy as a Model of the Human Science, *Research in Phenomenology*, Vol. IX, 1979, p. 78.
52. Hans-Georg Gadamer, 'Replik zu "Hermeneutik und Ideologienkritik"', *Wahrheit und Methode II. Ergänzungen*, Tübingen: Mohr Siebeck, 1993, p. 255.
53. In the context of the present book I would like to emphasise that despite hermeneutics' relevance for encountering the new and strange I do not want to suggest that conflict arises out of the unfamiliarity of the other.
54. Hans-Georg Gadamer, 'Vom Zirkel des Verstehens', *Wahrheit und Methode II. Ergänzungen*, Tübingen: Mohr Siebeck, 1993, p. 57.
55. Hubert Dreyfus, 'Beyond Hermeneutics. Interpretation in Late Heidegger and Recent Foucault', in Gary Shapiro and Alan Sica, eds, *Hermeneutics. Questions and Prospects*, Amherst: University of Massachusetts Press, 1988, p. 73.
56. Hans-Georg Gadamer, *Wahrheit und Methode I. Grundzüge einer philosophischen Hermeneutik*, Tübingen: Mohr Siebeck, 1993, p. 277.
57. Ibid., p. 299.
58. Jacob Samuel, *Zwischen Gespräch und Diskurs. Untersuchung zur sozialhermeneutischen Begründung der Agogik anhand einer Gegenüberstellung von Hans-Georg Gadamer und Jürgen Habermas*, Stuttgart: Paul Haupt, 1985, p. 58.
59. Gadamer, *Wahrheit und Methode I*, p. 9 (translation cited in Alan How, *The Habermas-Gadamer Debate and the Nature of the Social*, Aldershot: Avebury, 1995, p. 48).
60. Ibid., p. 275.
61. Ibid., p. 305.
62. Ibid.
63. Georgia Warnke, *Hermeneutics, Tradition and Reason*, Oxford: Blackwell, 1987, p. 80.
64. Gadamer, *Wahrheit und Methode I*, p. 307.
65. Ibid., p. 309 (translated in Hans-Georg Gadamer, *Truth and Method*, New York: Seabury, 1975, p. 304).
66. Hans-Georg Gadamer, 'Was ist Wahrheit?' *Wahrheit und Methode II. Ergänzungen*, Tübingen: Mohr Siebeck, 1993, p. 47.
67. Gadamer, *Wahrheit und Methode I*, p. 311 (translated in Gadamer, *Truth and Method*, p. 273).
68. Hans-Georg Gadamer, 'Dialogues in Capri', in Jacques Derrida and Gianni Vattimo, eds, *Religion*, Cambridge: Polity Press, 1998.
69. Gadamer, *Wahrheit und Methode I*, p. 299.
70. Michel Foucault, *The Order of Things*, New York: Vintage Books, 1973, p. 372.
71. Vattimo, *Beyond Interpretation*, p. 10.
72. Ibid., p. 76.
73. Ibid.

74. Ibid., p. 78.
75. Ibid.
76. Ibid., p. 80.
77. Ibid., p. 81.
78. Hermann Braun, 'Zum Verhältnis von Hermeneutik und Ontologie', in Rüdiger Bubner, et al., eds, *Hermeneutik und Dialektik. Aufsätze II*, Tübingen: Mohr Siebeck, 1970, p. 203.
79. Vattimo, *Beyond Interpretation*, p. 81.
80. Ibid., p. 82.
81. Ibid. Emphasis added.
82. So the title of a chapter in *Beyond Interpretation*.
83. Vattimo, *Beyond Interpretation*, p. 10.
84. John Caputo, *Radical Hermeneutics. Repetition, Deconstruction and the Hermeneutic Project*, Bloomington and Indianapolis: Indiana University Press, 1987, p. 130.
85. Campbell, *Why Fight*, p. 520.
86. Ignatieff, *The Warrior's Honour*, p. 178.
87. Frank Kermonde, Places of Memory, *Index on Censorship*, Vol. 30, No. 1, 2001, p. 87.
88. Kundera, *Testaments Betrayed*, p. 128.
89. Friedrich Nietzsche, 'On the Uses and Disadvantages of History for Life', *Untimely Meditations*, Cambridge: University Press, 1983, p. 62.
90. Ibid.
91. Ibid., p. 63.
92. Ibid.
93. Quoted in Joseph R. LLobera, *The Role of Historical Memory in (Ethno)Nation-Building*, London: Goldsmith College, 1996, p. 5.
94. I am very grateful for the discussions at the ECPR workshop on *The Political Use of Narrative* in Mannheim from 26–31 March 1999 which led to the development of this argument.
95. Kundera, *Testaments Betrayed*, p. 128.
96. Hans-Georg Gadamer, *Philosophical Apprenticeships*, New York: Seabury, 1985, p. 16.
97. Again, these thoughts have been inspired by the group discussions at the ESRC workshop in Mannheim.
98. Gadamer, *Truth and Method*, p. 295.
99. Hannah Arendt, *The Life of the Mind. One/Thinking*, London: Secker & Warburg, 1978, p. 203.
100. Hannah Arendt, *Between Past and Future. Eight Essays on Political Thought*, Harmondsworth: Penguin, 1968, p. 14.
101. Vattimo, *Beyond Interpretation*, p. 82.
102. See also Buckley-Zistel, In-Between War and Peace.

3 Effective history and the beginning of the Teso Insurgency

1. Richards, *No Peace, No War*, p. 15.
2. OXFAM, *OXFAM Kumi District Agricultural Rehabilitation Project: Final Evaluation*, Uganda: OXFAM, 1993.
3. Augusto Pazzaglia, *The Karimojong: Some Aspects*, Bologna: EMI, 1982, p. 35.

4. Jan Jelmert Jorgensen, *Uganda. A Modern History*, London: Croon Helm, 1981, p. 102.
5. N.N. 'Security in Grazing Areas and Villages', Paper presented at the Conference on Strategies for Peace and Sustainable Development in Karamoja and Neighbouring Districts, Kampala, 18–22 July 1994.
6. David Pulkol, 'Karamoja Cattle Rustling – A National Dilemma: Myths and Realities', Paper presented at the Conference on Strategies for Peace and Sustainable Development in Karamoja and Neighbouring Districts, Kampala, 18–22 July 1994.
7. Interview Michael Griffith, London, 12 January 2000.
8. Interview Owmony Owjok, Arapai, 20 March 2000.
9. It is however important to note that raiding is not a feature of all ethnic groups in Karamoja, nor of all members of a particular group. Only Karamojong warriors cattle rustle, and not every Karamojong, as it is widely believed.
10. This was partly based on the structure of indigenous leadership and Baganda overrule, as we shall see in the following.
11. Joan Vincent, *Teso in Transformation*, Berkley: University of California Press, 1982, p. 10.
12. Joanna de Berry, *Life After Loss: An Anthropological Study of Post-War Recovery, Teso, Uganda, with Special Reference to Young People*, London School of Economics (doctoral thesis), 2000, p. 75.
13. Ibid., p. 79.
14. Vincent, *Teso in Transformation*, p. 10.
15. Mahmood Mamdani, *Imperialism and Fascism in Uganda*, London: Heineman, 1983, p. 6.
16. Winfred K. Byanyima, 'How Guerrillas Became Peace Builders', in Elise Boulding, ed. *New Agendas for Peace Research. Conflict and Security Re-Examined*, London/Boulder: Lynne Rienner, 1992, p. 131.
17. Jorgensen, *Uganda. A Modern History*, p. 176.
18. Terence Ranger, 'The Invention of Tradition in Colonial Africa', in Eric Hobsbawm and Terence Ranger, eds, *The Invention of Tradition*, Cambridge: Cambridge University Press, 2000, p. 229.
19. Mahmood Mamdani, *Politics and Class Formation in Uganda*, London: Heinemann, 1976, p. 41.
20. Buganda refers to the region, Baganda to the people and Luganda to the language.
21. M. Louise Pirout, *Historical Dictionary of Uganda*, London: The Scarecrow Press, 1995, p. 96.
22. *Kabaka* signifies king in Luganda.
23. Pirout, *Historical Dictionary of Uganda*, p. 97.
24. Apolo Nsimbambi, 'The Land Question and Conflict', in Kumar Rupesinghe, ed. *Conflict Resolution in Uganda*, London: James Curry, 1989, p. 233; Pirout, *Historical Dictionary of Uganda*, p. 97.
25. Mamdani, *Imperialism and Fascism in Uganda*, p. 9.
26. Vincent, *Teso in Transformation*, p. 145.
27. Memorandum by Johnston, No. 13, East African Confidential, London, 2 March 1903, quoted in Mamdani, *Politics and Class Formation*, p. 42.

28. As stated by Apolo Nsimbambi, 'The Restoration of Traditional Rulers', in Holger Berndt Hansen and Michael Twaddle, eds, *From Chaos to Order. The Politics of Constitution Making in Uganda*, Kampala/London: Foutain/James Currey, 1995, p. 43.
29. Ranger, 'The Invention of Tradition', p. 221.
30. G.P. McGreagor (1967): *King's College, Budo: The First Sixty Years*. London; quoted in Ranger, 'The Invention of Tradition'.
31. Ibid., p. 225.
32. Ibid., p. 212.
33. Samwiri Lwanga-Lunyiigo, 'The Colonial Roots of Internal Conflict', in Kumar Rupesinghe, ed. *Conflict Resolution in Uganda*, London: James Curry, 1989, p. 31.
34. Jorgensen, *Uganda. A Modern History*, p. 90.
35. Yoweri K. Museveni, *Speech Given at a Consultation Organised by International Alert, 25th September 1987*, Kampala: Makerere University, 1987.
36. Jorgensen, *Uganda. A Modern History*, p. 94.
37. Mamdani, *Politics and Class Formation*, p. 133.
38. Ibid.
39. Jorgensen, *Uganda. A Modern History*, p. 106.
40. Mamdani, *Politics and Class Formation*, p. 209.
41. A.G. Gingyera-Pinycwa, *Milton Obote and His Time*, London: NOK Publishers, 1987, p. 22.
42. Susan Dicklitch, *The Elusive Promise of NGOs in Africa. Lessons from Uganda*, Basingstoke/London: Macmillan, 1998, p. 38.
43. Gingyera-Pinycwa, *Milton Obote and His Time*, p. 127.
44. Athur Gakwandi, *Uganda Pocket Facts*, Kampala: Fountain, 1999, p. 22.
45. Pirout, *Historical Dictionary of Uganda*, p. 296.
46. Dicklitch, *The Elusive Promise*, p. 40.
47. Ibid.
48. Human Rights Watch, *Hostile to Democracy. The Movement System and Political Repression in Uganda*, NYC/Washington/London/Brussels: Human Rights Watch, 1999, p. 31.
49. Phares Mutibwa, *Uganda Since Independence. A Story of Unfulfilled Hope*, London: Hurst & Company, 1992, p. 9.
50. Thomas P. Ofcansky, *Uganda. Tarnished Pearl of Africa*, Boulder: WestView Press, 1996, p. 43.
51. Mutibwa, *Uganda Since Independence*, p. 86.
52. It is estimated that between 100,000 and 500,000 people were killed in Amin's eighth year presidency. Persecuted were mainly supporters of Obote from Lango and Acholi, as well as Baganda. Watch, *Hostile to Democracy*, p. 32.
53. James J. Busuttil et al. (1991): *Uganda at the Crossroads – A Report on Current Human Rights Conditions. The Record*, October 1991; quoted in Watch, *Hostile to Democracy*.
54. Ibid., p. 33.
55. Mutibwa, *Uganda Since Independence*, p. 128.
56. Obote's second presidency is commonly referred to as Obote II.
57. Mutibwa, *Uganda Since Independence*, p. 154.
58. A.M. Babu, quoted in Ondoga ori Amaza, *Museveni's Long March from Guerrilla to Statesman*, Kampala: Fountain, 1998, p. 1.

59. E.A. Brett, 'Rebuilding War Damaged Communities in Uganda', in Tim Allen, ed. *In Search of Cool Ground. War, Flight and Homecoming in Northeast Africa*, London/Trenton: James Curry/Africa World Press, 1996, p. 208.
60. Inside the NRM cadre Museveni's long-term supporters were critical of this policy because to co-operate with the politicians against whom they had fought so fiercely in the Luwero Triangle went against their conception of victory. It was also felt that many opponents, especially from the UPC, had joined the NRM for opportunist reasons and that they were only waiting for power relations to change again to continue with their own political agenda.
61. Interview with Dennis Pain, London 13 January 2000.
62. It has been suggested that the reorganisation was imposed by IMF and World Bank as part of the Structural Adjustment Programme. Interview with Grace Akello, Portsmouth 6 January 2000.
63. Yoweri K. Museveni, *Sowing the Mustard Seeds: The Struggle for Freedom and Democracy in Uganda*, Basingstoke/London: Macmillan, 1996, p. 174.
64. Interview with Dennis Pain.
65. Interview with Musa Echweru.
66. Col. Omaria himself commented once that after having received special training at home as well as abroad it is difficult for a professional soldier to 'retire' forcefully.
67. Museveni, *Sowing the Mustard Seeds*, p. 58.
68. As discussed in Berdal, How 'New' Are 'New Wars'? Global Economic Change and the Study of Civil War; Richards, *Fighting for the Rain Forests. War, Youth and Resources in Sierra Leone*.
69. As argued by Joan Vincent, 'War in Uganda: North and South' in R.E. Downs and Stephen P. Reyna, eds, *Deadly Developments. Capitalism, State and War*, New York/London: Routledge, 1999.
70. Interview with Michael Obwaatum.
71. Interview with Joseph Okello.
72. 'Ugandan President Responds to "Concentration Camps" Allegations', *Radio Uganda*, Kampala, 1 March 1990.
73. Interview with Musa Echweru.
74. The RCs were later replaced by very similar Local Councils (LCs).
75. Brett, 'Rebuilding War', p. 210.
76. 'Museveni Wins Presidential Elections with 74.2 Per Cent of Vote', *Radio Uganda*, Kampala, 11 May 1996.
77. For a discussion see E. Hauser, Ugandan Relations with Western Donors in the 1990: What Impact on Democratisation? *Journal of Modern African Studies*, Vol. 37, No. 4, 1999.
78. See Susanne Buckley-Zistel and Bernard Tabaire, 'Preventing Violent Conflicts? UK Policy on Uganda. London: ISIS Policy Paper 87, March 2003.' London: ISIS Policy Paper 87, 2003.
79. They include *inter alia* Sweden, Britain, Norway, Ireland and the Netherlands.
80. United Nations, 'Report of the panel of experts on the illegal exploitation of natural resources and other forms of wealth of the Democratic Republic of the Congo (S/2001/357).' New York: United Nations, 2002.

81. Office of the Prime Minister, 'IDP Profiling in Lango and Teso Subregions. Preliminary Results', Kampala: Office of the Prime Minister, 2006, p. 8.
82. 'Northern Uganda "world's biggest neglected crisis"'. 22 October 2004, *The Guardian*, London.

4 Mediation and the creation of peace in Teso

1. Tarja Vayrynen, Going Beyond Similarity: The Role of the Facilitator in Problem-Solving Workshop Conflict Resolution, *Paradigms*, Vol. 9, No. 2, 1995, p. 73.
2. Sara Cobb, 'A Narrative Perspective on Mediation. Towards the Materialization of the "Storyteller" Metaphor', in Joseph P. Folgner and S. Tricia Jones, eds, *New Directions in Mediation. Communication Research and Perspectives*, Thousand Oaks/London/New Delhi: Sage, 1994; John Winslade and Gerald Monk, *Narrative Mediation*, San Francisco: Jossey-Bass Publishers, 2000, p. xi.
3. For a similar argument see Suganami, *On the Causes of War*.
4. See also Chabal and Daloz, *Culture Troubles*, p. 83.
5. Winslade and Monk, *Narrative Mediation*, p. 5.
6. Sara Cobb, Negotiation Pedagogy: Learning to Learn, *Negotiation Journal*, Vol. 16, No. 4, 2000, pp. 316–17.
7. For reviews of mediation literature see Jabri, *Discourses on Violence*; Deiniol Lloyed-Jones, Mediation, Conflict Resolution and Critical Theory, *Review of International Studies*, Vol. 26, No. 4, 2000.
8. The etymology of the Greek word *poetic* reveals its ancient meaning as 'creating' or 'making'.
9. Gilles Deleuze, *Negotiations 1972–1990*, New York: Columbia University Press, 1995, p. 125.
10. Vattimo, *Beyond Interpretation*, p. 38.
11. Fred-Mensah, 'Conflict Management Practises', p. 35.
12. John Maitland, 'Suffering of the People form Teso', *The Independent*, London, 25 July 1989, p. 15.
13. 'Ugandan President Responds to "Concentration Camps" Allegations'.
14. Interview with Grace Akello.
15. Interviews with Grace Akello and Ateker Ejalu.
16. Interview with Grace Akello.
17. Interview with Ateker Ejalu. A further indication of the little importance Museveni gave to the Teso insurgency is that it does not find any mentioning in his autobiography, Museveni, *Sowing the Mustard Seeds*.
18. Interview with Ateker Ejalu.
19. Ibid.
20. International Alert, 'Uganda – International Seminar on Internal Conflict, 21–25 September 1987', Kampala: Makerere University, 1987. Appendix G. The general Amnesty Statute expired after a few years and has been replaced by a series of presidential pardons.
21. 'Reporter' is the NRM/A jargon for ex-rebels who have reported to the authorities and handed in their guns. 'Reporters' became the term commonly used for surrendering rebels; it was considered more neutral then 'dissident' or 'ex-rebel'. Interview with James Eceret.
22. Interview with Ateker Ejalu.

23. Interview with Kenneth Olumia (brother to the late minister's wife), Soroti 24 February 2000.
24. Egoing James Peter Olupot, *The Bitter Price*, Kumi/Teso, 2000, p. 185.
25. Interview with Peter Olupot, Kumi 1 May 2000.
26. 'Uganda Presidential Commission to Investigate Rebellion in Eastern Districts', *Radio Uganda*, Kampala, 17 October 1990.
27. Interview with Grace Akello.
28. Dan Ochyang, 'Proposal for the Restoration of Stability, Peace and Progress to Teso', Kampala: UPC, 1991, p. 2.
29. PCT, 'Rehabilitation and Development Plan for Teso Region 1991/2–2000/1. Vol. 1: Guidelines/Strategies', Kampala: Ministry for Planning and Economic Development, Republic of Uganda, 1991, p. 48.
30. Ibid., pp. 48–9.
31. Interview with James Eceret.
32. Interview with George Oguli.
33. Ibid.
34. Interview with Peter Kalagala.
35. Faure, 'Traditional Conflict Management', p. 158.
36. Amnesty International, *Uganda. The Failure to Safeguard Human Rights*, London: Amnesty International, 1992.
37. Interviews with Sam Otai and Musa Echweru.
38. Interview with Michael Obwaatum.
39. Interview with Musa Echweru.
40. Ibid.
41. Deborah Ajulu and Sara Gibbs, *The Role of the Church in Advocacy: Case Studies from Southern and Eastern Africa*, Oxford: INTRAC, 1999, p. 4.
42. Chukwudum B. Okolo, *The Liberating Role of the Church in Africa Today*, Eldoret: AMECEA Gaba Publishers, 1991, p. 64.
43. Paul Gifford, *African Christianity. Its Public Role*, London: Hurst & Company, 1998, p. 133.
44. Wilson M. Mande, 'The Role of the Churches in the Political Reconstruction of Uganda in the 1990s', in J.N.K. Mugambi, ed. *The Church and Reconstruction of Africa*, Nairobi: All African Council of Churches, 1997, p. 180.
45. This comment was made by Prof. Opio-Epelu, Vice-President of Makerere University and former head of the PCT at Bishop Illukor's retirement service at the bishop's home in Kumi district, 8 April 2000.
46. Interview with Musa Echweru.
47. Interview with Richard Okiria.
48. Speech by Bishop Illukor, Church of Uganda at a Seminar of Bukedia Development Trust on Peace and Development, Feburary 1991.
49. Interview with Richard Okiria.
50. Pius Okiria, 'Personal Experience', in CECORE, ed. *Experiences and Best Practices of Peace-Builders*, Kampala: CECORE, 2000, p. 4.
51. Interview with George Oguli.
52. With reference to renewed cattle raiding in spring 2000, Ilukor was quoted saying: 'The Iteso went to the bush because of their cows and they were accused of being misled to the bush. The Iteso should, therefore, not continue to suffer without effective government intervention. "Ilukor Advises Teso"', *New Vision*, Kampala, 10 April 2000, p. 6.

53. Elizabeth G. Ferris, 'Women as Peace Makers', in Aruna Gnanadason, et al., eds, *Women, Violence and Non-Violent Change*, Geneva: WCC, 1996, p. 8.
54. Murithi, 'Final Report of the All-African Conference', p. 37.
55. World Vision quoted in Luckham et al., 'Conflict and Poverty in Sub-Sahara Africa', p. 44.
56. ISIS, 'Women's Experience in Armed Conflict. Situations in Uganda 1980–86: Luwero District. A Research Report', Kampala: ISIS – International Cross Cultural Exchange, 1998. In countries like Rwanda, for instance, where rape was a common instrument of degradation during the 1994 genocide, the HIV/AIDS prevalence amongst the survivors is shockingly high. Before the war, 45–60 per cent of Rwandan soldiers and army officers were infected with HIV, and, allegedly, they violated Rwandan women in full knowledge of their infection (see Clotilde Twagiramariya and Meredeth Turshen, ' "Favours" to Give and "Consenting" Victims: The Sexual Politics of Survival in Rwanda', in Clotilde Twagiramariya and Meredeth Turshen, eds, *What Women Do in Wartime. Gender and Conflict in Africa*, London/New York: Zed Books, 1998, p. 110).
57. Interview with Alfred Aruo.
58. For instance, the London based conflict resolution NGO International Alert runs a global advocacy project with the title: 'Women Building Peace: From the Village Council to the Negotiating Table' (www.international-alert.org).
59. Interview with Terence Achia and Thomas Okoth, Moroto 14 April 2000.
60. African Rights, *Rwanda – Not So Innocent. When Women Become Killers*, London: African Rights, 1995.
61. Sharon MacDonald, *Gender, Peace and War: Anthropological Perspectives*, Oxford: Oxford Project for Peace Studies, 1991, p. 5.
62. Interview with Mary Epechu and Richard Okiria.
63. Interview with Stella Sabiiti, Kampala 9 February 2000.
64. Interview with Musa Echweru.
65. 'Ugandan Minister Says for Rebel Army to Dissolve, Calls for Exiles to Return', *Radio Uganda*, Kampala, 6 July 1992; 'Rebel Leader Surrenders', *Radio Uganda*, Kampala, 2 February 1993.
66. See also Ledearch, *Building Peace*, p. 39.
67. Jabri, *Discourses on Violence*, p. 157.
68. See for instance Fred-Mensah, *Conflict Management Practises*, p. 31. A similar point is made by Böge, 'Traditional Approaches'.
69. PCT, 'Rehabilitation and Development Plan Vol. 1', p. 48.
70. Interview with Grace Akello.
71. Zartman, 'Changes in the New Order', p. 222.
72. Interview with Grace Akello.
73. Connolly, *Identity/Difference*, p. 67.
74. Gadamer, *Wahrheit und Methode I*, p. 311.

5 Narrating the cause of the Teso Insurgency

1. '17 Die of Hunger in Eastern Uganda', *Xinhua News Agency*, Kampala, 24 January 1994; 'Famine Threatening Eastern Uganda', *Xinhua News Agency*, Kampala, 14 March 1995.

Unfortunately, the most recent figures on development in the Teso sub-region, rather than the whole of Uganda, dates back to 1996 and 1998. See CDRN, 'A Study of Poverty in Selected Districts of Uganda: Apac, Kampala, Kapchorwa, Kibaale, Kisoro, Kumi and Nebbi', Kampala: CDRN, 1996; UNDP, 'Uganda Development Report', New York: UNDP, 1998. Poverty in Teso worsened dramatically due to the incursion of LRA soldiers into the region in 2001 as a result of which large parts of the population moved to IDP camps from which they are now slowly returning home. Moreover, the floods that swept over northern Uganda in 2007 had further serious repercussions for the Teso region.

2. PCT, 'Rehabilitation and Development Plan Vol. 1', p. 48.
3. Interview with James Eceret.
4. Interview with Itesö at Cafe Amigos, Soroti town, 29 April 2000.
5. Interview with John Olweny, Kampala 8 February 2000.
6. On 18 January 2000, the MP for Kabremaido (Soroti district), former Attorney General and Minister of Justice Joseph Ekemu was sentenced to two years in prison for embezzling 113 Million Ugenden Shilling dedicated for restocking.
7. Interview with Moses Omiat, Soroti, 21 March 2000.
8. Brett, 'Rebuilding War', p. 205.
9. Ibid., p. 209.
10. UNDP, 'Uganda Development Report'.
11. For a general overview see Alcira Kreimer and John Eriksson, 'The World Bank's Experience with Post-Conflict Reconstruction', Washington: World Bank, 1998, p. 65. For a critical assessment see Fumihiko Saito, Decentralisation Theories Revisited: Lessons from Uganda, *Ryukoku RISS Bulletin*, No. 31, 2001.
12. Interview with Richard Okiria.
13. See, for instance, David Campbell, MetaBosnia: Narratives of the Bosnian War, *Review of International Studies*, Vol. 24, No. 2, 1998; Hidemi Suganami, Stories of War Origins: A Narrative of the Cause of War, *Review of International Studies*, Vol. 23, No. 4, 1997.
14. Lewis P. Hinchman and Sandra K. Hinchman, 'Introduction', in Lewis P. Hinchman and Sandra K. Hinchman, eds, *Memory, Identity, Community*, Albany: State of New York Press, 1997, p. xvi.
15. Campbell, *Politics Without Principles*, p. 7.
16. Mikail Bakhtin, *The Dialogic Imagination*, Austin: University of Texas Press, 1981, p. 255.
17. Richard Baumann, *Story, Performance, and Event. Contextual Studies of Oral Narratives*, Cambridge: Cambridge University Press, 1986, p. 6.
18. Paul Antze and Michael Lambek, 'Introduction. Forecasting Memory', in Paul Antze and Micheal Lambek, eds, *Tense Past. Cultural Essays in Trauma and Memory*, New York, London: Routledge, 1996, p. xviii.
19. Halbwachs, *On Collective Memory*, p. 43.
20. Campbell, *National Deconstruction*, p. 37.
21. Cobb, 'A Narrative Perspective on Mediation', p. 54.
22. Impression gained during a workshop at a secondary school in Soroti in May 2000.
23. Interview with James Eceret, economist at the Presidential Commission for Teso, Kampala, 9 February 2000.

24. Interview with James Eceret.
25. OXFAM, 'OXFAM Kumi District Agricultural Rehabilitation Project: Final Evaluation', p. 13.
26. Museveni, *Sowing the Mustard Seeds*, p. 177.
27. Interview with Frieda Ediamo, Soroti 25 February 2000.
28. Peter Henriques, 'Peace without Reconciliation. War, Peace and Experience among the Iteso of East Uganda' , University of Copenhagen (doctoral thesis), 2000, p. 47.
29. Musa Echweru, 'Iteso Love Museveni – Ex-Rebel', *The Monitor*, Kampala, 22–26 April 1994, p. 8.
30. Among the targets were for instance Col. Omaria (MP for Soroti Central from 1980, and Minister of State for Internal Affairs in Obote II) (*New Vision* (Kampala) 18 November 1986, p. 16) as well as the Director of the Flying School George Oguli.
31. Olupot, 'The Bitter Price', p. 60.
32. Fidle Omunyokol, 'The Day a Helicopter Landed in Mukongoro', Soroti, 2000, p. 5.
33. Interview with Omax Omega.
34. Interview with Musa Echweru.
35. David Turton, 'Introduction: War and Ethnicity', in David Turton, ed. *War and Ethnicity. Global Connections and Local Violence*, Rochester: University of Rochester Press, 1997, pp. 3–4.
36. Henriques, 'Peace Without Reconciliation', p. 32.
37. For a description of different cultures see Richard Nzita, *Peoples and Cultures of Uganda*, Kampala: Fountain Publishers, 1995.
38. A.G. Gingyera-Pinycwa, 'Is there a Northern Question?' in Kumar Rupesinghe, ed. *Internal Conflicts and Their Resolution: The Case of Uganda*, London: James Curry, 1989, p. 49.
39. Museveni, 'Speech', p. 62. See also Gifford, *African Christianity*, p. 133; Gingyera-Pinycwa, 'Is There a Northern Question?'; Vincent, 'War in Uganda', p. 125.
40. Museveni, 'Speech', p. 62.
41. Brig. Chefe Ali, 'Preaching Peace against War', Paper presented at the Conference on Strategies for Peace and Sustainable Development in Karamoja and Neighbouring Districts, Kampala, 18–22 July 1994.
42. 'Defeating the Rebels and Cattle Rustlers', *Tarehe Sita*, Kampala, May/June 1987, pp. 3–5.
43. The number of troops reduced very suddenly in 1990 when Uganda supported the invasion of exile-Rwandans into Rwanda. This might have had a very strong effect on the ending of the insurgency as argued in interviews by Grace Akello, John Maitland (London 15 January 2000) and Dennis Pain.
44. Interview with John Maitland.
45. The prime reason for the Rebel High Command not to collaborate with Kony was that the Acholi rebels were considered to be too violent and cruel towards their own people. Interview with Sam Otai.
46. Donald Brenneis, 'Telling Troubles: Narrative, Conflict, and Experience', in Charles Briggs, ed. *Disorderly Discourse. Narrative, Conflict and Inequality*, New York/Oxford: Oxford University Press, 1996, p. 42.

47. Carolyn Nordstrom, 'War on the Front Lines', in Carolyn Nordstrom and Antonius C.G.M. Robben, eds, *Fieldwork under Fire: Contemporary Studies in Violence and Survival*, Berkley: University of California Press, 1995, p. 131.
48. Vincent, 'War in Uganda', p. 124.
49. Ibid.
50. J. Cole, 'The Use of Defeat: Memory and Political Morality in East Madagascar', in Richard Webner, ed. *Memory and the Postcolonial. African Anthropology and the Crisis of Power*, London/New York: Zed, 1998, p. 121.
51. Vakim Volkan, On Chosen Trauma, *Mind and Human Interaction*, Vol. 3, No. 13, 1991, p. 13. However, this can also be said for not remembering, or chosen amnesia. See Buckley-Zistel, Remembering to Forget.
52. Connolly, *Identity/Difference*, p. 67.

6 Facing past and future after the Teso Insurgency

1. Testimony of survivor recorded by Henriques, 'Peace Without Reconciliation', pp. 245–6.
2. 'Uganda: 47 Dead due to "Gross Negligence" after Rebel Round-up', *BBC Summary of World Broadcast*, London, 24 July 1989.
3. 'Uganda Museveni Promise Compensation for Mukura Deaths', *Radio Uganda*, Kampala, 25 August 1989.
4. Brandon Hamber, 'Repairing the Irreparable: Dealing with Double-binds of Making Reparations for Crimes of the Past', Johannesburg: Centre for the Study of Violence and Reconciliation, 1998. See also Pablo de Greiff, ed. *Reparations*, Oxford: Oxford University Press, 2006; Ruth Rublo-Marìn, ed. *What Happened to the Women? Gender and Reparations for Human Rights Violations*, New York: SSRC, 2006.
5. Rodger Mulindwa, 'Kumi to Deny Movt Votes Over Schools', *The Monitor*, Kampala, 9 January 2000.
6. 'Museveni Commissions Schools', *New Vision*, Kampala, 26 February 2001, p. 5.
7. Susanne Kuechler, 'The Place of Memory', in Adrian Forty and Susanne Kuechler, eds, *The Art of Forgetting*, Oxford/New York: Berg, 1999, p. 130.
8. Barbara Harell-Bond, *Imposing Aid. Emergency Assistance to Refugees*, Oxford: Oxford University Press, 1986, p. 293.
9. Ibid.
10. The wagons are not the remainders of the Mukura incident, they have been left behind much later. And yet their representation is much more powerful than that of the white house with the list of (incorrect) names.
11. Richard P. Werbner, 'Smoke from the Barrel of a Gun: Postwars of the Dead, Memory and Reinscription in Zimbabwe', in Richard P. Werbner, ed. *Memory and the Postcolonial. African Anthropology and the Critique of Power*, London/New York: Zed Publications, 1998, p. 78.
12. David Middleton and Derek Edwards, 'Introduction', in David Middleton and Derek Edwards, eds, *Collective Remembering*, London/Newbury Park/New Delhi: Sage, 1990, p. 8.
13. Odiya L'Pajule, 'What Are These People Apologising about?' *The Monitor*, Kampala, 21 January 2000; Obalell Omoding, 'Mukura: Lessons after

10 Years', *The Monitor*, Kampala, 11 July 1999; Obalell Omoding, 'Uganda Dead Remembered in Canada, UK', *The Monitor*, Kampala, 15 July 1999; Leo SSebweze, 'Uganda still Lives with Museveni's 12 Crimes', *The Monitor*, Kampala, 3 January 2001.

14. Nicolas Argenti, 'Ephemeral Monuments, Memory and Royal Sempiternity in a Grassfield Kingdom', in Adrian Forty and Susanne Kuechler, eds, *The Art of Forgetting*, Oxford/New York: Berg, 1999, p. 23.
15. Kuechler, 'The Place of Memory', p. 55.
16. Iona Irwin-Zarecka, *Frames of Remembrance. The Dynamics of Collective Memory*, London/New Brunswick: Transaction Publisher, 1994, p. 5.
17. Hans-Georg Gadamer, *Zukunft ist Herkunft*, Jena: Universität Jena, 1997, p. 55.
18. Nsimbambi, 'The Restoration of Traditional Rulers', p. 47.
19. Interview with Alfred Aruo, Soroti 7 May 2000.
20. The mandate coincides with the stated aims and objectives of the ICU Steering Committee of the Iteso Cultural Union in ICU, 'Iteso Cultural Union. A Cultural Union Development', Soroti: ICU, 1997.
21. I had the pleasure to personally attend the ceremony.
22. 'Teso Crowns Emorimor', *New Vision*, Kampala, 1 May 2000, p. 2.
23. In this period Museveni danced repeatedly all over Uganda. His public appearances were mostly related to his Movement referendum campaign.
24. 'Teso Crowns Emorimor'.
25. Eric Hobsbawm, 'Inventing Traditions', in Eric Hobsbawm and Terence Ranger, eds, *The Invention of Tradition*, Cambridge: Cambridge University Press, 2000, p. 1.
26. Ibid., p. 2.
27. Ranger, 'The Invention of Tradition', p. 213.
28. 'Promote Iteso Culture – Emorimor', *New Vision*, Kampala, 2 May 2000, p. 3.
29. As argued during a workshop with rural youth in Serere district, 8 May 2000.
30. Interview with Grace Akello.

7 Conflict termination and the absence of transformation in Teso

1. Lederach, 'Just Peace – The Challenge of the 21st Century', p. 33.
2. Giddens, *The Constitution of Society*, p. 26. See also Chapter 2 of this book.
3. Antze and Lambek, 'Forecasting Memory', p. xviii.
4. Vattimo, *Beyond Interpretation*, p. 82. Emphasis added.
5. Interview with Iteso at Cafe Amigos, Soroti town, 29 April 2000.
6. See, for instance, Joseph P. Folgner and Robert A. Baruch Bush, 'Ideology, Orientations, and Discourse', in Joseph P. Folgner and Tricia S. Jones, eds, *New Directions in Mediation. Communication Research and Perspectives*, Thousand Oaks/London/New Delhi: Sage, 1994; Anne Griffiths, Mediation, Gender and Justice in Botswana, *Mediation Quarterly*, Vol. 15, No. 4, 1998; Vivienne Jabri, Agency, Structure and the Question of Power in Conflict Resolution, *Paradigms*, Vol. 9, No. 2, 1995; Lloyed Jensen, Negotiations and Power Asymmetries: The Case of Bosnia, Northern Ireland and Sri Lanka, *International Negotiation*, Vol. 2, No. 2, 1997; Michael Roloff et al., The Interpretation of Coercive Communication: The Effects of Mode of Influence, Powerful

Speech and Speaker Authority, *International Journal of Conflict Management*, Vol. 9, No. 2, 1998; Nadim N. Rouhana and Susan H. Korper, Dealing with the Dilemmas Posed by Power Asymmetry in Intergroup Conflict, *Negotiation Journal*, Vol. 12, No. 4, 1996; Heinz Waelchli and Dhavan Shah, Crisis Negotiation Between Unequals: Lessons from a Classic Dialogue, *Negotiation Journal*, Vol. 10, No. 2, 1994; Margaret Wetherell, Positioning and Interpretative Repertoires: Conversation Analysis and Post-Structuralism in Dialogue, *Discourse & Society*, Vol. 9, No. 3, 1998.

7. Robert A. Baruch Bush and Joseph P. Folgner, The Promise of Mediation. Responding to Conflict through Empowerment and Recognition, San Francisco: Jossey-Bass Publishers, 1994, pp. 84–6.
8. Ibid., p. 87.
9. Winslade and Monk, *Narrative Mediation*, p. 5.
10. Michel Foucault, *The Archaeology of Knowledge and the Discourse on Language*, Translated by A.M. Sheridan Smith, New York: Pantheon Books, 1972, p. 216.
11. Cornelia Ilie, The Ideological Remapping of Semantic Roles in Totalitarian Discourses, or, How to Paint a White Rose Red, *Discourse & Society*, Vol. 9, No. 1, 1998, p. 76.
12. This process of poetic imagination, of course, is heavily dependent on the attitude and actions of the particular other, in our case the Museveni government, to which this book has paid only limited attention.
13. Robert Cox and Timothy Sinclair, *Approaches to World Order*, Cambridge: Cambridge University Press, 1996, p. 67.
14. For attempts to provide an ethics based on deconstruction see Critchley, *The Ethics of Deconstruction*; Jacques Derrida, *Adieu: To Emmanuel Levinas*, Stanford: Stanford University Press, 1999.
15. Hans-Georg Gadamer, 'Destruction and Deconstruction', in Diane P. Michelfelder and Richard E. Palmer, eds, *Dialogue and Deconstructions*, Albany: State University of New York, 1989, p. 113.
16. As also argued in Böge, 'Traditional Approaches'; Buckley-Zistel, 'The Truth Heals'; Faure, 'Traditional Conflict Management'. Even though this notion of justice is itself highly questionable.
17. Faure, 'Traditional Conflict Management'. See also Volker Böge, 'Von Muschelgeld und Blutdiamanten. Traditionale Konfliktbearbeitung in zeitgenössischen Gewaltkonflikten', Hamburg: Deutsches Übersee-Institut, 2004, p. 53.
18. Osaghae, 'Applying Traditional Methods', p. 216.
19. Zartman, 'Changes in the New Order', p. 228.

8 Dealing with the past of violent conflicts

1. Again, this is in inversion of Carolyn Nordstrom's work. Nordstrom, *A Different Kind of War Story*.
2. Oliver P. Richmond, *The Transformation of Peace*, Basingstoke: Palgrave Macmillan, 2005, p. 87.
3. Chester Crocker, 'Truth Commissions, Transitional Justice and Civil Society', in Robert I. Rotberg and Dennis Thompson, eds, *Truth v. Justice. The Morality of Truth Commissions*, Princeton: Princeton University Press, 2000.

4. David Crocker, Transitional Justice and International Civil Society: Towards a Normative Framework, *Constellations*, Vol. 5, No. 4, 1998, p. 496. See also Susanne Buckley-Zistel, 'Transitional Justice', Berlin: Plattform für zivile Konfliktbearbeitung, 2007.

5. Pablo de Greiff, 'Addressing the Past: Reparations for Gross Human Rights Abuses', in Agnes Hurwitz, ed. *Rule of Law and Conflict Management: Towards Security, Development and Human Rights*, NY: International Peace Academy, forthcoming, p. 2. Alexandra Barahona de Brito et al., 'Introduction', in Alexandra de Brito, et al., eds, *The Politics of Memory. Transitional Justice in Democratizing Societies*, Oxford: Oxford University Press, 1997.

6. de Greiff, 'Addressing the Past', p. 3.

7. Heidy Rombouts, Importance and Difficulties of Victim-Based Research in Post-Conflict Societies, *European Journal of Crime, Criminal Law and Criminal Justice*, Vol. 10, Nos. 2–3, 2002; Jenny Edkins, *Trauma and the Memory of Politics*, Cambridge: Cambridge University Press, 2003; Ian Wilkinson, Thinking with Suffering, *Cultural Values*, Vol. 5, No. 4, 2001; Joanna Zylinska, Mediating Murder: Ethics, Trauma and the Price of Death, *Journal for Cultural Research*, Vol. 8, No. 3, 2004.

8. GTZ, 'Vergangenheits- und Versöhnungsarbeit. Wie die TZ Aufarbeitung von gemeinsamen Konflikten unterstützen kann', Eschborn: GTZ, 2002, p. 30.

9. See, for example, Peter Bouckaert, 'South Africa: The Negotiated Transition from Apartheid to Nonracial Democracy', in Melanie Greenberg, et al., eds, *Words Over War. Mediation and Arbitration to Prevent Deadly Conflict*, Lanham, Boulder, New York, Oxford: Rowman & Littlefield Publishers, 2000; Jamie Frueh, *Political Identity and Social Change. The Remaking of the South African Social Order*, Albany: SUNY, 2003; Courtney Jung, *Then I Was Black. South African Political Identities in Transition*, New Haven/London: Yale University Press, 2000; Mahmood Mamdani, 'From Justice to Reconciliation: Making Sense of the African Experience', in Colin Leys and Mahmood Mamdani, eds, *Crisis and Reconstruction – African Perspective*, Uppsala: Nordiska Afrikainstitutet, 1997; Kogila Moodley and Heribert Adam, Race and Nation in Post-Apartheid South Africa, *Current Sociology*, Vol. 48, No. 2, 2000; Anika Oettler, *Erinnerungsarbeit und Vergangenheitspolitik in Guatemala*, Frankfurt: Vervuert, 2004; Eric Stover and Weinstein Harvey M., eds, *My Neighbour, My Enemy. Justice and Community in the Aftermath of Mass Atrocities*, Cambridge: Cambridge University Press, 2004; Christian Tomuschat, 'Vergangenheitsbewältigung durch Aufklärung: Die Arbeit der Wahrheitskommission in Guatemala', in Ulrich Fastenrath, ed. *Internationaler Schutz der Menschenrechte. Entwicklung – Geltung – Durchsetzung – Aussöhnung der Opfer mit den Tätern*, Dresden/München: Dresden University Press, 2000; Hugo Van der Merwe, 'National and Community Reconciliation: Competing Agendas in the South African Truth and Reconciliation Commission', in Nigel Biggar, ed. *Burying the Past. Making Peace and Doing Justice after Civil Conflict*, Washington: Georgetown University Press, 2001.

10. Van der Merwe, 'National and Community Reconciliation'.

11. Laurel E. Fletcher and Harvey M. Weinstein, Violence and Social Repair: Rethinking the Contribution of Justice to Reconciliation, *Human Rights Quarterly*, Vol. 24, No. 3, 2002, p. 637.

12. Ibid.; Mamdani, 'From Justice to Reconciliation: Making Sense of the African Experience'; Rama Mani, *Beyond Retribution. Seeking Justice in the Shadows of War*, Cambridge/Oxford: Polity Press, 2002.
13. Martha Minow, *Between Vengeance and Forgiveness. Facing History after Genocide and Mass Violence*, Boston: Beacon Press, 1998, p. 26.
14. Andrew Rigby, ' "Forgiving the Past": Paths towards a Culture of Reconciliation', Coventry: Coventry University/Centre for the Study of Forgiveness and Reconciliation, 2000, p. 5.
15. Nigel Biggar, 'Making Peace and Doing Justice: Must We Choose?' in Nigel Biggar, ed. *Burying the Past. Making Peace and Doing Justice after Civil Conflict*, Washington: Georgetown University Press, 2001, p. 13.
16. Fletcher and Weinstein, Violence and Social Repair, p. 585.
17. This argument is central to Buckley-Zistel, 'The Truth Heals'; Ledearch, *Building Peace*; Andrew Rigby, *Justice and Reconciliation. After the Violence*, London: Lynne Rienner, 2001.
18. See, for instance, Carlos Santiago Nino, *Radical Evil on Trial*, New Haven: Yale University Press, 1996; Diane F. Orentlicher, Settling Accounts: The Duty to Prosecute Human Rights Violations of a Prior Regime, *Yale Law Journal*, Vol. 100, No. 8, 1991.
19. Karl Jaspers, *The Question of German Guilt*, Translated by E.B. Ashton, New York: The Dial, 1947.
20. Buckley-Zistel, Remembering to Forget, p. 145; Susanne Buckley-Zistel, Frieden entwickeln? Eine kritische Analyse der Strategien der Internationalen Gebergemeinschaft zur Friedenskonsolidierung in gespaltenen Staaten, *Sicherheit + Frieden*, 2007.
21. Julie Merturs, 'Truth in a Box: The Limits of Justice through Judicial Mechanisms', in Ifi Amadiume and Abdullahi An-Na'im, eds, *The Politics of Memory. Truth, Healing and Social Justice*, London: Zed Books, 2000.
22. The list of truth commissions so far includes Argentina, Bolivia, Chad, Chile, East Timor, Ecuador, El Salvador, Germany, Ghana, Guatemala, Haiti, Morocco, Nepal, Nigeria, Panama, Peru, Philippines, Serbia and Montenegro, Sierra Leone, South Africa, South Korea, Sri Lanka, Uganda, Uruguay and Zimbabwe, while groups and individuals in Afghanistan, Angola, Bosnia-Herzegovina, Cambodia, Colombia, Indonesia, Jamaica, Kenya, Mexico, Morocco, Philippines, Uganda, Venezuela and Zimbabwe have asked for establishing new or similar bodies. For a more general overlook see Priscilla B. Hayner, *Unspeakable Truths. Confronting State Terror and Atrocity*, New York: Routledge, 2001.
23. Michael Humphrey, From Terror to Trauma: Commissioning Truth for National Reconciliation, *Social Identities*, Vol. 6, No. 1, 2000, p. 8.
24. Restorative justice stands in contrast to retributive justice. It 'revolves around the ideas that crime is, in essence, a violation of a *person* by another person (rather than a violation of legal rules); that in responding to a crime our primary concerns should be to make offenders aware of the harm they have caused, to get them to understand and meet their liability to repair such harm, and to ensure that further offences are prevented; that the form and amount of reparation from the offender to the victim and the measure to be taken to prevent re-offending should be decided collectively by offenders, victims and members of their communities through constructive

dialogue in an informal and consensual process; and that efforts should be made to improve the relationship between the offender and victim and to reintegrate the offender into the law-abiding community'. Gerry Johnstone, *Restorative Justice. Ideas, Values, Debates*, Cullompton: Willian, 2002, p. ix.

25. Whether a nation, as opposed to an individual, can have a cathartic experience, or whether the notion of catharsis is generally useful, is however questionable. See, for instance, Michael Ignatieff, Articles of Faith, *Index on Censorship*, Vol. 25, No. 5, 1996.

26. Reed Brody, 'Justice: The First Casualty of Truth?' *The Nation*, 30 April 2001. See also Gunnar Theissen, Mehrere Wahrheiten: Die südafrikanische Wahrheits- und Versöhnungskommission im Spiegelbild von Meinungsumfragen, *Welt-Trends*, Vol. 37, No. Winter 2002/2003, 2002.

27. Fletcher and Weinstein, Violence and Social Repair, p. 587; Ignatieff, Articles of Faith.

28. Van der Merwe, 'National and Community Reconciliation', p. 102.

29. Susanne Buckley-Zistel and Bernhard Moltmann, 'Versöhnung: Balance zwischen Wahrheit und Gerechtigkeit', in Reinhard Mutz, et al., eds, *Friedensgutachten*, Berlin: LIT Verlag, 2006, p. 171.

30. Vasuki Nesiah and Paul van Zyl, Response to Richard Wilson, *Human Rights Dialogue*, Vol. 2, No. 7, 2002.

31. Buckley-Zistel, 'The Truth Heals'? pp. 117–18.

32. TRC, 1998, Truth and Reconciliation Commission of South Africa Report, Vol. 1, TRC, www.news24.com/Content_Diplay/TRY_Report/1chap5.html (accessed 15 June 2005).

33. David Mendeloff, Truth-Seeking, Truth-Telling, and Post-Conflict Peace-Building: Curb the Enthusiasm, *International Studies Review*, Vol. 6, No. 3, 2004. In this context, Ignatieff questions the possibility of ever reaching a shared truth, since the parties to the conflict will never agree on whether an incidence was an act of aggression or self-defense. Similarly, he denies the possibility of shared suffering, since, even though people might have been subjected to similar pain they will always disagree over who bares the responsibility. Ignatieff, Articles of Faith, pp. 114–15.

34. Louis Kriesberg, 'Coexistence and the Reconciliation of Communal Conflicts', in Eugen Weiner, ed. *The Handbook of Interethnic Coexistence*, New York: The Continuum Publishing Company, 2000, p. 184.

35. John Borneman, Reconciliation after Ethnic Cleansing: Listening, Retribution, Affiliation, *Public Culture*, Vol. 14, No. 2, 2002, p. 281.

36. Hans-Richard Reuter, 'Ethik und Politik der Versöhnung', in Gerhard Beestermöller and Hans-Richard Reuter, eds, *Politik der Versöhnung*, Stuttgart: W. Kohlhammer Verlag, 2002, p. 29.

37. See, for instance, Ronald Fisher, 'Social-Psychological Processes in Interactive Conflict Analysis and Reconciliation', in Ho-Won Jeong, ed. *The New Agenda for Peace Research*, Ashgate: Aldershot, 1999, p. 3.

38. Aletta J. Norval, The (Im)possibility of Reconciliation, *Constellations*, Vol. 5, No. 2, 1998.

39. Jean Bethke Elshtain, 'Politics and Forgiveness', in Nigel Biggar, ed. *Burying the Past: Making Peace and Doing Justice after Civil Conflict*, Washington: Georgetown University Press, 2001, p. 52.

40. Ibid.
41. Nina Scherge, 'Gesamtbericht', Eschborn: GTZ/FES, 2005, pp. 2–3.
42. Hayner, *Unspeakable Truths. Confronting State Terror and Atrocity*, p. 155.
43. David Bloomfield, 'Reconciliation: An Introduction', in David Bloomfield, et al., eds, *Reconciliation after Violent Conflict. A Handbook*, Stockholm: IDEA, 2003, p. 11.
44. Van der Merwe, 'National and Community Reconciliation', p. 97.
45. Björn Pettersson, 'Post-Conflict Reconciliation in Sierra Leone: Lessons Learned', in IDEA, ed. *Reconciliation Lessons Learned from United Nations Peacekeeping Missions*, Stockholm: IDEA, 2005, p. 18.
46. See his quote in LLobera, *The Role of Historical Memory in (Ethno)Nation-Building*, p. 5.
47. Stanley Cohen, State Crimes and Previous Regimes: Knowledge, Accountability, and the Policing of the Past, *Law and Social Inquiry*, Vol. 20, No. 1, 1995. In analogy, the term *chosen amnesia* has been introduced to refer to the deliberate eclipsing of disturbing memories by a community in order to cope with the present realities of day-to-day life. This suggests an immediate benefit of not remembering: to chose amnesia serves a particular function deriving from particular needs of the present: the past is distorted to establish group coherence. A traumatic event is deliberately excluded from the discourse in order to prevent a sense of closure and to undermine the drawing of fixed boundaries of who is inside and who is outside a particular we-group. Through not referring to the underlying social cleavages they seek to reduce their impact and subvert their dividing powers. Buckley-Zistel, Remembering to Forget.
48. Etienne Balibar, 'The Nation Form: History and Ideology', in Geoff Eley and Ronald Grigor Suny, eds, *Becoming National*, Oxford: Oxford University Press, 1996, p. 140.
49. Hobsbawm, 'Inventing Traditions'.
50. Benedict Anderson, *Imagined Communities. Reflections on the Origin and Spread of Nationalism*, London/New York: Verso, 1991.
51. Barahona de Brito et al., 'Introduction', p. 38.
52. Balibar, 'The Nation Form: History and Ideology'.
53. Jürgen Habermas, 'What Does Working Off the Past Mean?' in Jürgen Habermas, ed. *A Berlin Republic: Writings on Germany*, Oxford: Polity, 1997. Pablo de Greiff, Trial and Punishment, Pardon and Oblivion: On Two Inadequate Policies of Dealing with Human Rights Abuses, *Philosophy and Social Criticism*, Vol. 22, No. 3, 1996. See also, Susanne Buckley-Zistel, Living in the Shadows [of Genocide], *Index on Censorship*, Vol. 34, No. 2, 2005.
54. Susanne Buckley-Zistel, Dividing and Uniting. The Use of Citizenship Discourses in Conflict and Reconciliation in Rwanda, *Global Society*, Vol. 20, No. 1, 2006, p. 111.
55. Coker, How Wars End, p. 621.

Bibliography

African Rights, *Rwanda – Not So Innocent. When Women Become Killers*, London: African Rights, 1995.

Ajulu, Deborah and Sara Gibbs, *The Role of the Church in Advocacy: Case Studies from Southern and Eastern Africa*, Oxford: INTRAC, 1999.

Ali, Brig. Chefe, 'Preaching Peace Against War', Paper presented at the Conference on Strategies for Peace and Sustainable Development in Karamoja and Neighbouring Districts, Kampala, 18–22 July 1994.

Amnesty International, *Uganda. The Failure to Safeguard Human Rights*, London: Amnesty International, 1992.

Anderson, Benedict, *Imagined Communities. Reflections on the Origin and Spread of Nationalism*, London/New York: Verso, 1991.

Antze, Paul and Michael Lambek, 'Introduction. Forecasting Memory', in Paul Antze and Micheal Lambek, eds. *Tense Past. Cultural Essays in Trauma and Memory*, New York, London: Routledge, 1996, pp. xi–xxxviii.

Arendt, Hannah, *Between Past and Future. Eight Essays on Political Thought*, Harmondsworth: Penguin, 1968.

Arendt, Hannah, *The Life of the Mind. One/Thinking*, London: Secker & Warburg, 1978.

Argenti, Nicolas, 'Ephemeral Monuments, Memory and Royal Sempiternity in a Grassfield Kingdom', in Adrian Forty and Susanne Kuechler, eds. *The Art of Forgetting*, Oxford/New York: Berg, 1999, pp. 21–52.

Ashley, Richard and R.B.J. Walker, 'Reading Dissidence/Writing the Discipline: Crisis and the Question of Sovereignty in International Studies', *International Studies Quarterly*, Vol. 34, No. 3, 1990, pp. 367–415.

Avruch, Kevin, 'Type I and Type II Errors in Culturally Sensitive Conflict Resolution Practice', *Conflict Resolution Quarterly*, Vol. 20, No. 3, 2003, pp. 351–71.

Bakhtin, Mikail, *The Dialogic Imagination*, Austin: University of Texas Press, 1981.

Balibar, Etienne, 'The Nation Form: History and Ideology', in Geoff Eley and Ronald Grigor Suny, eds. *Becoming National*, Oxford: Oxford University Press, 1996, pp. 132–49.

Barahona de Brito, Alexandra, Paloma Aguilar and Carmen Gonzales-Eriquez, 'Introduction', in Alexandra de Brito, Paloma Aguilar and Carmen Gonzales-Eriquez, eds. *The Politics of Memory. Transitional Justice in Democratizing Societies*, Oxford: Oxford University Press, 1997, pp. 1–39.

Baumann, Richard, *Story, Performance, and Event. Contextual Studies of Oral Narratives*, Cambridge: Cambridge University Press, 1986.

Berdal, Mats, 'How New Are "New Wars"? Global Economic Change and the Study of Civil War', *Global Governance*, Vol. 9, No. 4, 2003, pp. 477–502.

Berdal, Mats and David Keen, 'Violence and Economic Agendas in Civil Wars: Some Policy Implications', *Millennium*, Vol. 26, No. 3, 1997, pp. 795–818.

Berdal, Mats and David Malone, eds. *Greed and Grievance: Economic Agendas in Civil Wars*, New York: International Peace Academy, 2000.

Biggar, Nigel, 'Making Peace and Doing Justice: Must We Choose?' in Nigel Biggar, ed. *Burying the Past. Making Peace and Doing Justice after Civil Conflict*, Washington: Georgetown University Press, 2001, pp. 6–22.

Bloomfield, David, 'Reconciliation: An Introduction', in David Bloomfield, Teresa Barns and Luc Huyse, eds. *Reconciliation after Violent Conflict. A Handbook*, Stockholm: IDEA, 2003, pp. 10–18.

Böge, Volker, *Neue Kriege und traditionelle Konfliktbearbeitung*, Duisburg: INEF, 2004.

Böge, Volker, *Von Muschelgeld und Blutdiamanten. Traditionale Konfliktbearbeitung in zeitgenössischen Gewaltkonflikten*, Hamburg: Deutsches Übersee-Institut, 2004.

Böge, Volker, *Traditional Approaches to Conflict Transformation – Potential and Challenges*, Berlin: Berghof Center for Constructive Conflict Management, 2006.

Borneman, John, Reconciliation after Ethnic Cleansing: Listening, Retribution, Affiliation, *Public Culture*, Vol. 14, No. 2, 2002, pp. 281–304.

Bouckaert, Peter, 'South Africa: The Negotiated Transition from Apartheid to Nonracial Democracy', in Melanie Greenberg, John Barton and Margaret McGuinness, eds. *Words Over War. Mediation and Arbitration to Prevent Deadly Conflict*, Lanham, Boulder, New York, Oxford: Rowman & Littlefield Publishers, 2000, pp. 237–61.

Braun, Hermann, 'Zum Verhältnis von Hermeneutik und Ontologie', in Rüdiger Bubner, Konrad Cramer and Reiner Wiehl, eds. *Hermeneutik und Dialektik. Aufsätze II*, Tübingen: Mohr Siebeck, 1970, pp. 201–18.

Brenneis, Donald, 'Telling Troubles: Narrative, Conflict, and Experience', in Charles Briggs, ed. *Disorderly Discourse. Narrative, Conflict and Inequality*, New York/Oxford: Oxford University Press, 1996, pp. 41–52.

Brett, E.A., 'Rebuilding War Damaged Communities in Uganda', in Tim Allen, ed. *In Search of Cool Ground. War, Flight and Homecoming in Northeast Africa*, London/Trenton: James Curry/Africa World Press, 1996, pp. 203–19.

Brock-Utne, Birgit, 'Indigenous Conflict Resolution in Africa', Paper presented at the Indigenous Solutions to Conflicts, University of Oslo, Institute for Educational Research, 2001.

Buckley-Zistel, Susanne, 'Development Assistance and Conflict Assessment Methodology', *Journal for Conflict, Security and Development*, Vol. 3, No. 1, 2003, pp. 117–25.

Buckley-Zistel, Susanne, 'Living in the Shadows [of Genocide]', *Index on Censorship*, Vol. 34, No. 2, 2005, pp. 43–7.

Buckley-Zistel, Susanne, 'The Truth Heals'? – Gacaca Jurisdiction and the Consolidation of Peace in Rwanda, *Die Friedens Warte*, Vol. 80, No. 1–2, 2005, pp. 113–29.

Buckley-Zistel, Susanne, Dividing and Uniting. 'The Use of Citizenship Discourses in Conflict and Reconciliation in Rwanda', *Global Society*, Vol. 20, No. 1, 2006, pp. 101–13.

Buckley-Zistel, Susanne, In-Between War and Peace. 'Identities, Boundaries and Change after Violent Conflict', *Millennium*, Vol. 35, No. 1, 2006, pp. 3–21.

Buckley-Zistel, Susanne, 'Remembering to Forget. Chosen Amnesia as a Strategy for Local Coexistence in Post-Genocide Rwanda', *Africa*, Vol. 76, No. 2, 2006, pp. 131–50.

Buckley-Zistel, Susanne, 'Frieden entwickeln? Eine kritische Analyse der Strategien der Internationalen Gebergemeinschaft zur Friedenskonsolidierung in gespaltenen Staaten', *Sicherheit + Frieden*, 2007, pp. 77–81.

Buckley-Zistel, Susanne, *Transitional Justice*, Berlin: Plattform für zivile Konfliktbearbeitung, 2007.

Buckley-Zistel, Susanne and Bernhard Moltmann, 'Versöhnung: Balance zwischen Wahrheit und Gerechtigkeit', in Reinhard Mutz, Bruno Schoch, Corinna Hauswedell, Jochen Hippler and Ulrich Ratsch, eds. *Friedensgutachten*, Berlin: LIT Verlag, 2006, pp. 168–76.

Buckley-Zistel, Susanne and Bernard Tabaire, 'Preventing Violent Conflicts? UK Policy on Uganda. London: ISIS Policy Paper 87, March 2003', London: ISIS Policy Paper 87, 2003.

Burton, John, *Conflict: Resolution and Provention*, New York: St. Martin's Press, 1990.

Bush, Robert A. Baruch and Joseph P. Folgner, *The Promise of Mediation. Responding to Conflict Through Empowerment and Recognition*, San Francisco: Jossey-Bass Publishers, 1994.

Byanyima, Winfred K., 'How Guerrillas Became Peace Builders', in Elise Boulding, ed. *New Agendas for Peace Research. Conflict and Security Re-examined*, London/Boulder: Lynne Rienner, 1992, pp. 129–45.

Campbell, David, *Writing Security: United States Foreign Policy and the Politics of Identity*, Manchester: Manchester University Press, 1992.

Campbell, David, *Politics without Principles. Sovereignty, Ethics and the Narrative of the Gulf War*, Boulder/London: Lynne Rienner, 1993.

Campbell, David, 'The Politics of Radical Interdependence: A Rejoinder to Daniel Warner', *Millennium*, Vol. 25, No. 1, 1996, pp. 129–44.

Campbell, David, MetaBosnia: Narratives of the Bosnian War, *Review of International Studies*, Vol. 24, No. 2, 1998, pp. 261–81.

Campbell, David, *National Deconstruction. Violence, Identity, and Justice in Bosnia*, Minnesota: University Press, 1998.

Campbell, David, 'Why Fight: Humanitarianism, Principles, and Post-Structuralism', *Millennium*, Vol. 27, No. 3, 1998, pp. 497–523.

Caputo, John, *Radical Hermeneutics. Repetition, Deconstruction and the Hermeneutic Project*, Bloomington and Indianapolis: Indiana University Press, 1987.

CDRN, *A Study of Poverty in Selected Districts of Uganda: Apac, Kampala, Kapchorwa, Kibaale, Kisoro, Kumi and Nebbi*, Kampala: CDRN, 1996.

Chabal, Patrick and Jean-Pascal Daloz, *Culture Troubles. Politics and the Interpretation of Meaning*, London: Hurst, 2006.

Cobb, Sara, 'A Narrative Perspective on Mediation. Towards the Materialization of the "Storyteller" Metaphor', in Joseph P. Folgner and S. Tricia Jones, eds. *New Directions in Mediation. Communication Research and Perspectives*, Thousand Oaks/London/New Delhi: Sage, 1994, pp. 49–63.

Cobb, Sara, 'Negotiation Pedagogy: Learning to Learn', *Negotiation Journal*, Vol. 16, No. 4, 2000, pp. 315–21.

Cohen, Ira J., *Structuration Theory. Anthony Giddens and the Structuration of Social Life*, Basingstoke/London: Macmillan, 1989.

Cohen, Stanley, State Crimes and Previous Regimes: Knowledge, Accountability, and the Policing of the Past., *Law and Social Inquiry*, Vol. 20, No. 1, 1995, pp. 7–50.

Coker, Chris, How Wars End, *Millennium*, Vol. 26, No. 3, 1997, pp. 615–30.

Cole, J., 'The Use of Defeat: Memory and Political Morality in East Madagascar', in Richard Webner, ed. *Memory and the Postcolonial. African Anthropology and the Crisis of Power*, London/New York: Zed, 1998, pp. 105–24.

Collier, Paul and Anke Hoeffer, On the Incidences of Civil War in Africa, *Journal of Conflict Resolution*, Vol. 46, No. 1, 2002, pp. 13–28.

Connolly, William E., *Identity/Difference. Democratic Negotiations of Political Space*, Ithaca/London: Cornell University Press, 1991.

Council, Soroti District Resistance, 'Memorandum on Uganda National Constitutional Affairs', Soroti: Soroti District National Constitution Affairs, 1991.

Cox, Robert and Timothy Sinclair, *Approaches to World Order*, Cambridge: Cambridge University Press, 1996.

Cramer, Chris, Homo Economicus Goes to War: Methodological Individualism, Rational Choice and the Political Economy of War, *World Development*, Vol. 30, No. 11, 2002, pp. 1845–64.

Critchley, Simon, *The Ethics of Deconstruction. Derrida and Levinas*, Edinburgh: Edinburgh University Press, 1999.

Crocker, Chester, 'Truth Commissions, Transitional Justice and Civil Society', in Robert I. Rotberg and Dennis Thompson, eds. *Truth v. Justice. The Morality of Truth Commissions*, Princeton: Princeton University Press, 2000, pp. 322–35.

Crocker, David, Transitional Justice and International Civil Society: Towards a Normative Framework, *Constellations*, Vol. 5, No. 4, 1998, pp. 492–517.

Curle, Adam, *Making Peace*, London: Tavistock, 1971.

de Berry, Joanna, 'Life After Loss: An Anthropological Study of Post-war Recovery, Teso, Uganda, with Special Reference to Young People', London School of Economics (doctoral thesis), 2000.

de Greiff, Pablo, Trial and Punishment, Pardon and Oblivion: On Two Inadequate Policies of Dealing with Human Rights Abuses, *Philosophy and Social Criticism*, Vol. 22, No. 3, 1996, pp. 93–111.

de Greiff, Pablo, ed. *Reparations*, Oxford: Oxford University Press, 2006.

de Greiff, Pablo, 'Addressing the Past: Reparations for Gross Human Rights Abuses', in Agnes Hurwitz, ed. *Rule of Law and Conflict Management: Towards Security, Development and Human Rights*, NY: International Peace Academy, 2008, pp. 163–189.

de Waal, Alex, *Sudan: What Kind of State? What Kind of Crisis?* London: LSE Crisis States Research Centre, 2007.

Deleuze, Gilles, *Negotiations 1972–1990*, New York: Columbia University Press, 1995.

Der Derian, James, ed. *International Theory. Critical Investigations*, London/Basingstoke: Macmillan, 1995.

Der Derian, James and Michael J. Shapiro, eds. *International/Intertextual Relations. Postmodern Reading of World Politics*, New York: Lexington Books, 1989.

Derrida, Jacques, *Adieu: To Emmanuel Levinas*, Stanford: Stanford University Press, 1999.

Dicklitch, Susan, *The Elusive Promise of NGOs in Africa. Lessons from Uganda*, Basingstoke/London: Macmillan, 1998.

Dreyfus, Hubert, 'Beyond Hermeneutics. Interpretation in Late Heidegger and Recent Foucault', in Gary Shapiro and Alan Sica, eds. *Hermeneutics. Questions and Prospects*, Amherst: University of Massachusetts Press, 1988, pp. 66–83.

Duffield, Mark, *Global Governance and the New Wars: The Merging of Development and Security*, London: Zed Books, 2001.

Edkins, Jenny, *Trauma and the Memory of Politics*, Cambridge: Cambridge University Press, 2003.

Elshtain, Jean Bethke, 'Politics and Forgiveness', in Nigel Biggar, ed. *Burying the Past: Making Peace and Doing Justice after Civil Conflict*, Washington: Georgetown University Press, 2001, pp. 40–57.

Faure, Guy Oliver, 'Traditional Conflict Management in Africa and China', in William I. Zartman, ed. *Traditional Cures for Modern Conflicts. African Conflict 'Medicine'*, Boulder: Lynne Rienner, 2000, pp. 153–74.

Ferris, Elizabeth G., 'Women as Peace Makers', in Aruna Gnanadason, Musimbi Kanyoro and Lucia Ann McSpadden, eds. *Women, Violence and Non-Violent Change*, Geneva: WCC, 1996, pp. 2–28.

Fisher, Roger, Elisabeth Kopelman and Andres Schneider, *Beyond Machiavelli: Tools for Coping with Conflict*, Cambridge: Harvard University Press, 1994.

Fisher, Roger, William Ury and Bruce Patton, *Getting to Yes: Negotiating Agreement without Giving In*, New York: Penguin Books, 1983.

Fisher, Ronald, *Interactive Conflict Resolution*, Syracuse: Syracuse University Press, 1997.

Fisher, Ronald, 'Social-Psychological Processes in Interactive Conflict Analysis and Reconciliation', in Ho-Won Jeong, ed. *The New Agenda for Peace Research*, Ashgate: Aldershot, 1999, pp. 81–104.

Fletcher, Laurel E. and Harvey M. Weinstein, 'Violence and Social Repair: Rethinking the Contribution of Justice to Reconciliation', *Human Rights Quarterly*, Vol. 24, No. 3, 2002, pp. 573–639.

Folgner, Joseph P. and Robert A. Baruch Bush, 'Ideology, Orientations, and Discourse', in Joseph P. Folgner and Tricia S. Jones, eds. *New Directions in Mediation. Communication Research and Perspectives*, Thousandoaks/London/New Delhi: Sage, 1994, pp. 3–26.

Foucault, Michel, *The Archaeology of Knowledge and the Discourse on Language*, Translated by A.M. Sheridan Smith, New York: Pantheon Books, 1972.

Foucault, Michel, *The Order of Things*, New York: Vintage Books, 1973.

Foucault, Michel, 'Two Lectures', in Michael Kelly, ed. *Critique and Power. Recasting the Foucault/Habermas Debate*, Cambridge, MA/London: MIT Press, 1994, pp. 17–46.

Fred-Mensah, Ben K., 'Conflict Management Practices in Buem-Kator', in William I. Zartman, ed. *Traditional Cures for Modern Conflicts: African Conflict 'Medicine'*, Boulder: Lynne Rienner, 2000, pp. 31–45.

Frueh, Jamie, *Political Identity and Social Change. The Remaking of the South African Social Order*, Albany: SUNY, 2003.

Gadamer, Hans-Georg, *Truth and Method*, New York: Seabury, 1975.

Gadamer, Hans-Georg, 'Practical Philosophy as a Model of the Human Science', *Research in Phenomenology*, Vol. IX, 1979, pp. 74–86.

Gadamer, Hans-Georg, *Philosophical Apprenticeships*, New York: Seabury, 1985.

176 *Bibliography*

Gadamer, Hans-Georg, 'Destruction and Deconstruction', in Diane P. Michelfelder and Richard E. Palmer, eds. *Dialogue and Deconstructions*, Albany: State University of New York, 1989, pp. 102–13.

Gadamer, Hans-Georg, 'Replik zu "Hermeneutik und Ideologienkritik"', *Wahrheit und Methode II. Ergänzungen*, Tübingen: Mohr Siebeck, 1993, pp. 251–76.

Gadamer, Hans-Georg, 'Vom Zirkel des Verstehens', *Wahrheit und Methode II. Ergänzungen*, Tübingen: Mohr Siebeck, 1993, pp. 57–65.

Gadamer, Hans-Georg, *Wahrheit und Methode I. Grundzüge einer philosophischen Hermeneutik*, Tübingen: Mohr Siebeck, 1993.

Gadamer, Hans-Georg, 'Was ist Wahrheit?' *Wahrheit und Methode II. Ergänzungen*, Tübingen: Mohr Siebeck, 1993, pp. 44–56.

Gadamer, Hans-Georg, *Zukunft ist Herkunft*, Jena: Universität Jena, 1997.

Gadamer, Hans-Georg, 'Dialogues in Capri', in Jacques Derrida and Gianni Vattimo, eds. *Religion*, Cambridge: Polity Press, 1998, pp. 200–11.

Gakwandi, Athur, *Uganda Pocket Facts*, Kampala: Fountain, 1999.

Galtung, Johan, *Peace by Peaceful Means: Peace and Conflict, Development and Civilisation*, London: Sage, 1996.

Garcia, Ed, 'Addressing Social Change in Situations of Violent Conflict: A Practitioner's Perspective', in David Bloomfield and Beatrix Schmelzle, eds. *Social Change and Conflict Transformation*, Berlin: Berghof Center for Constructive Conflict Management, 2006, pp. 39–48.

Gasche, Rodolphe, *The Tain of the Mirror: Derrida and the Philosophy of Reflection*, Cambridge, MA/London: Harvard University Press, 1986.

Giddens, Anthony, *The Constitution of Society. Outline of the Theory of Structuration*, Cambridge: Polity Press, 1984.

Gifford, Paul, *African Christianity. Its Public Role*, London: Hurst & Company, 1998.

Gingyera-Pinycwa, A.G., *Milton Obote and His Time*, London: NOK Publishers, 1987.

Gingyera-Pinycwa, A.G., 'Is there a Northern Question?' in Kumar Rupesinghe, ed. *Internal Conflicts and Their Resolution: The Case of Uganda*, London: James Curry, 1989, pp. 44–65.

Gluckman, Max, *Custom and Conflict in Africa*, Oxford: Blackwell, 1955.

Griffiths, Anne, 'Mediation, Gender and Justice in Botswana', *Mediation Quarterly*, Vol. 15, No. 4, 1998, pp. 335–44.

Group, HSR, 'Human Security Report': HSR Group, 2006.

GTZ, 'Vergangenheits-und Versöhnungsarbeit. Wie die TZ Aufarbeitung von gemeinsamen Konflikten unterstützen kann', Eschborn: GTZ, 2002.

Habermas, Jürgen, 'What Does Working Off the Past Mean?' in Jürgen Habermas, ed. *A Berlin Republic: Writings on Germany*, Oxford: Polity, 1997, pp. 17–40.

Halbwachs, Maurice, *On Collective Memory*, Chicago/London: University of Chicago Press, 1992.

Hamber, Brandon, *Repairing the Irreparable: Dealing with Double-binds of Making Reparations for Crimes of the Past*, Johannesburg: Centre for the Study of Violence and Reconciliation, 1998.

Harell-Bond, Barbara, *Imposing Aid. Emergency Assistance to Refugees*, Oxford: Oxford University Press, 1986.

Hauser, E., 'Ugandan Relations with Western Donors in the 1990: What Impact on Democratisation?', *Journal of Modern African Studies*, Vol. 37, No. 4, 1999, pp. 621–41.

Hayner, Priscilla B., *Unspeakable Truths. Confronting State Terror and Atrocity*, New York: Routledge, 2001.

Henriques, Peter, 'Peace Without Reconciliation: War, Peace and Experience among the Iteso of East Uganda', University of Copenhagen (doctoral thesis), 2000.

Hinchman, Lewis P. and Sandra K. Hinchman, 'Introduction', in Lewis P. Hinchman and Sandra K. Hinchman, eds. *Memory, Identity, Community*, Albany: State of New York Press, 1997, pp. xiii–xxxii.

Hobsbawm, Eric, 'Inventing Traditions', in Eric Hobsbawm and Terence Ranger, eds. *The Invention of Tradition*, Cambridge: Cambridge University Press, 2000, pp. 1–15.

Hoffman, Mark, 'Defining and Evaluating Success: Facilitative Problem-Solving Workshops in an Interconnected Context', *Paradigms*, Vol. 9, No. 2, 1995, pp. 150–63.

Holmes, Tim, *A Participatory Approach in Practice: Understanding Fieldworkers' Use of Participatory Rural Appraisal in Action Aid the Gambia*, Brighton: Institute of Development Studies, 2001.

How, Alan, *The Habermas-Gadamer Debate and the Nature of the Social*, Aldershot: Avebury, 1995.

Howarth, David, 'Discourse Theory and Political Analysis', in David Howarth, Aletta J. Norval and Yannis Stravrakakis, eds. *Discourse Theory and Political Analysis. Identities, Hegemonies and Social Change*, Manchester: Manchester University Press, 2000.

Human Rights Watch, *Hostile to Democracy. The Movement System and Political Repression in Uganda*, NYC/Washington/London/Brussels: Human Rights Watch, 1999.

Humphrey, Michael, 'From Terror to Trauma: Commissioning Truth for National Reconciliation', *Social Identities*, Vol. 6, No. 1, 2000, pp. 7–27.

ICU, *Iteso Cultural Union. A Cultural Union Development*, Soroti: ICU, 1997.

Ignatieff, Michael, 'Articles of Faith', *Index on Censorship*, Vol. 25, No. 5, 1996, pp. 110–22.

Ignatieff, Michael, *The Warrior's Honour. Ethnic War and the Modern Conscience*, London: Chatto & Windus, 1998.

Ilie, Cornelia, 'The Ideological Remapping of Semantic Roles in Totalitarian Discourses, or, How to Paint a White Rose Red', *Discourse & Society*, Vol. 9, No. 1, 1998, pp. 57–80.

International Alert, *Uganda – International Seminar on Internal Conflict, 21th–25th September 1987*, Kampala: Makerere University, 1987.

Irani, George E. and Nathan C. Funk, 'Rituals of Reconciliation: Arab-Islamic Perspectives', *Arab Studies Quarterly*, Vol. 20, No. 4, 1998, pp. 53–74.

Irwin-Zarecka, Iona, *Frames of Remembrance. The Dynamics of Collective Memory*, London/New Brunswick: Transaction Publisher, 1994.

ISIS, 'Women's Experience in Armed Conflict. Situations in Uganda 1980–86: Luwero District. A Research Report', Kampala: ISIS – International Cross Cultural Exchange, 1998.

Jabri, Vivienne, 'Agency, Structure and the Question of Power in Conflict Resolution', *Paradigms*, Vol. 9, No. 2, 1995, pp. 53–71.

Jabri, Vivienne, *Discourses on Violence. Conflict Analysis Reconsidered*, Manchester: Manchester University Press, 1996.

Jabri, Vivienne, 'Revisiting Change and Conflict: On Underlying Assumptions and the De-Politicisation of Conflict Resolution', in David Bloomfield and Beatrix Schmelzle, eds. *Conflict Transformation and Social Change*, Berlin: Berghof Center for Constructive Conflict Management, 2006, pp. 69–76.

Jaspers, Karl, *The Question of German Guilt*, Translated by E.B. Ashton, New York: The Dial, 1947.

Jensen, Lloyed, 'Negotiations and Power Asymmetries: The Case of Bosnia, Northern Ireland and Sri Lanka', *International Negotiation*, Vol. 2, No. 2, 1997, pp. 21–41.

Johnstone, Gerry, *Restorative Justice. Ideas, Values, Debates*, Cullompton: Willian, 2002.

Jorgensen, Jan Jelmert, *Uganda. A Modern History*, London: Croon Helm, 1981.

Jung, Courtney, *Then I Was Black. South African Political Identities in Transition*, New Haven/London: Yale University Press, 2000.

Kaldor, Mary, *New and Old Wars: Organized Violence in a Global Era*, Cambridge: Polity Press, 1999.

Kaldor, Mary, *Global Insecurity: Vol. III of Restructuring the Global Military Sector*, Cassell: Pinter, 2000.

Kermonde, Frank, 'Places of Memory', *Index on Censorship*, Vol. 30, No. 1, 2001, pp. 87–96.

Kreimer, Alcira and John Eriksson, *The World Bank's Experience with Post-Conflict Reconstruction*, Washington: World Bank, 1998.

Kriesberg, Louis, 'Coexistence and the Reconciliation of Communal Conflicts', in Eugen Weiner, ed. *The Handbook of Interethnic Coexistence*, New York: The Continuum Publishing Company, 2000, pp. 182–98.

Kuechler, Susanne, 'The Place of Memory', in Adrian Forty and Susanne Kuechler, eds. *The Art of Forgetting*, Oxford/New York: Berg, 1999, pp. 53–72.

Kundera, Milan, *Testaments Betrayed*, London: Faber and Faber, 1995.

Ledearch, John Paul, *Building Peace. Sustainable Reconciliation in Divided Societies*, Washington: United States Institute of Peace, 1997.

Lederach, John Paul, 'Just Peace – The Challenge of the 21st Century', in European Platform for Conflict Prevention, eds. *People Building Peace*, Utrecht: European Platform for Conflict Prevention, 1999, pp. 27–36.

Linklater, Andrew, *The Transformation of Political Community. Ethical Foundations of the Post-Westphalian Era*, Cambridge/Oxford: Polity Press, 1998.

LLobera, Joseph R., *The Role of Historical Memory in (Ethno)Nation-Building*, London: Goldsmith College, 1996.

Lloyed-Jones, Deiniol, 'Mediation, Conflict Resolution and Critical Theory', *Review of International Studies*, Vol. 26, No. 4, 2000, pp. 645–62.

Luckham, Robin, Ismail Ahmed, Robert Muggah and Sarah White, 'Conflict and Poverty in Sub-Sahara Africa: An Assessment of the Issues and Evidence', Brighton: Institute of Development Studies, 2001.

Lwanga-Lunyiigo, Samwiri, 'The Colonial Roots of Internal Conflict', in Kumar Rupesinghe, ed. *Conflict Resolution in Uganda*, London: James Curry, 1989, pp. 24–43.

MacDonald, Sharon, *Gender, Peace and War: Anthropological Perspectives*, Oxford: Oxford Project for Peace Studies, 1991.

Malan, Jannie, 'Traditional and Local Conflict Resolution', in Paul van Tongeren, Malin Brenk, Marte Hellema and Juliette Verhoeven, eds. *People Building Peace II: Successful Stories of Civil Society*, Boulder: Lynne Rienner, 2005.

Malkki, Liisa H., *Purity and Exile. Violence, Memory, and National Cosmology among Hutu Refugees in Tanzania*, Chicago: University of Chicago Press, 1995.

Mamdani, Mahmood, *Politics and Class Formation in Uganda*, London: Heinemann, 1976.

Mamdani, Mahmood, *Imperialism and Fascism in Uganda*, London: Heineman, 1983.

Mamdani, Mahmood, 'From Justice to Reconciliation: Making Sense of the African Experience', in Colin Leys and Mahmood Mamdani, eds. *Crisis and Reconstruction – African Perspective*, Uppsala: Nordiska Afrikainstitutet, 1997, pp. 17–25.

Mande, Wilson M., 'The Role of the Churches in the Political Reconstruction of Uganda in the 1990s', in J.N.K. Mugambi, ed. *The Church and Reconstruction of Africa*, Nairobi: All African Council of Churches, 1997, pp. 180–202.

Mani, Rama, *Beyond Retribution. Seeking Justice in the Shadows of War*, Cambridge/Oxford: Polity Press, 2002.

Mendeloff, David, 'Truth-Seeking, Truth-Telling, and Post-Conflict Peace-Building: Curb the Enthusiasm', *International Studies Review*, Vol. 6, No. 3, 2004, pp. 355–80.

Merturs, Julie, 'Truth in a Box: The Limits of Justice Through Judicial Mechanisms', in Ifi Amadiume and Abdullahi An-Na'im, eds. *The Politics of Memory. Truth, Healing and Social Justice*, London: Zed Books, 2000, pp. 142–61.

Miall, Hugh, Oliver Ramsbotham and Tom Woodhouse, *Contemporary Conflict Resolution*, Cambridge: Polity Press, 1999.

Miall, Hugh, *Conflict Transformation: A Multi-Dimensional Task*, Berlin: Berghof Centre for Constructive Conflict Management, 2004.

Middleton, David and Derek Edwards, 'Introduction', in David Middleton and Derek Edwards, eds. *Collective Remembering*, London/Newbury Park/New Delhi: Sage, 1990, pp. 1–22.

Minow, Martha, *Between Vengeance and Forgiveness. Facing History after Genocide and Mass Violence*, Boston: Beacon Press, 1998.

Moodley, Kogila and Heribert Adam, 'Race and Nation in Post-Apartheid South Africa', *Current Sociology*, Vol. 48, No. 3, 2000, pp. 51–69.

Murithi, Tim, 'Final Report of the All-African Conference on African Principles of Conflict Resolution and Reconciliation', Addis Ababa: UNITAR, 1999.

Murithi, Tim, 'African Approaches to Building Peace and Social Solidarity', *African Journal for Conflict Resolution*, Vol. 6, No. 2, 2006, pp. 9–34.

Museveni, Yoweri K., 'Speech given at a consultation organised by International Alert, 25 September 1987', Kampala: Makerere University, 1987.

Museveni, Yoweri K., *Sowing the Mustard Seeds: The Struggle for Freedom and Democracy in Uganda*, Basingstoke/London: Macmillan, 1996.

Mutibwa, Phares, *Uganda since Independence. A Story of Unfulfilled Hope*, London: Hurst & Company, 1992.

Nations, United, 'Report of the Panel of Experts on the Illegal Exploitation of Natural Resources and Other Forms of Wealth of the Democratic Republic of the Congo (S/2001/357)', New York: United Nations, 2002.

Nesiah, Vasuki and Paul van Zyl, 'Response to Richard Wilson', *Human Rights Dialogue*, Vol. 2, No. 7, 2002, pp. 2–3.

Newman, Edward and Oliver P. Richmond, eds. *Challenges to Peacebuilding: Managing Spoilers During Conflict Resolution*, New York/Tokyo: United Nations University Press, 2006.

Nietzsche, Friedrich, 'On the Uses and Disadvantages of History for Life', *Untimely Meditations*, Cambridge: University Press, 1983, pp. 57–124.

Nino, Carlos Santiago, *Radical Evil on Trial*, New Haven: Yale University Press, 1996.

N.N., 'Security in Grazing Areas and Villages', Paper presented at the Conference on Strategies for Peace and Sustainable Development in Karamoja and Neighbouring Districts, Kampala, 18–22 July 1994.

Nordstrom, Carolyn, 'War on the Front Lines', in Carolyn Nordstrom and Antonius C.G.M. Robben, eds. *Fieldwork Under Fire: Contemporary Studies in Violence and Survival*, Berkley: University of California Press, 1995, pp. 129–54.

Nordstrom, Carolyn, *A Different Kind of War Story*, Philadelphia: University of Pennsylvania Press, 1997.

Nordstrom, Carolyn and Antonius C.G.M. Robben, 'Anthropology and Ethnography of Violence and Sociopolitical Conflict', in Carolyn Nordstrom and Antonius C.G.M. Robben, eds. *Fieldwork Under Fire. Contemporary Studies of Violence and Survival*, Berkley/Los Angeles/London: University of California Press, 1995, pp. 1–24.

Norval, Aletta J., 'The (Im)possibility of Reconciliation', *Constellations*, Vol. 5, No. 2, 1998, pp. 250–65.

Nsimbambi, Apolo, 'The Land Question and Conflict', in Kumar Rupesinghe, ed. *Conflict Resolution in Uganda*, London: James Curry, 1989, pp. 233–49.

Nsimbambi, Apolo, 'The Restoration of Traditional Rulers', in Holger Berndt Hansen and Michael Twaddle, eds. *From Chaos to Order. The Politics of Constitution Making in Uganda*, Kampala/London: Foutain/James Currey, 1995, pp. 41–60.

Nzita, Richard, *Peoples and Cultures of Uganda*, Kampala: Fountain Publishers, 1995.

Ochyang, Dan, *Proposal for the Restoration of Stability, Peace and Progress to Teso*, Kampala: UPC, 1991.

Oettler, Anika, *Erinnerungsarbeit und Vergangenheitspolitik in Guatemala*, Frankfurt: Vervuert, 2004.

Ofcansky, Thomas P., *Uganda. Tarnished Pearl of Africa*, Boulder: WestView Press, 1996.

Office of the Prime Minister, *IDP Profiling in Lango and Teso Subregions. Preliminary Results*, Kampala: Office of the Prime Minister, 2006.

Okiria, Pius, 'Personal Experience', in CECORE, ed. *Experiences and Best Practices of Peace-Builders*, Kampala: CECORE, 2000, pp. 3–9.

Okolo, Chukwudum B., *The Liberating Role of the Church in Africa Today*, Eldoret: AMECEA Gaba Publishers, 1991.

Olupot, Egoing James Peter, *The Bitter Price*, Kumi/Teso: PN Press, 2000.

Omunyokol, Fidle, *The Day a Helicopter Landed in Mukongoro*, Soroti: Etesot, 2000.

Orentlicher, Diane F., 'Settling Accounts: The Duty to Prosecute Human Rights Violations of a Prior Regime', *Yale Law Journal*, Vol. 100, No. 8, 1991, pp. 2537–615.

ori Amaza, Ondoga, *Museveni's Long March from Guerrilla to Statesman*, Kampala: Fountain, 1998.

Osaghae, Egohosa E., 'Applying Traditional Methods to Modern Conflict: Possibilities and Limits', in William I. Zartman, ed. *Traditional Cures for Modern Conflicts. African Continent 'Medicine'*, Boulder: Lynne Rienner, 2000, pp. 201–18.

OXFAM, 'OXFAM Kumi District Agricultural Rehabilitation Project: Final Evaluation', Uganda: OXFAM, 1993.

Paris, Roland, *At War's End. Building Peace after Civil Conflict*, Cambridge: Cambridge University Press, 2005.

Pazzaglia, Augosto, *The Karimojong: Some Aspects*, Bologna: EMI, 1982.

PCT, 'Rehabilitation and Development Plan for Teso Region 1991/2–2000/1. Vol. 1: Guidelines/Strategies', Kampala: Ministry for Planning and Economic Development, Republic of Uganda, 1991.

Pettersson, Björn, 'Post-Conflict Reconciliation in Sierra Leone: Lessons Learned', in IDEA, eds *Reconciliation Lessons Learned from United Nations Peacekeeping Missions*, Stockholm: IDEA, 2005, pp. 7–31.

Pirout, M. Louise, *Historical Dictionary of Uganda*, London: The Scarecrow Press, 1995.

Porter, Elisabeth, Gillian Robinson, Marie Smyth, Albrecht Schnabel and Eghosa Osaghe, *Researching Conflict in Africa. Insights and Experiences*, Tokyo/New York: United Nations University Press, 2005.

Pulkol, David, 'Karamoja Cattle Rustling – a National Dilemma: Myths and Realities', Paper presented at the Conference on Strategies for Peace and Sustainable Development in Karamoja and Neighbouring Districts, Kampala, 18–22 July 1994.

Ranger, Terence, 'The Invention of Tradition in Colonial Africa', in Eric Hobsbawm and Terence Ranger, eds. *The Invention of Tradition*, Cambridge: Cambridge University Press, 2000, pp. 211–63.

Reimann, Cordula, *Assessing the State of the Art in Conflict Transformation*, Berlin: Berghof Research Center for Constructive Conflict Management, 2001.

Reuter, Hans-Richard, 'Ethik und Politik der Versöhnung', in Gerhard Beestermöller and Hans-Richard Reuter, eds. *Politik der Versöhnung*, Stuttgart: W. Kohlhammer Verlag, 2002, pp. 15–36.

Richards, Paul, *Fighting for the Rain Forests. War, Youth and Resources in Sierra Leone*, London: James Currey: African Issues, 1996.

Richards, Paul, *No Peace, No War. An Anthropology of Contemporary Armed Conflict*, Oxford: James Currey, 2005.

Richmond, Oliver P., 'A Genealogy of Peacemaking: The Creation and Re-Creation of Order', *Alternatives*, Vol. 26, No. 3, 2001, pp. 317–48.

Richmond, Oliver P., *Maintaining Order, Making Peace*, Basingstoke: Palgrave Macmillan, 2002.

Richmond, Oliver P., *The Transformation of Peace*, Basingstoke: Palgrave Macmillan, 2005.

Rigby, Andrew, ' "Forgiving the Past": Paths Towards a Culture of Reconciliation', Coventry: Coventry University/Centre for the Study of Forgiveness and Reconciliation, 2000.

Rigby, Andrew, *Justice and Reconciliation. After the Violence*, London: Lynne Rienner, 2001.

Ringmar, Eric, *Identity, Interest, Action. A Cultural Explanation of Sweden's Intervention in the Thirty Years War*, Cambridge: Cambridge University Press, 1996.

Roloff, Michael, Gaylen Paulson and Jennifer Vollbrecht, 'The Interpretation of Coercive Communication: The Effects of Mode of Influence, Powerful Speech and Speaker Authority', *International Journal of Conflict Management*, Vol. 9, No. 2, 1998, pp. 139–61.

Rombouts, Heidy, 'Importance and Difficulties of Victim-Based Research in Post-Conflict Societies', *European Journal of Crime, Criminal Law and Criminal Justice*, Vol. 10, Nos 2–3, 2002, pp. 216–32.

Ropers, Norbert, *Roles and Functions of Third Parties in the Constructive Management of Ethnopolitical Conflicts*, Berlin: Berghof Research Centre for Constructive Conflict Management, 1997.

Ross, Marc Howard and Jay Rothman, 'Issues of Theory and Practice in Ethnic Conflict Resolution', in Marc Ross and Jay Rothman, eds. *Theory and Practice in Ethnic Conflict Resolution. Theorizing Success and Failure*, Basingstoke/London: Macmillan, 1999, pp. 1–23.

Ross, Mark Howard, 'Creating Conditions for Peacemaking: Theories of Practice in Ethnic Conflict Resolution', *Ethnic and Racial Studies*, Vol. 23, No. 6, 2000, pp. 1002–34.

Rothman, Jay, 'Action Evaluation and Conflict Resolution: Theory and Practice', *Mediation Quarterly*, Vol. 15, No. 2, 1997, pp. 119–31.

Rouhana, Nadim N. and Susan H. Korper, 'Dealing with the Dilemmas Posed by Power Asymmetry in Intergroup Conflict', *Negotiation Journal*, Vol. 12, No. 4, 1996, pp. 353–66.

Rubin, Jeffrey, 'Western Perspectives on Conflict Resolution', in Paul E. Salem, ed. *Conflict Resolution in the Arab World: Selected Essays*, Beirut: American University of Beirut, 1997, pp. 3–10.

Rublo-Marìn, Ruth, ed. *What Happened to the Women? Gender and Reparations for Human Rights Violations*, New York: SSRC, 2006.

Saito, Fumihiko, 'Decentralisation Theories Revisited: Lessons from Uganda', *Ryukoku RISS Bulletin*, No. 31, 2001, pp. 30–47.

Salem, Paul E., 'A Critique of Western Conflict Resolution from a Non-Western Perspective: Selected Essays', in Paul E. Salem, ed. *Conflict Resolution in the Arab World*, Beirut: American University of Beirut, 1997, pp. 11–27.

Samuel, Jacob, *Zwischen Gespräch und Diskurs. Untersuchung zur sozialhermeneutischen Begründung der Agogik anhand einer Gegenüberstellung von Hans-Georg Gadamer und Jürgen Habermas*, Stuttgart: Paul Haupt, 1985.

Scherge, Nina, *Gesamtbericht*, Eschborn: GTZ/FES, 2005.

Shapiro, Michael J., *Violent Cartographies. Mapping Cultures of War*, Minneapolis: University of Minnesota Press, 1997.

Speckmann, Thomas, 'Frieden schaffen nur mit Waffen. Vom Wiederaufbau gescheiterter Staaten', *Merkur*, Vol. 59, No. 5, 2005, pp. 388–98.

Spittal, Patricia, ' "We are Dying. It is Finished". Linking an Ethnographic Research Design to an HIV/AIDS Participatory Approach in Uganda', in Susan E. Smith, Dennis Willms and Nancy Johnson, eds. *Nurtured by Knowledge. Learning to do Participatory Action Research*, Ottawa: International Development Research Centre, 1997, pp. 86–110.

Stedman, John Stephen, Donald Rothschild and Cousens Elisabeth, *Ending Civil War: The Implementation of Peace Agreements*, Boulder: Lynne Reiner, 2002.

Stover, Eric and Weinstein Harvey M., eds. *My Neighbour, My Enemy. Justice and Community in the Aftermath of Mass Atrocities*, Cambridge: Cambridge University Press, 2004.

Suganami, Hidemi, *On the Causes of War*, Oxford: Clarendon, 1996.

Suganami, Hidemi, 'Stories of War Origins: A Narrative of the Cause of War', *Review of International Studies*, Vol. 23, No. 4, 1997, pp. 401–18.

Theissen, Gunnar, 'Mehrere Wahrheiten: Die südafrikanische Wahrheits- und Versöhnungskommission im Spiegelbild von Meinungsumfragen', *WeltTrends*, Vol. 37, No. Winter 2002/2003, 2002, pp. 65–80.

Tomuschat, Christian, 'Vergangenheitsbewältigung durch Aufklärung: Die Arbeit der Wahrheitskommission in Guatemala', in Ulrich Fastenrath, ed. *Internationaler Schutz der Menschenrechte. Entwicklung – Geltung – Durchsetzung – Aussöhnung der Opfer mit den Tätern*, Dresden/München: Dresden University Press, 2000.

Tongeren, Paul van, Malin Brenk, Marte Hellema and Juliette Verhoeven, eds. *People Building Peace II: Successful Stories of Civil Society*, Boulder: Lynne Rienner, 2005.

Torfing, Jacob, *New Theories of Discourse. Laclau, Mouffe and Zizek*, Oxford: Blackwell, 1999.

TRC, 1998, 'Truth and Reconciliation Commission of South Africa Report', Vol. 1, TRC, www.news24.com/Content_Diplay/TRY_Report/1chap5.html. (accessed 15.6.2005).

Turton, David, 'Introduction: War and Ethnicity', in David Turton, ed. *War and Ethnicity. Global Connections and Local Violence*, Rochester: University of Rochester Press, 1997, pp. 1–46.

Twagiramariya, Clotilde and Meredeth Turshen, ' "Favours" to Give and "Consenting" Victims: The Sexual Politics of Survival in Rwanda', in Clotilde Twagiramariya and Meredeth Turshen, eds. *What Women Do in Wartime. Gender and Conflict in Africa*, London/New York: Zed Books, 1998, pp. 101–18.

UNDP, 'Uganda Development Report', New York: UNDP, 1998.

Uwazie, Ernest E., 'Social Relations and Peacekeeping Among the Igbo', in William I. Zartman, ed. *Traditional Cures for Modern Conflict: African Conflict 'Medicine'*, Boulder: Lynne Rienner, 2000, pp. 15–29.

Van der Merwe, Hugo, 'National and Community Reconciliation: Competing Agendas in the South African Truth and Reconciliation Commission', in Nigel Biggar, ed. *Burying the Past. Making Peace and Doing Justice after Civil Conflict*, Washington: Georgetown University Press, 2001, pp. 85–106.

Vandeginste, Stef and Filip Reijntjens, 'Traditional Approaches to Negotiation and Mediation. Burundi, Rwanda, and Congo', in Luc Reychler and Thania Paffenholz, eds. *Peacebuilding. A Field Guide*, London: Lynne Rienner, 2001, pp. 128–37.

Vasquez, John A., 'War Endings: What Science and Constructivism Can Tell Us', *Millennium*, Vol. 26, No. 3, 1997, pp. 651–78.

Vattimo, Gianni, *Beyond Interpretation. The Meaning of Hermeneutics for Philosophy*, Translated by D. Webb, Cambridge/Oxford: Polity Press, 1997.

Vayrynen, Raimo, 'To Settle or to Transform. Perspectives on the Resolution of National and International Conflicts', in Raimo Vayrynrn, ed. *New Directions in Conflict Theory. Conflict Resolution and Conflict Transformation*, London/Newbury Park/New Delhi: Sage, 1991, pp. 1–25.

Vayrynen, Tarja, 'Going Beyond Similarity: The Role of the Facilitator in Problem-Solving Workshop Conflict Resolution', *Paradigms*, Vol. 9, No. 2, 1995, pp. 71–86.

Vincent, Joan, *Teso in Transformation*, Berkley: University of California Press, 1982.

Vincent, Joan, 'War in Uganda: North and South', in R.E. Downs and Stephen P. Reyna, eds. *Deadly Developments. Capitalism, State and War*, New York/London: Routledge, 1999, pp. 107–32.

Volkan, Vakim, 'On Chosen Trauma', *Mind and Human Interaction*, Vol. 3, No. 13, 1991, pp. 3–19.

Volkan, Vakim and Norman Itzkowitz, 'Modern Greek and Turkish Identities and the Psychodynamics of Greek-Turkish Relations', in Antonius C.G.M. Robben and Marcelo M. Suárez-Orozco, eds. *Cultures under Siege. Collective Violence and Trauma*, Cambridge: Cambridge University Press, 2000, pp. 227–47.

Waelchli, Heinz and Dhavan Shah, 'Crisis Negotiation Between Unequals: Lessons from a Classic Dialogue', *Negotiation Journal*, Vol. 10, No. 2, 1994, pp. 129–41.

Walker, R.B.J., *Inside/Outside: International Relations as Political Theory*, Cambridge: Cambridge University Press, 1993.

Warnke, Georgia, *Hermeneutics, Tradition and Reason*, Oxford: Blackwell, 1987.

Werbner, Richard P., 'Smoke from the Barrel of a Gun: Postwars of the Dead, Memory and Reinscription in Zimbabwe', in Richard P. Werbner, ed. *Memory and the Postcolonial. African Anthropology and the Critique of Power*, London/New York: Zed Publications, 1998, pp. 71–104.

Wetherell, Margaret, 'Positioning and Interpretative Repertoires: Conversation Analysis and Post-Structuralism in Dialogue', *Discourse & Society*, Vol. 9, No. 3, 1998, pp. 387–415.

Wilkinson, Ian, 'Thinking with Suffering', *Cultural Values*, Vol. 5, No. 4, 2001, pp. 421–44.

Wilmer, Franke, 'The Social Construction of Conflict and Reconciliation in the Former Yugoslavia', *Social Justice*, Vol. 25, No. 4, 1998, pp. 90–113.

Winslade, John and Gerald Monk, *Narrative Mediation*, San Francisco: Jossey-Bass Publishers, 2000.

Wittgenstein, Ludwig, *Philosophical Investigation*, Translated by G.E.M. Ancombe, Oxford: Basil Blackwell, 1993.

Zartman, William I., 'Changes in the New Order and the Place for the Old', in William I. Zartman, ed. *Traditional Cures for Modern Conflicts. African Conflict 'Medicine'*, Boulder: Lynne Rienner, 2000, pp. 219–30.

Zartman, William I., 'Introduction', in William I. Zartman, ed. *Traditional Cures for Modern Conflict: African Conflict 'Medicine'*, Boulder: Lynne Rienner, 2000, pp. 1–11.

Zylinska, Joanna, 'Mediating Murder: Ethics, Trauma and the Price of Death', *Journal for Cultural Research*, Vol. 8, No. 3, 2004, pp. 227–46.

Newspapers

Brody, Reed, 'Justice: The First Casualty of Truth?' *The Nation*, 30 April 2001.

Echweru, Musa, 'Iteso Love Museveni – Ex-rebel', *The Monitor*, Kampala, 22–26 April 1994, p. 8.

L'Pajule, Odiya, 'What are these People Apologising about?' *The Monitor*, Kampala, 21 January 2000.

Maitland, John, 'Suffering of the People form Teso', *The Independent*, London, 25 July 1989, p. 15.

Mulindwa, Rodger, 'Kumi to Deny Movt Votes Over Schools', *The Monitor*, Kampala, 9 January 2000.

Omoding, Obalell, 'Mukura: Lessons after 10 Years', *The Monitor*, Kampala, 11 July 1999.

Omoding, Obalell, 'Uganda Dead Remembered in Canada, UK', *The Monitor*, Kampala, 15 July 1999.

SSebwezze, Leo, 'Uganda still Lives with Museveni's 12 Crimes', *The Monitor*, Kampala, 3 January 2001.

'Defeating the Rebels and Cattle Rustlers', *Tarehe Sita*, Kampala, May/June 1987, pp. 3–5.

'17 Die of Hunger in Eastern Uganda', *Xinhua News Agency*, Kampala, 24 January 1994.

'Famine Threatening Eastern Uganda', *Xinhua News Agency*, Kampala, 14 March 1995.

'Ilukor Advises Teso', *New Vision*, Kampala, 10 April 2000, p. 6.

'Museveni Commissions Schools', *New Vision*, Kampala, 26 February 2001, p. 5.

'Northern Uganda "World's Biggest Neglected Crisis".' 22 October 2004, *The Guardian*, London.

'Promote Iteso Culture – Emorimor', *New Vision*, Kampala, 2 May 2000, p. 3.

'Teso Crowns Emorimor', *New Vision*, Kampala, 1 May 2000, p. 2.

Radio Broadcasts

'Museveni Wins Presidential Elections with 74.2 Per Cent of Vote', *Radio Uganda*, Kampala, 11 May 1996.

'Rebel Leader Surrenders', *Radio Uganda*, Kampala, 2 February 1993.

'Uganda: 47 Dead due to "Gross Negligence" after Rebel Round-up', *BBC Summary of World Broadcast*, London, 24 July 1989.

'Uganda Museveni Promise Compensation for Mukura Deaths', *Radio Uganda*, Kampala, 25 August 1989.

'Uganda Presidential Commission to Investigate Rebellion in Eastern Districts', *Radio Uganda*, Kampala, 17 October 1990.

'Ugandan Minister Says for Rebel Army to Dissolve, Calls for Exiles to Return', *Radio Uganda*, Kampala, 6 July 1992.

'Ugandan President Responds to "Concentration Camps" Allegations', *Radio Uganda*, Kampala, 1 March 1990.

Index

accountability, 50, 135
actors, 8, 18, 22–3, 26, 31, 35, 69, 76, 92, 132
Africa, 5–6, 13–15, 23–8, 35, 58–62, 86–9, 91, 103–4
Akello, Grace, 78, 81, 87, 92–4, 96–7, 118, 158–9, 159–65
Amin, Idi, 2, 50, 57, 63–4, 66–7, 89–90, 93, 96, 136, 138–9
amnesty, 79, 134
    amnesty Statute, 79, 84, 159
Amuria district, 54, 72
Anderson, Benedict, 142
Anglican Church of Uganda, 87
Anglo-German Agreement of 1890, 58
antagonism, 5, 8, 10, 37–8, 50, 54, 66, 124–5, 134, 139–44
    antagonistic relationship, 1–4, 10, 21–2, 28, 30, 38, 48, 115, 122–3, 125, 131, 133, 143–4
anthropology, 54, 60, 90, 103
Aporu, Okol, 80
atrocity, 13, 28, 48, 49, 67, 77, 86, 101, 108–9, 112, 114, 135, 137–8
authority, 21, 23, 27, 35, 42, 93, 102, 131, 142
    authoritative power, 35

Bantu, 36, 104
Banyankole, 104
Battle of Mengo, 63
Berdal, Mats, 35
Besigye, Kizza, 70–2
Binaisa, Godfrey, 64
boundaries, 1, 4, 14, 33–8, 46–54, 56, 59, 76, 85, 123, 125–6, 129
    challenging and changing, 37, 52, 92, 111, 126, 129
British Foreign and Commonwealth Office, 78

British Protectorate, 58
Buganda, 58–64, 117
burial, 114
    funeral customs, 114
    mourning, 90, 113
Burton, John, 17

Campbell, David, 4, 34, 36–7, 129
camps, 68, 72, 104, 107
capitalism, 24, 59, 61
    cash crops, 55, 59, 61–2, 77, 104, 132
    class division, 19, 59–62, 71, 76
Catholic Church, 87
cattle, 55, 77, 96, 100–1, 105
    cattle herding, 55–6
    cattle rustling, 2, 56–7, 66–8, 73, 82, 89, 100–1, 104–6, 108–10
    restocking, 84, 96
Christianity, 23, 45, 59, 87, 113, 137, 139
    churches, 2, 68, 76, 86–8, 92, 95, 107–8, 129, 141
citizenship, 14, 141, 143
civil society, 18
co-existence, 47, 51–2, 130, 136, 139
cognition, 23, 26, 115
colonialism, 5, 8, 13–14, 23–4, 54–71, 103–5, 124
    indirect rule, 14, 58–9, 69
    labour reservoirs, 58, 61, 63
commemoration, 113, 114–16, 142
communication, 6–8, 35, 47, 75
conflict
    causes of, 5, 13, 15, 17–19, 28, 99–105, 108–9, 125, 127, 135, 138, 140, 142–3
    cleavages, social and political, 5, 7–8, 14–15, 54, 61, 69, 124, 127, 134, 136, 141, 170